LIGHTS OF CREATION & TRANSCENDENCE

David Birnbaum / Mesorah Matrix Series

www.MesorahMatrix.com

MESORAH
MATRIX
VOLUME 8

LIGHTS OF CREATION & TRANSCENDENCE
David Birnbaum / Mesorah Matrix Series

U-VACHARTA BA-CHAYIM

EXPLORING HIGHER DIMENSIONS

Editors

David
Birnbaum & Cohen
Martin S.

Associate Editor: **Saul J. Berman**

New Paradigm Matrix®

Published by NEW PARADIGM MATRIX

COPYRIGHT © 2018
NEW PARADIGM MATRIX FOUNDATION

Library of Congress Cataloging-in-Publication Data

Birnbaum, David.

U-vacharta Ba-chayim / David Birnbaum and Martin S. Cohen.

ISBN 978-0-9961995-5-1

1. U-vacharta Ba-chayim.   2. Jewish Spirituality.   I. Title.

21st CENTURY PUBLISHING

New Paradigm Matrix
att: David Birnbaum
Tower 49
Twelve E. 49th St.,
11th Floor,
New York, NY 10017

www.NewParadigmMatrix.com

Direct contact to Editor-in-Chief

David.Birnbaum.NY@gmail.com

Washofsky
Cohen
Kosman
Graetz
Poupko
Maged
Treiger-Bar-Am
Rothstein
Jacobson-Maisels
Thiede
Greyber
Dorff
Goodfriend
Cook
Bulka
Cardin
Grumet
Goldberg
Weiss
Glazer

U-vacharta Ba-chayim

"And thou shalt choose life!"

David Birnbaum and Martin S. Cohen

Editors

NEW PARADIGM MATRIX

www.NewParadigmMatrix.com

David Birnbaum & Martin S. Cohen

U-vacharta
Ba-chayim

"And thou shalt choose life!"

with essays by

Reuven P. Bulka, Nina Beth Cardin, Martin S. Cohen, Michael J. Cook,
Elliot N. Dorff, Aubrey L. Glazer, Edwin C. Goldberg, Elaine Goodfriend,
Michael Graetz, Daniel Greyber, Zvi Grumet, James Jacobson-Maisels,
Admiel Kosman, Alex Maged, Gidon Rothstein, Barbara Shulamit Thiede,
Kim Treiger-Bar-Am, Mark Washofsky and Shira Weiss

Saul J. Berman
Associate Editor

New Paradigm Matrix Publishing
New York
2018

21st CENTURY PUBLISHING

From the Editor-in-Chief

May 10, 2018

It is a privilege to be serving as Editor-in-Chief of this unique 10-theme series. I am honored to be working with world-class editors Benjamin Blech, Martin S. Cohen, Saul J. Berman, and Shalom Carmy.

It is our hope and prayer that the series be a catalyst for intellectual and spiritual expansion – as well as a unifying force both for our people as well as for individuals of good will globally.

Sincerely,

David Birnbaum

דוד אריה בן אברהם יעקב הלוי   25 אייר 5778

Mesorah Matrix series

jewish thought & spirituality

10-theme

10-volume

200+ original essays

150+ global thought leaders

a decade-long unified endeavor

genre: *applied scholarship*

www.MesorahMatrix.com

21st CENTURY PUBLISHING

Mesorah Matrix series

A POTENTIALLY ICONIC LEGACY SERIES
FOR THE 21ST CENTURY

10-VOLUME SERIES……200+ ESSAYS……A GLOBAL EFFORT

150+ ESSAYISTS….SPANNING THE WORLD'S TOP JEWISH THOUGHT
LEADERS

A DYNAMIC CONTEMPORARY GLOBE-SPANING ENDEAVOR AND
COLLECTION

ESSAYISTS COVER A VERY WIDE SPECTRUM OF JUDAISM:

THE COMPLETE SERIES TO DATE IS AVAILABLE ON-LINE GRATIS
IN FLIP-BOOK FORM……AND DOWNLOAD-ABLE GRATIS
+
AVAILABLE IN SOFTCOVER VIA AMAZON
+
AVAILABLE IN E-BOOK FORM VIA VARIOUS MODALITIES

A UNIQUE STUDY AND REFERENCE TOOL FOR CLERGY, ACADEMICS,
STUDENTS & LAY INTELLIGENSIA

A STELLAR CORE COURSE OF STUDY – WHETHER FOR ONE SEMESTER
OR MULTI-YEAR

AND… AS AN UNINTENDED CONSEQUENCE, THE SERIES HAS
BROKEN DOWN BARRIERS - AND SERVED AS A FORCE-MULTIPLIER –
IN UNIFYING THE JEWISH PEOPLE

IN DEPTH & BREADTH……SCOPE & SPECTRUM
A LANDMARK SERIES
UNIQUE ACROSS THE 3,500+ YEAR SPAN OF JEWISH HISTORY

a unique, timeless and potentially multi-semester

Contemporary Jewish Thought

Course Text

a *sui generis* series • all original essays • broad spectrum authorship

a potentially iconic Jewish resource

Am ha-Sefer

This New Paradigm Matrix work
is available via multiple modalities:

amazon: www.AmazonX1000.com

eBooks: www.eReader1000.com

online: www.MesorahMatrix.com

contact: NPM1000@yahoo.com

The ten volumes of the Mesorah Matrix series amount to a contemporary encyclopedia of the best of traditional and new creative thinking on the central issues of Jewish Spirituality for the 21st century. People grappling with the place of truth, personal virtues and social values in their lives, will find multiple essays which challenge them to grow intellectually and spiritually in their Jewish identity. The ideas are all deeply rooted in Jewish texts in ways that enlighten the early texts and brighten the path into the future of the Jewish People.

- Rabbi Saul Berman
  Yeshiva University
  Chanukah, 2018

About the Editors

Martin S. Cohen has been a Senior Editor of the inter-denominational Mesorah Matrix series since 2012.

From 2000-2014, he served as Chairman of the Editorial Board of the quarterly journal *Conservative Judaism*, which was published under the joint auspices of the Jewish Theological Seminary and the Rabbinical Assembly.

Rabbi Cohen also served as the senior editor of *The Observant Life*, a landmark compendium of Jewish law and custom published by the Rabbinical Assembly in 2012.

His weekly blog can be viewed at www.TheRuminativeRabbi.blogspot.com. He has served as rabbi of the Shelter Rock Jewish Center in Roslyn, New York, since 2002.

Rabbi Cohen was educated at the City University of New York and at the Jewish Theological Seminary, where he was ordained a rabbi and received his Ph.D. in Ancient Judaism. He is the recipient of fellowships at the Hebrew University in Jerusalem in 1983 and Harvard University in 1993.

Martin Cohen has taught at Hunter College, the Jewish Theological Seminary, the Institute for Jewish Studies of the University of Heidelberg, as well as at the University of British Columbia and the Vancouver School of Theology.

His published works include *The Boy on the Door on the Ox* (2008) and *Our Haven and Our Strength: A Translation and Commentary on the Book of Psalms* (2004), as well as four novels and four books of essays.

Rabbi Cohen is currently writing a translation and commentary on the Torah and the Five Megillot.

MARTIN S. COHEN MAJOR WORKS

As Senior Editor

Mesorah Matrix series 2012 - present

Conservative Judaism 2000 - 2014

The Observant Life 2012

As Author (Non-Fiction)

Travels on the Private Zodiac: Reflections on Jewish Life, Ritual and Spirituality (1995)

In Pursuit of Wholeness: The Search for Spiritual Integrity in a Delusional World (1996)

Travels on the Road Not Taken: Towards a Bible-Based Theology of Jewish Spirituality (1997)

Sefer Ha-ikarim Li-z'maneinu (2000)

Our Haven and Our Strength: The Book of Psalms (2004)

Siddur Tzur Yisrael (2005)

Zot Nechamati for the House of Mourning (2006)

Riding the River of Peace (2007)

The Boy on the Door on the Ox (2008)

As Author (Fiction)

The Truth About Marvin Kalish (1992)

Light from Dead Stars (1996)

The Sword of Goliath (1998)

Heads You Lose (2002)

About the Editors

David Birnbaum is a philosophical writer, historical chronicler and *conceptual theorist*. His first work *God and Evil* (KTAV, 1988) is considered by many to be a breakthrough *modern day classic* in the field of theodicy. See God-And-Evil.com.

Editor-in-Chief Birnbaum is known globally as "the architect of Potentialism Theory" – a unified philosophy/cosmology/metaphysics. The paradigm-challenging theory (see ParadigmChallenge.com) is delineated in Birnbaum's 3-volume *Summa Metaphysica* series (1988, 2005, 2014). See Philosophy1000.com.

A riposte to *Summa Theologica* of (St.) Thomas Aquinas, the Birnbaum treatise challenges both the mainstream Western philosophy of Aristotelianism and the well propped-up British/atheistic cosmology of Randomness. See Potentialism Theory.com.

The focus of 150+ reviews/articles, Summa Metaphysica has been an assigned Course Text at over 15 institutions of higher learning globally. See SummaCoverage.com.

Summa Metaphysica was the focus of an international academic conference on Science & Religion in April 16-19 2012 (see Conference1000.com). The work has been very widely covered globally. See RewindSumma.com.

David Birnbaum is the Editor-in-Chief of the *Mesorah Matrix* series on Jewish thought and spirituality. The *sui generis* series spans 10-volumes and 10 themes. The entire series is comprised of 200+ specially commissioned original pieces from 150-180 global Jewish thought leader essayists. See Mesorah1000.com.

In the history realm, David Birnbaum is the author/chronicler of the 2-volume *The Crucifixion – of the Jews*, and of the 7-volume *Jews, Church & Civilization*. His Crucifixion series, in particular, traces a direct trajectory from the Canonical Gospels in the First Century to Auschwitz in the Twentieth. See History1000.com.

David Birnbaum has served on the faculty of the New School for Social Research in Manhattan. He is a graduate of Yeshiva University High School (Manhattan), CCNY (City College of New York) and Harvard. His commentary blog is www.ManhattanObserver.com.

DAVID BIRNBAUM MAJOR WORKS

As Author

4-volume *Summa Metaphysica** (www.philosophy1000.com)

2-volume *The Crucifixion* (www.crucifixion1000.com)

7-volume *Jews, Church & Civilization* (www.civilization1000.com)

As Editor-in-Chief

10-volume *Mesorah Matrix* (www.mesorah1000.com)

As Conceptualizer

3-volume *Summa Spinoffs* (www.Spinoffs1000.com)

8-volume *Potentialism Theory* via Graphic-Narrative
(www.TheoryGraphics1000.com)

As Commentator

www.ManhattanObserver.com

YouTube channels

Summa Metaphysica

Mesorah Matrix

*

Summa I: Religious Man / God and Evil
Summa II: Spiritual Man / God and Good
Summa III: Secular Man / The Transcendent Dynamic
Summa IV: Quantum Man / Morphed Cosmic Order

DAVID BIRNBAUM MAJOR WORKS

Summa Metaphysica series

presenting new paradigm
Potentialism Theory
a universal, unified, seamless & fully-integrated
overarching philosophy

www.SummaMetaphysica.com

Summa I:
Religious Man: God and Evil: focus: *theodicy & eternal origins* [1988]**

Summa II:
Spiritual Man: God and Good: focus: *metaphysics & teleology* [2005]

Summa III:
Secular Man: The Transcendent Dynamic: focus: *cosmology & evolution* [2014]

Summa IV:
Quantum Man: Morphed Cosmic Order: focus: *quantum-potential* [2020]

see also secondary site PotentialismTheory.com

see also: RewindSumma.com 222+ panel Scroll-Down tour

YouTube Channel: Summa Metaphysica

see also Supplement: Articles on Summa
(only online - on www.SummaMetaphysica.com)

** see also: www.GodOfPotential.com

** see special YouTube channel: www.UnifyingScienceSpirituality.com

www.BirnbaumAcademic.com

www.David1000.com

www.Major1000.com

U-vacharta Ba-chayim

U-vacharta Ba-chayim

TABLE OF CONTENTS

Free Will: Is There Anything Free About It?
MICHAEL GRAETZ

The modern social science of psychology presents a great challenge to earlier religious concepts of free will. If there are an almost limitless number of forces (some of which are not even in our consciousness) that impact on each decision we make, and if some of these forces may be coercive, this calls into question the very assumption of "free" will. This essay argues that rabbinic literature attempted to discover exactly what was free in a person's choice— that is, to assert that guilt or innocence depends not on some amorphous "will" (which may be a chimera), but on a more specific part of the thought process, namely, intention (which can be discerned and evaluated).

Preface

Martin S. Cohen

In one of his most famous poems, Robert Frost imagines himself standing at a crossroads in a "yellow wood" and having to decide which path forward to choose. The poem turns on the fact that neither path clearly recommends itself as the "better" one to choose: both are covered in yellow autumnal leaves, one is "just as fair" as the other, and both lead to destinations that Frost cannot see.[1] In just twenty lines, the poet thus suggests the plight of moderns who must make decisions in life that may eventually be perceived as matters of great importance, but that feel hardly even to matter much when they are actually being made. That is surely a challenge we all face, but how exactly to deal with it is challenging to say. It surely seems exaggerated to conclude from the poet's reverie that our decisions in life don't really matter at all simply because we cannot say at the outset where they may ultimately lead us—much less that they have no real importance because we will end up in the same place anyway. Those conclusions both feel just a bit irrational, but neither should we read the poem's famous conclusion—that the poet's decision to travel the path less taken has ended up making all the difference in his life—as suggesting that the wisest choices in life are invariably those spurned by the majority. Surely, for all the *oylem* may be a *goylem*, it can't always be unwise to make some specific decision in life merely because many others have previously chosen to make it!

(The Yiddish aphorism, one of my own father's favorites, conveys the same message as the one attributed, possibly spuriously, to Alexander Hamilton according to which "the masses are asses.")

The Torah offers a different take on the decision to choose one path forward in life over another. Speaking from the edge of his own life, Moses begins by imagining two paths stretching forth before the Israelites as they contemplate their future. And he knows their names, too: they are the paths of blessing and of curse, "a blessing if you obey all the commandments of the Eternal, your God, that I am commanding you this day, and a curse if you do not obey the commandments of the Eternal, your God, and swerve off the path that I am commanding you today…" (Deuteronomy 11:26–28).

Later in his speech, Moses returns to that same trope and describes that same choice in far greater detail:

> Behold, by commanding you today to love the Eternal, your God, and to walk in God's ways and to keep God's commandments and statutes and laws, I am placing before you today, on the one hand, life and goodness, and, on the other, death and evil. And so shall you live and flourish as the Eternal, your God, blesses you in the land that you are now entering to possess. If, however, your heart should turn away and you stop obeying—such that you actually turn to apostasy and prostrate yourself before alien gods and worship them— then I am telling you clearly today that you shall surely perish, that you will not live for long on the land that you are about to cross the Jordan to enter and possess. I call heaven and earth on this day as my witnesses that I am placing before you life and death, blessing and curse. Choose life, so that you live, you and your progeny. And love the Eternal, your God, by obeying God's voice and by cleaving unto God—for it is God who grants you your life and who determines how long shall last the days you dwell on the land that the Eternal

swore to grant to your ancestors Abraham, Isaac, and Jacob (Deuteronomy 30:15-20).

The title of the volume you are holding is taken from the end of this very passage, where the Torah presents Moses instructing the people how to deal with the choice that lies before them. *U-vaḥarta ba-ḥayyim* ("choose life"), he commands—and his meaning feels clear and unambiguous: to secure a long life for yourself and your progeny, *choose* to live in God's service, *choose* to devote yourself to obeying God's voice, and *choose* to cleave unto God all the days of your life. And the aggregate result of all that wise choosing will lead to the greatest choice of all: the choice to embrace life at its fullest and richest, both as individuals linked personally to the Almighty in covenantal intimacy *and* as citizens of a nation linked to the Almighty in exactly the same way.

There are countless ways to respond to the injunction to choose life, and each of the authors in this volume has chosen one to explore in his or her essay. Some are theoretical in nature and deal with the larger notion of how choice and obligation interact in the context of religion. Others are more practical and treat of the specific ways in which individuals might respond to the biblical obligation to choose life in the context of the consequential decisions that we find ourselves faced with in life. Still others are rooted in history and present the way the injunction to choose life was understood by different thinkers at different moments in Jewish history. And some have used the scriptural injunction to choose life as a jumping-off point for considering the notion of free will itself, and pondering how the theological notion that God is all-knowing can be reconciled with the sense people have of being able freely to make real, meaningful choices in life.

The authors who have contributed essays to this volume address all of these questions. Our authors come from a wide range of backgrounds: many are congregational rabbis, while others are teachers and academics, and still others work in the Jewish world in different capacities. They are a disparate group, our authors: men and women, older and younger, staunchly traditionalist and more liberally oriented, Israelis and Diaspora-based. Yet, for all they are different, they are also united by the common belief that the written word, and particularly in the form of the essay, is a useful and satisfying medium in which to explore Judaism and Jewishness itself in a deep and meaningful way.

This is not a book solely for Jews of any particular spiritual orientation; nor, for that matter, is it a book solely for Jewish readers. Rather, we hope that this anthology may open a door for all who possess the kind of curiosity about Jewish religion and culture that cannot be dealt with effectively by platitudes or even heartfelt op-ed pieces, but rather by thoughtful, text-based studies intended to inform, to persuade, and to inspire. I feel privileged to present the work of these authors to the reading public and I hope our readers will likewise feel that this is a remarkable collection.

Unless otherwise indicated, all translations here are the authors' own work. Biblical citations of the NJPS refer to the complete translation of Scripture first published under the title *Tanakh: The Holy Scriptures* by the Jewish Publication Society in 1985. The four-letter Hebrew name of God is rendered in this volume almost always as "the Eternal" or "Eternal God" (although authors have sometimes departed from this convention, as dictated by the constraints of their own writing).

I would like to take this opportunity to acknowledge the other senior editors of the Mesorah Matrix series, David Birnbaum and Benjamin Blech, as well as Saul J. Berman, our associate editor. They and our able staff have all supported me as I've labored to bring this volume together and I am grateful to them all.

As always, I must also express my gratitude to the men and women, and particularly to the lay leadership, of the synagogue I serve as rabbi, the Shelter Rock Jewish Center in Roslyn, New York. Possessed of the unwavering conviction that their rabbi's book projects are part and parcel of his service to them (and, through them, to the larger community of those interested in learning about Judaism through the medium of the well-written word), they are remarkably supportive of my literary efforts as author and editor. I am in their debt, and I am pleased to acknowledge that debt formally, here and whenever I publish my own work or the work of others.

Martin S. Cohen
Roslyn, New York
Erev Rosh Hashanah 5778
September 20, 2017

NOTES

[1] Robert Frost, "The Road Not Taken," first published in the author's *Mountain Interval* (New York: Henry Holt and Co., 1916), p. 9, and innumerable times since.

Abbreviations

A.T.	-	*Arba·ah Turim*
B.	-	Babylonian Talmud
M.	-	Mishnah
M.T.	-	*Mishneh Torah*
S.A.	-	*Shulhan Arukh*
T.	-	Tosefta
Y.	-	Yerushalmi

A Note from the Editors

Every effort has been made to retain a good level of consistency between the essays that appear here in terms of the translation and transliteration of Hebrew. Many of our decisions have, needs be, been arbitrary, but we have done our best to create a book that will be as accessible to newcomers to the study of Judaism as it is inspiring to cognoscenti. All translations are their authors' unless otherwise indicated.

Essays

Choose Life: Freedom and Obligation

Kim Treiger-Bar-Am

The Torah tells us to choose life:

> See, I have set before you this day life and good, and death
> and evil….
> This day I call heaven and earth as witnesses against you
> that I have set before you life and death, blessing and curse.
> Now **choose life**, so that you and your children may live.
> (Deuteronomy 30:15, 19)

U-vaḥarta ba-ḥayyim. The phrase indicates that we have a choice, and
yet obligates us. Is it, then, really a choice? Are we free to choose? The
Bible's offer of a choice of life has been described as a suggestion—
that we are "endowed with free choice and *urged* to choose life and
good."[1] Perhaps, though, we are forced to make that choice. Is the
choice an obligatory one?

It is both. In Judaism, both choice and obligation are central. The
people freely choose *and* are obligated by the Sinai covenant. They
freely interpret it subjectively, and continue to abide by it.

Jewish tradition sees freedom and obligation as one. The Talmud
suggests that the word *ḥarut*, used in the Bible (Exodus 32:16) to
describe the tablets at Sinai as "engraved" by God, should be read as
ḥeirut, "liberty." The two words sound similar and are spelled identi-
cally in Hebrew, differing only with respect to a single vowel.[2] The

word-play allows the rabbis to derive a les son: the commandments are said to bring freedom.

How do freedom and obligation function side by side? We can be held responsible only for acts that we are free to perform. Freedom affords us responsibility. Freedom also allows us to be moral. Judaism embraces responsible moral choice and action.

This essay will trace the ethos of freedom and obligation through Jewish tradition. We'll see first how Judaism accords freedom, and then its obligation. The two will then be shown to work together, under the covenant and in human relationships. The essay will close with a personal reflection about obligation alongside freedom in our lives.

Freedom

Freedom abounds in Jewish tradition. The biblical narrative exhibits freedom and choice. The formation of the covenant with the Jewish people portrays freedom, according to both biblical and post-biblical accounts. Freedom further stands out in the interpretation of the law that began at the time of the Bible and continues through to today.

Biblical Narrative

The Bible sees humans as God's partners in the work of creation. While the Torah states that the creation of the heavens and earth was finished (Genesis 2:1), a talmudic passage considering the verse says that people complete the creation (B. Shabbat 119b). The *Etz Hayim Torah and Commentary* explains: "God left the world a bit incomplete so that we might become God's partners in the work of Creation."[3] The idea of creation in partnership can also be found in the Book of Isaiah, where the prophet describes our task of feeding the hungry and caring for the poor (58:6, 10, and 12).[4] We are to bring God's spirit down to earth, as Rabbi Joseph Soloveitchik (1903–1993) taught.[5] We complete creation, and fix the world: *tikkun olam*.

God is free; and because humanity is created in the divine image, humanity is likewise free.[6] We find the first description of human freedom in the Garden of Eden, when Adam freely chooses names for the animals (Genesis 2:19–20). The biblical narrative continues to be replete with references to freedom. People freely argue with God: Abraham negotiates with God for the survival of the town of Sodom (Genesis 18:22), and Moses for the survival of the Jewish people (Exodus 32:9–14; Numbers 14:11–20, 16:19–23). The life praised in the Bible is the independent, free life of the shepherd.[7] The number seven, oft-repeated in the Torah, represents freedom: the seventh day is the Sabbath, when Jews do not work, and the seventh year is the Sabbatical year, *sh'nat ha-sh'mittah*, when the land is not to be tilled and slaves are to be freed.

The Covenant

The Bible relates that at Sinai God offered to the people of Israel the covenant, which they were free to accept. Yet the narrative records that the people responded by saying *na·aseh v'nishma*, "we will do and we will hear" (Exodus 24:7).[8] It has been argued that this statement shows a lack of independent consideration of the terms of the covenant before its acceptance: the phrase indicates that the people promise to fulfill the commandments even before considering them. Debates are recorded in the Talmud as to whether or not the covenant was freely accepted.[9]

Perhaps the people were not *really* free to reject the covenant. They were, after all, newly freed slaves still possessed of the mentality of slaves in the middle of the desert without other protection or resources. Moreover, the medieval commentator Rabbi Jacob ben

Meir, popularly called Rabbeinu Tam (1100–1171), wrote that the people were overwhelmed by the experience of direct divine revelation.[10] The biblical narrative relates that thunder and flames accompanied the direct word of God. Under such circumstances, who could say no?

The Talmud records a view that takes the Torah's description of the people "at the foot of the mountain" (Exodus 19:17) literally, seeing the people as having been *underneath* it. This was because God held Mount Sinai overhead as a barrel above the heads of the people (*kafah aleihem har k'gigit*), threatening to drop it if the people did not accept the covenant. The argument is brought forth that just as a debt that has been coerced may be voided by a rabbinical court, so too the giving of the Law at Mount Sinai should be voided because it was accepted under duress. The Talmud resolves the issue by pointing to the people's free acceptance of the Torah in the days of Mordechai and Queen Esther, as related in the *megillah* we read on Purim (Esther 9:27).[11]

Even before the events related in the Book of Esther, the biblical narrative contains examples of the covenant being accepted by free choice. For example, in Exodus 19:15 God is recorded as saying: "And now, *if* you obey Me and keep My covenant, you shall be to Me a treasure out of all peoples, for Mine is the entire earth"—demonstrating that the covenant is understood to depend on the people's conditional (and hence free) acceptance of it. Conditional language is also used by Moses in his recounting of the Sinai events, as he reminisces about the past on the plains of Moab. In Deuteronomy 11:27–28 and again in Deuteronomy 28:1, Moses reminds the people of the blessings they will receive *if* they hearken to the commandments, or the curses *if* they do not. The people's consent is also shown by their response of "Amen" to each of the instructions noted by Moses, when he directs Joshua what to tell them at the mountains of Gerizim and

Ebal after they have entered the Land of Canaan (Deuteronomy 27).

The books of the prophets record the giving and acceptance of the covenant in the Land of Canaan, as Moses had instructed—and the people are seen to willingly accept the covenant. In Shechem, Joshua asks the people to choose whether they will follow God, and the people respond: "we will serve the Eternal" (Joshua 24:14–15, 24:16–24); consequently, Shechem is dubbed "the city of the covenant" (Joshua 5:4–7).[12] Generations later, King Josiah stands to confirm the covenant with God, and all of the people stand as well (2 Kings 23:3). Even the people's actions, in the very act of crossing the Jordan River to the plains of Jericho for the circumcision ceremony signifying the covenant, show their consent.[13]

Today, after the Holocaust, the Jewish people's maintenance of their identity and practice has been described by Rabbi Irving Greenberg as a voluntary taking-on of the covenant.[14] Many understand bar and bat mitzvah likewise to demonstrate voluntarily taking on the covenant. Another example is the commandment that Jews wear fringes (known as *tzitzit*), which symbolize the taking on of commandments and duties by choice. The obligation to wear *tzitzit* is only in effect when four-cornered garments are worn.[15] Hence, when Jews do wear *tzitzit*, they can be seen as having *chosen* to do so; they obligate themselves.[16]

Interpretation

The people's interpretation of divine law further shows freedom with respect to the commandments. The phrase *na·aseh v'nishma*, uttered by the Israelites at the covenant ceremony on the slopes of Mount Sinai, can be understood as signaling the people's commitment to abide by the Torah and also to interpret it. *Nishma* comes from the verbal root *shin-mem-ayin*, which also yields the word *mishma·at*, meaning "discipline." Also derived from that root are words that have to do with "hearing," as well as the modern Hebrew word for "meaning" itself: *mashma·ut*. With *na·aseh v'nishma*, the people gave their commitment both to uphold and give meaning to the Torah, based on the subjective freedom to interpret God's word as best they could.[17]

Indeed, interpretation began at Sinai. All of the people were present (Exodus 19:8, Exodus 20:15, and Deuteronomy 29:13–14); rabbinic sources understand this to have included souls of future generations of the Jewish people.[18] The midrash holds that there are "seventy faces to the Torah," meaning that there are many different and valid interpretations.[19] Rabbi Solomon Luria (the Maharshal, c. 1510–1573) wrote that there are forty-nine paths or channels of understanding the Torah.[20] According to a sixth-century midrash, each and every Jew present at Sinai understood the Torah in his or her own way.[21]

Interpretation of the Torah again came with the editorial process of canonization by Ezra after the Babylonian Exile in the fifth century BCE.[22] The continued interpretation of the Torah and divine law is evidenced by the Talmud's recording of rabbis in constant controversy and debate.

The talmudic story of the Akhnai oven shows Jewish law (*halakhah*) being determined though human interpretation, and God's approval of the process.[23] In that story, the rabbis disagreed about whether a certain type of oven could become impure, with the majority ruling that it could. Rabbi Eliezer, the most brilliant sage of his generation, disagreed with the majority and he invoked a series of miracles to underscore the correctness of his view: a carob tree uprooted itself, a river ran backward, and walls of the study hall began to fall. Eventually, even a heavenly voice declared that Rabbi Eliezer was right. Rabbi Joshua quoted a biblical passage stating *lo ba-shamayim hi*, "It [i.e., the Torah] is not in heaven!" (Deuteronomy 30:12, which appears shortly before the text quoted at the beginning of this essay about choosing life). When the prophet Elijah was asked about God's reaction to this event, he responded: "God laughed [with joy], saying, 'My children have defeated Me, My children have defeated Me.'"

The biblical phrase *lo ba-shamayim hi* has been taken to mean that *halakhah* is to be interpreted by humans on earth, rather than by God in heaven.[24] In its biblical context, the phrase *lo ba-shamayim hi* reminds that the commandments are neither high in the heaven nor far in the sea, but near to the people, in our hearts and mouths (Deuteronomy 30:11–14).[25]

The development of *halakhah* from the time of the Talmud and on has continued to rely on interpretation. The interpretation of *halakhah* is subjective, and hence arises from human freedom. Rabbi Joseph Soloveitchik called it autonomy, writing that "the power of creative interpretation (*ḥiddush*) is the very foundation of the received tradition."[26]

The strong element of freedom in Jewish tradition—as we have seen in biblical narrative, the covenant, and the interpretation of *halakhah*—is suffused with ethical obligation.

Obligation to the Other and Others

While Judaism centrally involves the freedom of the Self, it also is founded upon the obligation to the Other—namely, God—as well as others—namely, other people. The covenant was (and continues to be) made with God, and hence entails obligations to God. Yet as it is made on behalf of the people acting together as a nation, it entails obligations to the people as well. The Jewish people's statement upon receiving the Torah at Mount Sinai, *na·aseh v'nishma*, is in the plural. The people are in fellowship with one another and are responsible for one another, an idea neatly encapsulated in the talmudic dictum *kol yisrael areivim zeh ba-zeh* ("every Jew is responsible for every other one").[27]

The divine law presents 613 commandments, or *mitzvot*—a term often understood today as meaning "good deeds." Indeed, many of the commandments require ethical behavior toward others. They demand that we show respect. When Hillel was asked in ancient times to explain the entire Torah law while his questioner stood on one foot, he replied: "That which is hateful to you do not do to your neighbor; this is the whole Torah, and the rest is commentary—go and learn it."[28] We have a duty to fulfill commandments of *g'milut hasadim* ("acts of lovingkindness"), such as caring for the sick and the needy, and educating the children in the community. A well-known biblical requirement is for one to "love thy neighbor as thyself" (Leviticus 19:18).[29]

In the words of the prominent Jewish philosopher Martin Buber (1878–1965), we are in an I-Thou relation with the Other and others. That relation is ethical. The ethical nature of freedom and obligation is reflected in the necessary responsibility of our choices, as we will now see.

Freedom *and* Obligation: The Interdependence

Freedom allows us to take on obligation. Reaching the age of bar or bat mitzvah marks the independence and freedom of the new adult through the taking on of obligations: literally, the Aramaic words *bar mitzvah* mean "a bearer of commandments." The link from freedom to obligation is affirmed in the Bible and throughout Jewish teaching. We can see the link as necessary in time, in responsible choice, in positive freedom, and in our covenantal partnership with God.

Temporality

The move from freedom to obligation can be seen in relation to time. The Bible's exodus story shows that, as humans, we are able to take upon ourselves legal obligation only once we are free. The Ten Commandments and the ensuing laws (Exodus 20–22) were given only after the Jews achieved their freedom from slavery—and indeed were possible only then.[30] Without having freedom, one cannot be held responsible for one's actions. As Maimonides (c. 1135–1204) wrote, without freedom, the notion of responsibility to law fails.[31]

The temporal relation has a twist. The Jewish people's choice of life, upon embracing the covenant, was made in the past and will be made in the future. The phrase *u-vaharta ba-hayyim* begins with a *vav*, a Hebrew letter that shifts the grammatical tense of a verb: what begins with a *vav* in describing the past can be seen as referring to the future. Further, the Talmud teaches that "there is no earlier and later [i.e., distinction in time] in the Torah"[32]; the well-known Torah commentator Rashi (1040–1105) referred to this principle frequently.[33] The phrase *u-vaharta ba-hayyim* is thus both a past tense description of events and an indication of future events, as well as a commandment. It says that we have *chosen life* in the *past*, that we are to *choose life* in the *future*, and also that we are *commanded* to *choose life*.

Responsible Choice

Not only does freedom come *before* obligation and *enable* it; freedom also *requires* obligation. As free beings we can take on obligation, and we must. The phrase *u-vaharta ba-hayyim* indicates moral responsibility: we are morally obligated to choose the good.

Because we are free, we can be held accountable. While God can command us to obey certain laws, only *we* bear responsibility for what we do. In the words of the prophet Ezekiel, "the righteousness of the righteous shall be his own, and the wickedness of the wicked shall be his own."[34] We bear responsibility, and we are obligated to make the responsible choice.

Maimonides underscored the ability of all to repent and choose good. We are not predestined to be righteous or wicked; the choice is within our free will. Maimonides wrote:

> Free choice (r'shut) is bestowed upon every human being. One who desires to turn toward the good way and be righteous has the power (ha-r'shut b'yado) to do so. One who wishes to turn towards the evil way and be wicked has the power to do so.[35]

Responsible choice is made when we repent from wrongdoing.

The U-netaneh Tokef prayer on the Days of Awe states: "On Rosh Hashanah it is written and on Yom Kippur it is sealed…who shall live and who shall die." Given God's foreknowledge, how is freedom possible? The prayer continues: "Repentance, prayer, and charity avert the severity of the decree." It is by our free choice and behavior that we can make the change.

Choice and responsibility are seen in the law regarding the parapet. The Torah requires that we build parapets on the roofs of our houses as guardrails to prevent someone from falling (Deuteronomy 22:8). But how does this rule square with free will? If God has planned or foreseen that someone will fall off a roof, then what does it matter whether we act to guard against that possibility? Rashi comments that we do so in order that no one fall off *our* roof and that we not be accountable for someone's injury or death. We are morally responsible to take care to guard others. Humans have the choice of being meritorious or guilty—namely, the choice of whether to build the parapet or not.[36]

The bottom line of the free will debate is that we are free to make choices, and we have the obligation to make responsible ones. Because the responsible choice is moral, it is obligatory that we choose it. As Hermann Cohen put it, we are not volunteers when it comes to morality.[37] That free will and a will under law are identical[38] will be further seen with our discussion of positive freedom.

Positive Freedom

Positive freedom is the freedom to choose the right thing. It is not license, nor the freedom to do what you *want* to do, but freedom to do what you *ought* to do. It is freedom to be a responsible, moral person. The Mishnah states that "the only free person is one who occupies oneself with the study of Torah" (M. Avot 6:2), which is considered responsible and moral action.

The obligations of the covenant have been seen by some as giving human beings freedom from nature. Rabbi Judah Halevi (c. 1075–1141), the great poet of medieval Spain, wrote that rather than being enslaved to time, servants of God are free.[39] In the twentieth century, the Jewish thinker Yeshayahu Leibowitz (1903–1994) highlighted the importance of obedience to the commandments[40] while also noting the freedom that they bring. Leibowitz wrote that the *mitzvot* allow an escape from slavery to natural inclinations, giving the ability to devote oneself wholly to God.[41]

Here Jewish thought is akin to theories put forward by a long tradition of philosophers, including Plato and Immanuel Kant, who consider a will to be free if it does not have ordinary desires, but the desires of a true self for its own good. Plato raised the question of whether freedom involves doing what one wants or doing what one would want if one possessed a clear understanding of the needs of the soul (*Gorgias* 468b–d). And it has been noted that "like Plato, Maimonides has a conception of the 'true' or rational self, the self which seeks truth about God and the universe He created."[42] Maimonides' thought also bears many resemblances to

Kantian theory. For Kant, autonomy is positive freedom, meaning the capability of choosing the moral law.[43]

Covenantal Partnership

Freedom and obligation are both present in the covenantal relationship, which is one of partnership. We choose to take it on. We complete God's creation of the world, together with God and together with others who have taken on the covenant. *Lo ba-shamayim hi*: the divine law is not far out of reach by humans, but indeed on earth. It is not in heaven, but upon our hearing it (*nishma*), we interpret it and lend it meaning (*mashma·ut*). Hence it is our law, made in partnership with God. As moral law, it is obligatory.

Freedom and Obligation, Personally

Seeing freedom and obligation as linked in this way impacts my understanding of liberalism, of Israel, and of the covenant.

Living as a modern Jew in a liberal society, the confluence of freedom and obligation is meaningful for me. Modern ethics in liberal democratic societies surround rights. Everything is about choice. Liberalism has been critiqued for focusing too heavily on the Self: the individual and his or her rights.[44] Given the priority lent to freedom and rights, the duty to others has fallen out of view.

A Jewish view may add a necessary layer to this slant on liberalism. Judaism shows the centrality of obligation in addition to freedom: the duty of the individual to others, and to the community. As Robert Cover wrote, while the reigning myth in the West is based in the rhetoric of individual rights, the myth of Sinai in Judaism is based in the rhetoric of communal obligations and fulfilling commands.[45] Morality involves not only liberty, but a view outside of oneself. Upon finding that duties are intrinsic to rights, and with the emphasis on obligation to others—such as the obligation of *g'milut ḥasadim*, acts of kindness—the picture of the Self and of society becomes rounded out.

Human beings have a fundamental right to be treated with respect, and a fundamental duty to respect the dignity of others. The right to dignity adjoins the obligation of respect. In Hebrew, the same word—*kavod*—means both "dignity" and "respect." That word's root (*kaf-bet-dalet*) is the same root for the word *kaveid*, meaning "heavy." Perhaps we can say that the lightness of dignity bears the weight of obligation. The right of dignity and obligation of respect come together.

Also as an Israeli, it brings me comfort to see freedom coupled with obligation. The State of Israel is defined constitutionally as both a Jewish and a democratic state, and those two sets of values are sometimes thought to conflict. Yet the values cohere in Judaism, as well as in democratic theory, based on the philosophical concept of positive freedom discussed above. Judaism sees as inextricably tied together the freedom of the individual, *and* one's obligation to God and to the Jewish people. Both rights and duties are of concern.[46]

What's more, freedom and obligation recall for me the closeness of the Jewish people's partnership in covenant with God, which bears both elements. The partnership of creation is recalled on Friday evenings at the Sabbath table, whose ritual includes the blessings on the wine and bread (challah). Thanks are given to God for them both. While God indeed creates the earth that gives grapes and wheat, it is human effort that produces the wine and bread. The blessings thus reflect both the human Self and the Other.[47]

The phrase considered here, *u-vaharta ba-ḥayyim*, appears in the Torah portion read each year on the Sabbath before the High Holy Days. As I write this, the hymn we sing in our prayer services on Yom Kippur resonates for me: "We are Your people, You are our Shepherd." We are in it together. We have chosen each other. The Yom Kippur prayers recall the joy of our partnership with God. In the *haftarah* portion chanted on Yom Kippur morning, Isaiah portrays God as saying that if we uphold the covenant and care for the downtrodden—to uphold our task in the partnership—we shall "delight in the Eternal" (58:14).

The covenantal relationship is one of both choice and obligation, both right and duty. We are obligated to choose life, and that obligation brings freedom.

NOTES

[1] This interpretive translation is put forward by Lenn E. Goodman, "Individuality," in *Judaic Sources and Western Thought: Jerusalem's Enduring Presence*, ed. Jonathan A. Jacobs (Oxford: Oxford University Press, 2011), pp. 238–261, esp. p. 244 (emphasis added).

[2] See B. Eiruvin 54a and M. Avot 6:2.

[3] *Etz Hayim Torah and Commentary*, eds. David Lieber et al. (New York: Rabbinical Assembly, United Synagogue of Conservative Judaism, and Jewish Publication Society, 2001), p. 11. Also discussing human partnership in creation, see Avivah Gottlieb Zornberg, *Genesis: The Beginning of Desire* (Philadelphia: Jewish Publication Society, 1995), p. 32. Zornberg further notes that the acceptance of the covenant is to prevent the destruction of the world, as seen in the sources cited in note 11 below. The conclusion of this essay recalls our acknowledgment of our helping God complete the work of creation when we recite the Kiddush blessing on Friday eve (see note 17 below).

[4] Cf. also Isaiah 43:12, in which God proclaims: "You are My witnesses." *Yalkut Shimoni* to Isaiah (§455) reads the passage to mean that without the people as witnesses, God is not, as it were, the Lord. See Irving Greenberg, "The Voluntary Covenant," in *Perspectives* (New York: National Jewish Resource Center, 1987), pp. 27–44, n. 27. Zornberg reads Vayikra Rabbah 36:4 (commenting on this verse in Isaiah) as saying that God becomes the Creator of the world "only when the question of meaning has been decided by man" (*Genesis*, p. 28). Later in this essay, I discuss "meaning" as humanity's contribution to creation. For more on the idea of creation in partnership in Isaiah, see also Zohar I 5a, which reads Isaiah 51:16 to say not "[you are] My people" (*ammi*) but "with me" (*immi*).

[5] Joseph B. Soloveitchik, *Halakhic Man* (Philadelphia: Jewish Publication Society, 1983), p. 108: "While mysticism repairs flaws in creation by 'raising it on high'…the Halakhah fills the 'deficiency' by drawing the Shekhinah, the Divine Presence, downward into the lowly world…" As partners in creation, humans also have the task of constructing a halakhic world and actualizing it in reality (pp. 71, 99).

[6] God is not bound by nature's laws. The biblical creation story shows God able to limit divine activities and rest on the Sabbath, whereas a force of nature (such as gravity) could not stop; see Jonathan Sacks, *Covenant and Conversation—Genesis: The Book of Beginnings* (Jerusalem: Koren, 2009), p. 21. Nor is God limited by the moral law. Rather, as a perfect agent, God's will must necessarily cohere with the moral law; see Kenneth Seeskin, "Autonomy and Jewish Thought," in *Autonomy and Judaism: The Individual and the Community in Jewish Philosophical Thought*, ed. Daniel H. Frank (Albany: State University of New York Press, 1992), p. 31.

[7] Yoram Hazony, *The Philosophy of Hebrew Scriptures* (Cambridge: Cambridge University Press, 2012), pp. 103–139.

[8] For *v'nishma*, see Zornberg, *Genesis*, pp. 27, 29 ("listen"). Other translations use "obey" (such as JPS 1917 edition). According to *Etz Hayim*, the phrase indicates obeying or seeking to understand. Yet Rabbi Jonathan Sacks has explained that there is not even a word in ancient Hebrew for the term "obedience"; for modern Hebrew a word was borrowed from Aramaic. See Jonathan Sacks, *Covenant and Conversation: Bo*, 28 January 2012 – 4 *Shevat* 5772, available online at http://rabbisacks.org/covenant-conversation-5772-bo-the-necessity-of-asking-questions/. *V'nishma* has been characterized as indicating the people's interpreting and lending meaning to the divine law, as I discuss below. Further below, I also discuss how the commandments are understood not to require strict obedience or subservience, but free and responsible action. For other phrases indicating the people's commitment, cf. Exodus 19:8 (*kol asher dibbeir Ha-shem na'aseh*; "All that God has spoken we will do"), Exodus 24:3 (*kol ha-d'varim asher dibbeir Ha-shem na'aseh*; "All the words which God has spoken will we do"). (Note that I am using *Ha-shem* in place of the four-letter name of God that appears in the biblical text itself.)

[9] See, e.g., the discussion surrounding the lesson of Rav Avdimi bar Ḥama bar Ḥasa at B. Shabbat 88a, and the similar lesson at B. Avodah Zarah 2b.

[10] Tosafot to B. Shabbat 88a, s.v. *moda rabba l'oraita*, as discussed by David Novak in *The Jewish Social Contract: An Essay in Political Theology* (Princeton, NJ: Princeton University Press, 2005), p. 73. The people were *b'al korham* ("overwhelmed").

[11] B. Shabbat 88a; see also Tanḥuma, *Va-y'ḥi* §8. Rabbi Jonathan Sacks translates Esther 9:27 (*kiyy'mu v'kibb'lu ha-y'hudim aleihem*) as "[the Jews] confirmed and took [it] upon themselves," thus showing willing acceptance of the covenant (see his blog for *Ki Tisa* [23 February 2008/5768], available online at http://rabbisacks.org/covenant-conversation-5768-ki-tisa-a-stiff-necked-people/). Recalling the discussion of humanity's partnership with God in creation of the world, Rashi took the talmudic discourse regarding Mount Sinai being held as a barrel over the heads of the people as a reminder of the responsibility that the Jewish people have for the world's continuance: if they had not accepted the Torah, the world would have been destroyed. See his comments to Exodus 19:17, s.v. *va-yityatz'vu b'taḥtit ha-har* and to Genesis 1:31, s.v. *yom ha-shishi*. See also Zornberg, *Genesis*, pp. 27 and 28. See above note 3.

[12] Haggai Ben-Arzi, "The Covenant on the Plains of Moab—*Ki Tavo* 5775" (Parshat Hashavua Study Center, Bar Ilan University, September 5, 2015), available online at www.biu.ac.il/JH/Parasha/eng/kitabo/1085BenArzi.doc

[13] Ibid.

[14] Greenberg, "The Voluntary Covenant," pp. 35–37.

[15] Maimonides, at M.T. Hilkhot Tzitzit 3:11, ruled as follows: "Even though one is not obligated to acquire a [four-cornered] garment and wrap oneself in it in order to [fulfill the commandment of] *tzitzit*, it is not fitting for a pious individual to exempt himself from this commandment."

[16] Jonathan Sacks, "Beyond the Fringe," *Covenant and Conversation-Shelach Lecha* (1 June 2013 / 23 Sivan 5773), reprint available online at http://www.chabad.org/parshah/article_cdo/aid/2230061/jewish/Beyond-the-Fringe.htm.

[17] *Shama*, the verb of which *nishma* is the passive form, is "untranslatable into English because it means [1] to listen, [2] to hear, [3] to understand, [4] to internalise, and [5] to respond" (Jonathan Sacks, *Covenant and Conversation: Bo*, 28 January 2012 / 4 *Shevat* 5772), available online at: http://rabbisacks.org/covenant-conversation-5772-bo-the-necessity-of-asking-questions/.

[18] In the Talmud (at B. Yoma 73b, Nedarim 8a), Moses' statement that the covenant is being forged with "those standing here with us today before God and also those who are not here with us today" (Deuteronomy 29:14) is taken to reference generations not yet born. Hence, all Israel was "foresworn from Sinai." Another talmudic text (B. Shevuot 39a) declares that the souls of all future generations were present at Sinai and freely gave their consent generations before they were born.

[19] Bemidbar Rabbah 13:15. Midrash is an interpretation of the biblical text by the use of illustrative stories, and commentaries through personal experience and human imagination. My thanks to Rabbi Susan Silverman for this insight into midrash.

[20] The Maharshal wrote that all souls were present at Mount Sinai and received the Torah via forty-nine conduits (*kol eḥad ra·ah derekh tzinnor shelo l'fi hassagato*) and in each generation continue to do so (*kol eḥad v'eḥad l'fi hotzeiv m'kor sikhlo*). See Michael Rosensweig, "*Eilu ve-Eilu Divrei Elohim Hayyim*: Halakhic Pluralism and Theories of Controversy," in *Rabbinic Authority and Personal Autonomy*, ed. Moshe Sokol (Northvale, NJ: Jason Aronson, 1992), p. 109, and Leon Wiener Dow, "Opposition to the 'Shulhan Aruch': Articulating a Common Law Conception of the *Halacha*," *Hebraic Political Studies* 3 (2008), esp. p. 352. Rabbi Luria opposed the idea of writing all of the laws into a Shulḥan Arukh, which would be tantamount to saying that the law was not to be debated. A passage from the Talmud of the Land of Israel (at Y. Sanhedrin 4:2, 22a) instructs that the Torah may be interpreted in forty-nine ways affirming an opinion and forty-nine ways opposing it. See Eliezer Berkovits, *Not in Heaven: The Nature and Function of Halakha* (New York: Ktav, 1983), p. 78.

[21] Pesikta D'rav Kahana (ed. Mandelbaum [New York: Jewish Theological Seminary, 1987], p. 224; trans. William G. Braude and Israel J. Kapstein [Philadelphia: Jewish Publication Society, 1975], p. 249); discussed by David Golinkin, "Is Judaism Really in Favor of Pluralism and Tolerance?" in *Responsa*

in a Moment 9.6 (11 Tammuz 5775 / June 2015), available online at: http://www.schechter.edu/is-judaism-really-in-favor-of-pluralism-and-tolerance/.

[22] The canonization and recording process is described in the Torah at Ezra 7 and Nehemiah 10. Regarding the notion that the canonization of the Bible was "the end of prophecy" and that "interpretation took the place of revelation," see David Weiss Halivni, *Revelation Restored: Divine Writ and Critical Responses* (Boulder, CO: Westview, 1997), p. 83.

[23] As preserved at B. Bava Metzia 59b.

[24] See Berkovits, *Not in Heaven*, p. 174.

[25] The full text reads: "Surely, this Instruction which I [God] enjoin upon you this day is not too baffling for you, nor is it beyond reach. It is not in the heavens.... Neither is it beyond the sea.... No, the thing is very close to you, in your mouth and in your heart, to observe it" (Deuteronomy 30:11–14, trans. NJPS). For interpretations regarding the approach to divine law as an internal journey, see Arthur Green, *Radical Judaism: Rethinking God and Tradition* (New Haven: Yale University Press, 2010), esp. pp. 36–37.

[26] Soloveitchik, *Halakhic Man*, p. 81. Soloveitchik wrote of the dialectical tension between human freedom and obedience, as symbolized by Adam 1 and Adam 2 in the creation narratives of Genesis 1 and 2; see his *Lonely Man of Faith* (New York: The Leaves, 1965), pp. 80–81.

[27] B. Sanhedrin 27b.

[28] B. Shabbat 31a.

[29] The obligations arising from this passage are discussed, for example, by Lenn E. Goodman in his "The Individual and the Community in the Normative Traditions of Judaism," in *Autonomy and Judaism*, ed. Daniel H. Frank (Albany, NY: State University of New York Press, 1992), p. 110, n. 48.

[30] Naḥmanides (1194–1270) noted in his comment to Exodus 21:2 (s.v. *ki tikneh eved ivri*) that the subject of the first biblical law is the requirement to free slaves in the seventh year—precisely because the Jews were slaves in Egypt. This notion is also referenced in the first of the Ten Commandments.

[31] Maimonides, M.T. Hilkhot Teshuvah, chap. 5. See Jonathan Sacks, *Covenant and Conversation—Genesis*, p. 22.

[32] B. Pesaḥim 6b.

[33] See, for example, Rashi on Genesis 6:3, s.v. *v'yihyu yamav mei·ah v'esrim shanah*.

[34] Ezekiel 18:20, as cited by Kenneth Seeskin, in his "Ethics, Authority, and Autonomy," in the *Cambridge Companion to Modern Jewish Philosophy*, eds. Michael L. Morgan and Peter Eli Gordon (Cambridge: Cambridge University Press, 2007), p. 192.

[35] M.T. Hilkhot Teshuvah 5.1. See Arthur Hyman, "Aspects of the Medieval Jewish and Islamic Discussion of 'Free Choice,'" in *Freedom and Moral*

Responsibility: General and Jewish Perspectives, eds. Charles H. Manekin and Menachem M. Kellner (Bethesda: University of Maryland, 1997), p. 143. The translation given here comes from the edition of the Mishneh Torah edited and translated by Moses Hyamson (Jerusalem: Boys Town, 1962), p. 86b.

[36] Rashi on Deuteronomy 22:8, s.v. *ki tivneh bayit ḥadash*. See the introductory essay by Charles H. Manekin, "Freedom and Moral Responsibility: A Guide for the Perplexed" in *Freedom and Moral Responsibility*, pp. 9-10. The mishnaic passage at Pirkei Avot 3:19 reads *ha-kol tzafui v'ha-r'shut n'tunah*, which can be translated as "Everything is *predicted* yet permission is granted," thus pointing to determinism. Alternatively, the passage can be translated as "Everything is *observed* and power is granted," meaning that humanity has free will while God watches human actions. See Manekin's introductory essay, p. 9, citing Efraim Elimelech Urbach, *The Sages: Their Concepts and Beliefs*, trans. Israel Abrahams (Jerusalem: Magnes Press, 1975), vol. 1, pp. 257–258.

[37] Kenneth Seeskin, *Autonomy in Jewish Philosophy* (Cambridge: Cambridge University Press, 2001), pp. 5–6.

[38] Ibid., p. 63; Seeskin, "Autonomy and Jewish Thought," p. 23.

[39] Halevi's "Servants" begins with these words: "The servants of time are servants of servants; / only God's servant alone is free." This is the English version by Thomas Kovach, Eva Jospe, and Gilya Gerda Schmidt of Franz Rosenzweig's German translation, as published in Franz Rosenzweig, *Ninety-Two Poems and Hymns of Yehudah Halevi*, ed. Richard A. Cohen (Albany: State University of New York Press, 2000), p. 124.

[40] Leibowitz called for total subservience to God's command, even without regard to its morality. He highlighted a talmudic discussion (B. Berakhot 33b) that one should fulfill the commandment not to remove eggs from the nest while the mother bird is watching (*shillu·aḥ ha-kein*, Deuteronomy 22:6-7) not because of ethics or compassion, but simply because it is commanded.

[41] "Emancipation from the bondage of nature can only be brought about by the religion of the Mitzvot." Yeshayahu Leibowitz, *Judaism, Human Values, and the Jewish State*, ed. Eliezer Goldman, trans. Eliezer Goldman, Yoram Navon, Zvi Jacobson, Gershon Levi, and Raphael Levy (Cambridge, MA: Harvard University Press, 1995), p. 22.

[42] Seeskin, "Autonomy and Jewish Thought," pp. 26–29.

[43] Kant, *Groundwork of the Metaphysics of Morals* 4:412 and 4:446. I explore this comparison further in my forthcoming book, *Positive Freedom in Kantian and Jewish Thought*.

[44] See, for example, Mary Ann Glendon, *Rights Talk: The Impoverishment of Political Discourse* (New York: Free Press, 1991).

[45] Robert M. Cover, "Obligation: A Jewish Jurisprudence of the Social Order," in *Law, Politics, and Morality in Judaism*, ed. Michael Walzer (Princeton:

Princeton University Press 2006), pp. 3–33.

[46] Rights are discussed not in the Torah but rather later, in rabbinic sources with regard to private law. See Haim H. Cohn, *Human Rights in Jewish Law* (New York: Ktav, 1984), as well as his Hebrew-language volume *Zekhuyyot Adam B'mikra U-v'talmud* (Tel Aviv: Israel's Ministry of Defense Books, 1988).

[47] Regarding the human partnership with God in creation, as seen above, the Talmud states: One who recites the verses Genesis 2:1-3 on Friday night, "acknowledging God as the Creator, helps God complete the work of Creation." B. Shabbat 119b, discussed in *Etz Hayim*, on Genesis 2:1, p. 12.

"Therefore, Choose Life" vs. *Carpe Diem*

Edwin C. Goldberg

Introduction

For many years, I thought the charge to "choose life" was an unbearable cliché. Except for the severely depressed, who would not choose life? The Latin phrase *carpe diem* ("seize the day") made much more sense to me. This may be due in part to that wonderful speech in the film *Dead Poets Society*, when the prep school teacher played by the late Robin Williams shows his young charges pictures of now-deceased former students and then declaims:

> They're not that different from you, are they? Same haircuts. Full of hormones, just like you. Invincible, just like you feel. The world is their oyster. They believe they're destined for great things, just like many of you, their eyes are full of hope, just like you. Did they wait until it was too late to make from their lives even one iota of what they were capable? Because, you see gentlemen, these boys are now fertilizing daffodils. But if you listen real close, you can hear them whisper their legacy to you. Go on, lean in. Listen, you hear it?—Carpe—hear it?—Carpe, carpe diem, seize the day boys, make your lives extraordinary.[1]

And the expression *carpe diem* also reminds me of the Saul Bellow novella of the same name (and also starring Robin Williams in the film version, ironically). In short, "seize the day" seems like sound advice, whereas "choose life" sounds, well, redundant.

As a Reform rabbi I am annually confronted with the need to make more sense out of "choose life," since these words are featured in our Yom Kippur morning Torah service, in the reading from Deuteronomy 29 and 30 (read instead of the traditional Torah reading from Leviticus 16). The passage appears in the final book of the Torah, which comprises a restatement of biblical law known by the Greek name "Deuteronomy" (meaning "second law"). Moses is here exhorting the people one last time before he dies and they enter the Promised Land. The phrase "choose life" appears at the end of the appeal (Deuteronomy 30:19), capping Moses' argument. My forebears in the Reform Movement were more interested in not focusing congregational attention on the scapegoat (described as found in the traditional reading) than they were in emphatically promoting the notion of choosing life. Nevertheless, I appreciate their desire to give their congregants a hopeful, positive message on Yom Kippur.

I do believe that an important message can be mined from the phrase "choose life" precisely when we compare it with the Latin *carpe diem*, a phrase first found in the Odes of Horace.[2] It is usually understood as something akin to "strike while the iron is hot" or "gather ye rosebuds while ye may." Horace's teaching reflects a very different sort of wisdom from the biblical exhortation to choose life. In this essay I will compare and contrast the Bible and Horace, in order to see if new life might be breathed into the old cliché of choosing life. It is not a new thing to compare Hebrew and Hellenistic outlooks. Matthew Arnold did so in his famous comparison of Hebraism and Hellenism,[3] and Erich Auerbach's stylistic contrast between the Bible and Homer offers another classic example of this method.[4] A similar approach to the current passage in Deuteronomy may allow us to dive more deeply into the biblical words, and allow us to appreciate the simple profundity of the message of choosing life.

"Therefore, Choose Life" and *Carpe Diem*

To some of the more mindful among us, "seize the day" might imply that we should practice living in the moment. The usual understanding is more akin to the admonition, preserved in Isaiah 22:13, that we should not be among those who say, "Let us eat and drink, for tomorrow we may die." In other words, seizing the day means not worrying about tomorrow. However, I don't think this was the lesson that the teacher in *Dead Poets Society* wanted to share with his young charges. He was arguing that the boys should not *only* worry about their future, but he did not mean that they should be irresponsible about the present or proud of the degree to which they ignore its exigencies.

Carpe diem can be seen as a corrective to putting off pleasure, not a negation of it. Seizing the day is practical only in balance with planning for the days ahead. Isaiah aside, it is not helpful to reduce *carpe diem* to an unholy call to hedonism.

Of course, if we need not reduce *carpe diem* to a cliché, then maybe there is also hope for *u-vaharta ba-hayyim*, "choose life." The context of this appeal, in Deuteronomy 30, is the need for each of us to decide what path in life to take: that of blessing or of curse, of life or of death. Life here is not the literal opting to not die, but rather the sum of all of our choices. The words are a general call to follow a good path. Not many people are going to argue against this appeal, even if their life choices do not always reflect this advice. So once again, we seem to be dealing with a cliché.

But let us not forget that the Hebrew *u-vaharta ba-hayyim* does not mean simply "choose life," but rather "*therefore*, choose life." Often overlooked, I am intrigued by this small word—the Hebrew conjunction *u-*, usually rendered in this verse as "therefore." In general, Hebrew is a much more compact language than English. One Hebrew word might be accurately rendered with several English words. The Hebrew letter *vav* (pronounced as *u-* in our passage) can be understood here to imply a logical conclusion to the argument. Consider, for instance, the translation from the Jewish 1917 edition of the Jewish Publication Society: "I call heaven and earth to witness against you this day, that I have set before thee life and death, the blessing and the curse; therefore choose [*u-vaḥarta*] life, that thou mayest live, thou and thy seed." Hebrew scholars connect the letter *vav* (rendered here as *u-*) with the image of a hook.[5] One might argue that the *vav* in our sentence is the "hook" that turns the cliché into an important message.

The implication is that God has made a case for choosing life—and in a way that goes beyond the oft-repeated parental phrase "Because I said so." So, what does "therefore" in the phrase suggest? What is the great argument that God makes for choosing life? In the biblical context, the exhortation to choose life is immediately preceded by the key declaration by God concerning free choice: "I call heaven and earth to record this day against you, that I have set before you life and death, blessing and cursing; therefore choose life, that both you and your seed may live" (Deuteronomy 30:19). Hence "therefore" indicates the power that each of us has to make any choice we want. Maimonides puts it like this:

> Freedom of choice has been granted to every person: if one desires to turn toward a good path and be righteous, the ability to do so is in one's hands; and if one desires to turn toward an evil path and be wicked, the ability to do so is in one's hands...

This concept is a fundamental principle and a pillar of the Torah and its commandments, as it is written: "See, I have set before you life [and good, and death and evil]" and "See, I set before you today [a blessing and a curse]" (Deuteronomy 30:15)….For were God to decree that a person be righteous or wicked, of if there were to exist something in the very essence of a person's nature that would compel a person toward a specific path, a specific conviction, a specific character trait or a specific deed…how could God command us through the prophets "do this" and "do not do this"?…What place would the entire Torah have? And by what measure of justice would God punish the wicked and reward the righteous?[6]

The teaching of Maimonides encapsulates precisely how we can see "therefore, choose life" as something other than a cliché. We are not prisoners of fate. Nothing is decided in advance. Our choices are freely ours to make, and the consequences that follow are our own as well. When Rabbi Akiva famously taught that "all is foreseen [by God] but free will is given" (M. Avot 3:15), he anticipated Maimonides' formulation by a millennium. The only way the world makes sense is for us to be free agents. Understood in this light, "therefore, choose life" is as hopeful as "seize the day" is pessimistic. Life is uncertain, of course, but we have much we can do to influence its course.

Fate and Free Choice

There are many medieval Jewish commentators who struggle with the contradiction between God knowing the future and our ability to influence our fate.[7] Such arguments are far beyond the scope of this essay. They tend to take Maimonides to task for suggesting that we humans are not equipped to understand how God can know what we will do, and yet insisting that we have free will. To me, and

I suppose many moderns, the argument is moot. We can only see reality through our limited perception, so we really have no rational choice but to "get over" suffering about it and accept things as they are. Indeed, I would argue that belief in our ability to make our own destiny is the only way that "therefore, choose life" makes sense. Any other speculation is at best impractical.

The takeaway from this reading of "therefore, choose life" is the dizzying reality of what it means to be completely free in our agency. If, from our human perspective, nothing is pre-ordained, then life can easily become overwhelming and chaotic—our choices are infinite. This is not a reassuring thought. Some of us do not even like visiting large grocery stores, due to the absurdly large number of choices before us. Now imagine that every moment beckons with complete freedom. If you really believed this to be true, would you seize the day...or plan for another day? Would you serve yourself or nurture others? And is the choice really up to us?

In recent years, some in the various fields of science have argued that free will is only an illusion: it is our biology that encumbers us, not our theology. For instance, Sam Harris wrote in his 2012 book *Free Will* that free will itself is an illusion, and he uses science and his own cognition to attempt to prove his thesis. Here is his conclusion:

> It is not that free will is simply an illusion—our experience is not merely delivering a distorted view of reality. Rather, we are mistaken about our experience. Not only are we not as free as we think we are—we do not feel as free as we think we do. Our sense of our own freedom results from our not paying close attention to what it is like to be us. The moment we pay attention, it is possible to see that free will is nowhere to be found, and our experience is perfectly compatible with this truth. Thoughts and intentions simply arise in the mind. What else could they do? The truth about us is stranger than many suppose: The illusion of free will is itself an illusion.[8]

Sam Harris is a writer who challenges belief in God (his book is dedicated to Christopher Hitchens), and now he appears to be challenging our belief in ourselves as well. I find it hard to argue against his reasoning, which is clever, but that does not mean I agree with him. In other words: I admire his way of arguing but since I believe that his premises are wrong, so too are his conclusions. I choose to believe in a world where there is free choice. (Ideally, I also want to believe in a Deity who cares about the choices I make.) Thus, the "therefore" in "therefore, choose life" to me means rejecting appeals to fatalism. It means expanding our awareness of the choices before us.

Consider the story of the hasid who has left the house of study and is hurrying home. A peasant on the way asks the student to help him with his spilled wares. He responds that he can't. The peasant rebukes the student: "Don't say you can't. Say you won't. You always have a choice." This tale, which I once heard Arthur Green tell in a lecture, is an appeal to stop lying to ourselves. Our actions are not predetermined or based on factors beyond our control. We are free moral agents, and that implies the great power before us. As Marianne Williamson wrote (and was cited by Nelson Mandela in his 1994 inaugural address), "Our deepest fear is not that we are inadequate. Our deepest fear is that we are powerful beyond measure."[9] When seen in this way, "therefore, choose life" ceases to become a cliché and instead can be seen to articulate a terrifying realization. Our responsibility for who we are is far greater than we imagined.

"Choose Life" and Yom Kippur

As a Reform rabbi who often preaches about this text on Yom Kippur, it strikes me as somewhat odd that the Bible presents us with the choice between blessing and curse at the end of Deuteronomy, when we were *already* given this same choice earlier in the book. In Deuteronomy 11:26–28, we read: "Behold I give you this day a blessing and a curse: the blessing, when you shall obey the commandments of the Eternal your God…and the curse if you do not obey the commandments." Why the repetition?

Rabbi Shlomo Riskin, reflecting the teaching of his mentor, Rabbi Joseph Soloveitchik, posits that the repetition is necessary because the context of the two verses is quite different.[10] The first choice happens before we transgress. The second choice is when we are asked to reverse course and return to the blessing. In other words, it is never too late to turn back toward the right path. Yom Kippur's power comes from the very fact that our ability to choose the right path is not at all constricted by the fact that we have already made so many wrong choices. As we read a few verses earlier in Deuteronomy, "the commandment [i.e., the injunction to return to the right path] is not far [from us]" (30:11).

I am haunted by the rabbinic treatment of the character of Elisha ben Abuyah, the heretic who is usually referred to only as "the other." His transgression was so bad, according to the Talmud, that God would not even consider accepting his repentance. And yet, even this transgressor finally achieves a measure of peace. We read in the Talmud:

> Some time later, Elisha ben Abuyah fell ill and Rabbi Meir was told: "Your master is ill." He went to visit him and said, "Repent!" Elisha asked, "Having gone so far, will I be accepted?" Rabbi Meir replied, "Is it not written, 'You allow a person to return, up to their being crushed' (Psalm 90:3), up to the time that life is being crushed out of them?" In that instant, Elisha ben Abuyah began to weep, and then he died. Rabbi Meir rejoiced, saying: "My master, it would appear,

departed in a state of repentance."

However, after he was buried, fire came forth from heaven to burn his grave. They went and told Rabbi Meir: "The grave of your master is on fire!" Rabbi Meir went out, spread his cloak over the grave, and said to him: "Stay this night" — in this world that is wholly night—"and it shall be in the morning"—the world-to-come, all of which is morning—"if the 'One who is good' will redeem you"—that is, the Holy One, who is good, of whom it is said, "The Eternal is good to all and God's mercies are on all God's works." But if God is not willing to redeem you, then I, Meir, will redeem you. "As the Eternal lives, lie down until morning." The fire was then extinguished.[11]

I must stress that this is the only case in classic Jewish literature of which I am aware in which a person's repentance is not accepted by God—at least, not until the very end. And then, ultimately, Elisha's repentance too is accepted. If there is hope for Elisha ben Abuyah, it stands to reason that there is hope for us all. It is never too late to choose to do the right thing, and it is in our power to make the right choice. Therefore, choose life.

Conclusion

Therefore, choose life. In practical terms, what does this actually mean? I would hope that is does not mean that we awake each morning in fear of all the choices before us. Were that the case, many would never rise from bed! Rather, our task as free moral agents is to follow the example set by the great essayist, E. B. White. When, upon retiring from his lengthy career at *The New Yorker*, he was asked for his life philosophy, he responded with these words: "If the world were merely seductive, that would be easy. If it were merely challenging, that would be no problem. But I arise in the morning torn between a desire to improve (or save) the world and a desire to enjoy (or savor) the world. This makes it hard to plan the day."[12]

Herein lies our path. We make ourselves aware of the choices, we determine how we want to divide our time between ourselves and the rest of the world, and—if we choose to live with integrity—we act accordingly. This, then, is the profound simplicity of choosing life. As Oliver Wendell Holmes, Jr. supposedly said: "For the simplicity that lies this side of complexity, I would not give a fig, but for the simplicity that lies on the other side of complexity, I would give my life."[13] Such is the essence of "therefore, choose life"—so simple, and yet so profound.

NOTES

[1] Tom Schulman, *Dead Poets Society* (Alexandria, VA: Alexandria Street Press, 2003).

[2] Horace, *Odes*, Book I. Horace lived from 65 BCE to 8 BCE. The literal meaning from the Latin is "pluck the day," as in "pluck the fruit when it is ripe." The extended version of the phrase is *carpe diem, quam minimum credula postero*, which means "pluck the day, trusting as little as possible in the future."

[3] "Hebraism and Hellenism" is a chapter from Arnold's *Culture and Anarchy* (London: Smith, Elder & Co, 1869); cited from Matthew Arnold, *Culture and Anarchy* (Lanham, MD: Start Publishing, 2017), pp. 99–110.

[4] Erich Auerbach, *Mimesis: The Representation of Reality in Western Literature*, trans. Willard R. Trask (Princeton, NJ: Princeton University Press, 1953), pp. 1–20.

[5] The name of the sixth letter, *vav*, means a nail or hook. It appears thirteen times in the description of the Tabernacle, in the Book of Exodus, where it is generally translated as "hook." This usage syncs with the grammar of the Hebrew language, where *vav* functions as the conjunctive Hebrew form of "and" when prefixed to a word. We might even say that *vav* "hooks" the words together.

[6] M.T. Hilkhot Teshuvah 5:1–3.

[7] For a summary of various Jewish philosophers of the period and their arguments, see Menachem Kellner, *Dogma in Medieval Jewish Thought: From Maimonides to Abravanel* (Oxford: Oxford University Press, 1986).

[8] Sam Harris, *Free Will* (New York: Free Press, 2012), p. 64.

[9] Marianne Williamson, *A Return to Love: Reflections on the Principles of "A Course in Miracles"* (New York: HarperCollins, 1992), p. 190.

[10] Shlomo Riskin, *Devarim: Moses Bequeaths Legacy, History and Covenant* (Jerusalem: Maggid, 2014), p. 344.

[11] Y. Talmud Ḥagigah 2:1, 77b–c; quoting Psalm 145:9 and Ruth 3:13.

[12] Israel Shenker, "E. B. White: Notes and Comment by Author," in *The New York Times* (July 11, 1969), p. 37.

[13] The earliest citation I found for this quote is in Max De Pree, *Leadership is an Art* (New York: Crown, 2004), p. 22.

Choose Life…Or Choose the Good—Which Is It

Reuven P. Bulka

Always Choosing

Life is full of choices. Literally everything we do is preceded by a choice, though most of these choices are subconscious, even spontaneous. We can, of course, choose not to breathe, but the regular breaths we take are not preceded by a choice prior to taking every breath. It would be almost impossible to live that way. Waking up every morning is likewise a choice, in that we can choose to sleep more or sleep the entire day. We do not necessarily explicitly choose to get up, but there is a subconscious element of choice at work.

There are other matters that are more closely linked to conscious choice, including what to eat for a meal, what clothing to wear, what career to choose, whom to marry, etc. We are constantly choosing, whether or not we realize this fact of life. Some choices, such as whether we put on a blue or white shirt, are not that critical; other choices, such as the city or neighborhood in which we choose to live, are more critical. And the life-mate we choose is undoubtedly the most important life-choice we will make.

The Most Critical Choice

Yet even the choice of life-mate is not ultimately the most important or most critical choice we make—it is certainly the most important *specific* choice, but not the most important *general* choice. The latter—the most foundational choice we are presented with—is the very choice of life itself. That imperative choice is spelled out in the Torah:

> Behold I have placed before you today life and the good, and death and the evil...life and death I have placed before you, the blessing and the curse; choose life so that you and your progeny live. (Deuteronomy 30:15, 19)

These are the "do or die" words of Moshe Rabbeinu, a vital component of Moses's parting legacy.[1] He sets the parameters of choice in front of the people in bold, dramatic, and concise terms. Between the beginning and the conclusion of this "either/or" option, there is a bit more articulation of what exactly this choice entails. It is a choice between loving God and following God's ways (including fulfilling God's obligations), on the one hand; and, on the other hand, going astray by embracing false gods and serving them (Deuteronomy 30:16–17).

Moshe Rabbeinu assures the people that although there is technically a choice for them to make, it is not a choice between alternatives of equal worth. In modern parlance, we would categorize it as a no-brainer. Embracing God and God's ways conduces to life; embracing idols conduces to death. What kind of person would knowingly choose death over life?

Lest one think this is merely a spiritual matter, Moshe Rabbeinu leaves no room for doubt. The choice of life includes living, proliferating, and prospering on the land (Deuteronomy 30:16). The choice of death brings with it a shortened life (Deuteronomy 30:18). The choice presented to the community of Israel thus boils down to a choice between longevity and premature death, between prosperity and misery, between good and evil. The choice they are urged to make is the life choice—that is, *u-vaharta ba-hayyim* (Deuteronomy 30:19).

Life or the Good?

One wonders why Moshe Rabbeinu specifically tells his listeners to "choose life" rather than to "choose the good." Why choose life? We correctly think of the Torah as the guide for life, the instructional manual for how to live, the recipe for what is good in life. Why, then, are we asked to base this crucial choice on "life," an ostensibly more material matter, rather than upon the more noble and spiritually uplifting choice of what is "good"?

Adding to this difficulty is the question of how exactly does the compact that we refer to as the covenant work? What choice do we really have? Can we opt out if we want? This is exactly what Moshe Rabbeinu is pleading that we avoid.

The life-good and death-evil equation is presented not as a threat, but instead as a fact of life. Life as designed by God is founded on this very equation. It is a matter of fact that, under normal circumstances, those who embrace a healthful lifestyle with all that it entails will prosper in the many dimensions of life.

The Charity Model

Consider, for example, the simple obligation to share with others, and the various ways we actualize our charity obligations. Tithing and other regulations, such as leaving the gleanings of the field and the corners of the field to the poor (Leviticus 19:9–10), are directed at the actual food supply. Our food must be shared with others. A conspicuous, gluttonous consumer with a voracious appetite might reject this obligation in order to have more to eat.

What are the more likely repercussions of such a choice? Spread out over an entire community, it could mean that more people will die of starvation. But it could also mean that more people will die from overeating. According to the Talmud, more people die from overeating than from famine.[2] This is no doubt due to the principle of cause and effect. The effect of overeating is higher cholesterol levels, obesity, higher blood pressure, attendant heart problems, diabetes, kidney failure, etc.—all of which can lead to premature death. But undereating, as occurs during times of famine, can result in malnourishment—and can likewise lead to premature death.

This is the way the world works. This is the way God made the world. Only a total fool, or a cruel person, does not see the dire consequences of being niggardly.

The connection of famine with the failure to carry out one's charity obligations is most graphically presented in Pirkei Avot, which sees the failure to tithe (among other breaches of the covenant) as directly connected to the severity of the ensuing famine (5:8–9).[3] Sharing, such as by giving *tzedakah*, is the "affirmative action" that counterbalances the imbalances in the world, and allows both the rich and the poor to live better, and longer.

Emotions in Giving

Consider, too, the emotional side of sharing. In its mandate to give charity, the Torah's language addresses the emotional side of giving even as it speaks of the material side, stating that "you must surely open your hand to the poor person" (Deuteronomy 15:8). What exactly is meant by "surely open your hand," as opposed to simply "give"? With a closed hand, one can hardly give anything.

The obligation contained in the verse goes beyond just giving. It is the obligation to engage in charity "with a good heart and with joy," in the words of Rabbi Eleazar Azikri (1533–1600), the author of the *Sefer Ḥareidim* and contemporary of both Rabbi Yosef Karo (1488–1575) and Rabbi Yitzḥak Luria (1534–1572).[4] The open hand is a metaphor for an open-hearted desire, as opposed to a tight-fisted, begrudging, less than enthusiastic attitude. In the end the poor person may have the exact same amount of money or goods, but his or her enjoyment of the gift will be undermined because of being upset at the callous attitude of the benefactor. Food eaten in despondency does not taste as good, does not digest as well, and does not nourish as effectively.

On the other hand, consider a poor person who has received charity that was given with joy, even the ultimate joy that is conveyed when the benefactor expresses genuine gratitude to the poor person for accepting the charity, thereby enabling the benefactor to share, and through that sharing to fulfill the obligation to be charitable. Such a person is uplifted, eats with much more positivity, and will be much more amply enhanced both physically and emotionally.

This is the way that one must engage in charity: with a joyous attitude. This is more than a homily, an added-on nicety; it is, in fact, the halakhic requirement. The end-result of charity bestowed in accordance with the *halakhah* is a society in which the have's and the have-not's appreciate each other, live well together, and enhance each other. The cause-effect is built into the halakhic DNA of the *mitzvah* of *tzedakah*.

Reward or Consequence?

Cause-and-effect is also built in to the very essence of the covenant.

Consider the following verses:

> If you walk in My statutes and keep My commandments and
> do them, then I will give you the rains in their season, so that
> the land shall yield its produce and the trees of the field shall
> yield their fruit...and you shall eat your bread to satisfaction
> and you will dwell in your land in tranquility. (Leviticus
> 26:3–5)

This passage seems to be based the idea of reward—that is, that the reward for following God's dictates is a bountiful life. However, it runs contrary to the well-known talmudic principle that "There is no reward for the fulfillment of the precepts in this world."[5] If the covenant is indeed reward-based, it would be a glaring contradiction of the notion that there is no reward in this world for observance of the commandments. What, then, is the underlying principle at work in the if-then statement in the biblical passage quoted above? If it is not about a reward, what exactly is it talking about?

Concerning the promise that "you shall eat your bread to satisfaction" (Leviticus 26:5), the noted commentator Rabbi Shlomo Yitzḥaki (1040–1135), popularly known as Rashi, explains that it means "you will eat a little bit, but it will be blessed in your digestive system."[6] The blessing is therefore not a promise of great bounty, as abundance will not be necessary. The blessing will instead derive from a mindset that is not fixated on excessive consumption, but rather on having what is necessary, with the rest being shared with others.

When everyone's focus reflects a balance of concerns, taking only what is needed but no more, sharing with others so they have enough, and not despoiling the environment in search of excess, then everything works out. People have what they need, the land is not abused, and tranquility reigns. This is not so much a "reward" for behaving responsibly as much as it is a natural consequence of doing so.

The Life Choice

Returning to the basic question of why we are asked to choose life (as opposed to choosing the good), we can now see the reason: being asked to choose life is a perpetual reminder that the primary value underlying God's commandments for us is affirmation of life. It is a subtle but clear reminder that the choice of good is a life-choice, since the Torah is designed to enhance life in terms of both quantity and quality. And this is consistent with the rabbinic understanding that when we are told to "live by them [i.e., the commandments]" (Leviticus 18:5), it means that we are "to live by them, and not to die by them."[7]

The discipline, the regulations, the full complement of obligations and prohibitions—burdensome as they might seem at times—were designed by God to affirm life. Should a lurking danger to life arise as a result of the fulfillment of a precept, such as a diabetic whose fasting on Yom Kippur is life-threatening, the obligation to fulfill the *mitzvah* is suspended.

The ultimate gauge of whether or not an action is "good" is whether or not it enhances life. Life affirmation is primary; good is secondary, insofar as it derives from life itself. The same dynamic that pertains regarding charity—its relatively clear connection to life and what establishes it as good—is at work in all the precepts of the Torah.

Other examples of this theme are found in many other *mitzvot*: Shabbat and its relaxation motif, bringing the first fruits and the gratitude thereby elicited, Torah study and its meditative focus. This is not to suggest that these are the only values underlying these (or other) precepts. Rather, I mean to suggest that no matter what the fundamental reason for any of the commands may be, they are all in some way an affirmation of life, either in quantity or in quality.

In choosing life, we affirm God and the plan that God has implemented for the world. We can reject this choice, but in so doing we are—in a significant, qualitative way—rejecting life, even as we are also expressing our desire to live. That makes little, if any, sense. In effect, there really is no choice, no viable alternative to life affirmation.

How Often?

We are urged to choose life, but exactly how often must we make that choice? Is it a once-and-for-all choice? Is it a daily choice? A yearly choice?

Consider the fascinating insight of Rabbi Eleazar Azikri in a passage in his *Sefer Ḥareidim*, dealing with how obligations imposed by the Torah relate to the various parts of the body—the heart, eyes, ears, mouth, hands, feet, etc. Seeing the imperative to "choose life" as itself being one of the precepts, he writes: "If a prohibition or potential prohibition presents itself and the individual refrains, that person fulfills the obligation to choose life."[8] This understanding opens up an entirely new window into the directive to choose life. Every time we are challenged by a tempting but forbidden opportunity, we are confronted with a choice. Do we take the easy route and allow what is prohibited, or do we reject the easy route and choose to affirm the obligation?

Every time we choose correctly, we not only fulfill the immediate obligation—be it regarding Shabbat, rejecting non-kosher foods, resisting the temptation unlawfully to acquire property, etc.—we also fulfill the over-arching *mitzvah* to choose life. The obligation to choose correctly (that is: the obligation to choose life) can appear at any time. In any situation when temptation lurks—such as the temptation to sleep in and miss reciting the Shema at its proper time, or the desire to eat on Yom Kippur when hunger pangs are very strong—choice is necessary.

This idea of choosing is at work in the rabbinic admonition that we "reckon the loss incurred in the performance of a commandment against its recompense and the gain obtained through the committing of a transgression against its loss." (M. Avot 2:1). With this formula, we are supplied with the right questioning tools to reach the right conclusion.

Every time the right choice is made, it is a faith-reinforcing endeavor, an honest and profound confrontation with alternatives, and an exercise in free will. There may be those who see a willingness to acknowledge the challenge *itself* as a vacillation in faith, basing themselves on the supposition that temptation so strong can only be a sign of weakness. Rabbi Azikri implicitly argues to the contrary, that facing down such a challenge is a singular opportunity to fulfill a critical *mitzvah*. The opportunity to "choose life" presents itself not once in a lifetime, but often.

Continuous choosing brings renewed vigor to our faith affirmation, and removes the danger that such faith affirmation becomes reduced to rote, mechanical, even meaningless behavior. "Choose life," says the biblical imperative. "Keep on choosing life" is the way to truly capture the heart and soul of the commandment.

NOTES

[1] Moshe Rabbeinu means "our teacher Moses" and it is a traditional epithet for the great biblical leader.

[2] B. Shabbat 33a.

[3] Rashi (to Avot 5:8) sees this as a measure-for-measure consequence.

[4] Eleazar ben Moshe Azikri, *Sefer Hareidim* §23. See further on this my *Best-Kept Secrets of Judaism* (Southfield, MI: Targum/Feldheim, 2002), pp. 99–101. The expression "with good heart and joy" is based on Kohelet 9:7, *leikh ekhol b'simhah lahmekha u-sh'teih v'leiv-tov yeinekha* ("go eat your bread in joy and drink your wine with a good heart").

[5] B. Kiddushin 31b.

[6] Rashi to Leviticus 26:5, s.v. *va-akhaltem lahm'khem la-sova*, citing Sifra, *B'hukotai* 1:7.

[7] B. Sanhedrin 74a.

[8] *Sefer Hareidim* §20, p. 57. And cf. further my *Best-Kept Secrets of Judaism*, pp. 198–200.

Choosing Life

James Jacobson-Maisels

The Torah teaches in Deuteronomy, "I call heaven and earth to witness against you this day: I have put before you life and death, blessing and curse. Choose life—if you and your offspring would live—by loving YHVH your God, heeding His commands, and holding fast to Him. For thereby you shall have life and shall long endure upon the soil that YHVH swore to your ancestors—Abraham, Isaac, and Jacob—to give to them" (Deuteronomy 30:19–20).[1] I recall sitting with my friend Jonathan in *shul* twenty years ago and joking with each other: "Hmm, life or death, blessing or curse...I think I'll take life, please!" Choosing life seems obvious; it doesn't seem like much of a choice.

But of course, the real question is much less obvious than that. Of course, we all want to live. Of course, we all want blessings. But what does it mean to really be alive? The Talmud teaches, "The righteous in their deaths are called alive...[whereas] the wicked in their lives are called dead."[2] All too often, we walk through the world not fully alive. We are not fully present; we have not fully claimed who we are. Instead of living fully, we live out a kind of living death, an inability to fully inhabit our lives. We are disconnected, we are numbed, we are lost in anxiety and stress, we are depressed, we are overwhelmed and frantic, we are zoned out on TV/Facebook/Twitter/surfing the internet, we are lost in fantasy, we are trapped in fulfilling someone else's expectation or vision for ourselves, and we are protecting ourselves from feeling anything too strongly. We are protecting ourselves from really feeling the fullness of life which is our joy, wonder, fullness, and our dance...and which is *also* our anger, fear, sorrow, and loss. What is the cure for the situation we find ourselves in, for a modern world that seems to cut us off from life? How do we choose life? By loving God, our verse tells us. By loving, more particularly, YHVH—that peculiar form of the Hebrew verb "to be" which is the divine name, that which was, is, and will be. We love this life, this very moment, this truth. And in loving life, we choose life and we become truly alive. We reconnect with our childlike delight and wonder in life, in my baby daughter's delight in her encounter with the world, with herself, with all that is new and all that she already knows. We reconnect with the delight of encounter itself, of meeting, of noticing, and of being awake to that which presents itself.

As adults, this does not come naturally. Rather, as the verse commands us, we have to choose. We can choose to be "wicked"— disconnected from life, from others and ourselves, and so act in ways that are harmful to ourselves and others, and therefore live a living death. Or we can choose to be "righteous"—profoundly connected to ourselves, to our life and to others, and so naturally compassionate and naturally engaged and alive. Choosing life is choosing to engage with life, to appreciate life, and to feel gratitude for life. A parallel source to the talmudic passage cited above reads: "The wicked in his life is considered as if dead because he sees the setting sun and does not bless 'the One who creates light' [the first blessing of the formal morning service]; [he sees the] setting [sun] and does not bless 'who brings the evening' [the first blessing of the evening service]; he eats and drinks and does not bless. But the righteous bless on every particular thing."[3] We walk through life too often with the wonders and majesty of nature before us, with the gifts of food and drink, yet we do not bless. And we do not bless in a way that actually connects us to the wonder of that moment. Even one who says the traditional prayers in the morning and evening, who actually does recite "the One who creates light" and "who brings the evening," does not necessarily connect that blessing to the actual experience of the encounter with the sun as it rises in the east and sets in the west. But the righteous individual, the one who is truly alive, recites the appropriate benediction whenever the possibility arises. Righteous people notice life as it presents itself to them, and they respond by choosing to engage with that life, by choosing to appreciate that life, by choosing to give thanks for that life. What is the difference between living and dying? It is the wonder and awe of life, the appreciation for this extraordinary thing that is life, that is the cycles of nature, and that is the food and drink we are gifted with each day.

The Polish hasidic master Rabbi Yehudah Leib Alter of Ger, called the Sefat Emet (1847–1905), takes this theme further in a teaching on the Torah portion *Ki Tissa*:

> It is written "Remember that you were a slave [in the land of Egypt and YHVH your God redeemed you]; therefore I command [this matter upon you today]" (Deuteronomy 15:15). "Remember that you were a slave in the land of Egypt [and YHVH your God freed you from there with a mighty hand and an outstretched arm; therefore YHVH your God has commanded you] to observe the Sabbath [day]" (Deuteronomy 5:15). For it [the Sabbath] is a testimony concerning the exodus from Egypt, by which the Israelites merited the aspect of liberation, that is, not to be enslaved to the body. For this is the essence of liberation. Therefore, Shabbat is connected to them [the Israelites].
>
> And it is written "It [Shabbat] shall be a sign for all time [between Me and the people of Israel]: (Exodus 31:17). For in truth God always gives the people Israel the capacity to act beyond nature and the modes of behavior of all creatures.

But [this quality] is hidden during the six days of creation and is revealed on Shabbat. Shabbat is the exception that teaches something about the general situation. We say "[we give thanks]…for Your miracles which are with us each day" [in the Modim blessing of the Amidah]. Similarly [we say], "into Your hand I deposit my spirit" [Psalm 31:6, paraphrased in Adon Olam]. For though nature continues on its course, the Israelite must be drawn after heavenly behavior. Concerning this, it is written: "Choose life" (Deuteronomy. 30:19).[4]

The teaching begins with two verses, both of which begin with the same words and address parallel subjects: the first verse, the obligation to free a slave at the Sabbatical year; and the second verse, the obligation to observe the Sabbath both for oneself, one's family, and one's servants. The teaching thus begins with the question of the connection between liberation and the Sabbath (whether every seven days or every seven years; and whether personal, agricultural, or cosmic). The Sefat Emet continues by describing this liberation as the ability to not be enslaved by the body. In hasidic parlance, drawing from medieval usage grounded in Neoplatonic teachings and language as imbibed from the Arabic world, the word "body" (*guf*) here does not literally denote our *actual* bodies, but rather something closer to our egos. For example, pride is classically referred to as a corporeal or embodied quality, while humility is a spiritual quality. But in fact pride is no more physical than humility: they are both mental/emotional qualities of an individual. Denoting pride as "bodily" in Jewish texts describes a certain relationship to the self. Bodily qualities are those that are connected to the ego, the self, and the illusion (according to these thinkers) of separation (versus the truth of non-duality in these approaches' understanding of the nature of the world). Spiritual qualities are those connected to self-release or annihilation, and the recognition of non-separation. Of course an ego-driven desire is often expressed through the body, and so this may be one reason for the development of the use of the term "body" in this way.

In particular, what Shabbat symbolizes and makes possible is the ability to "act beyond nature and the modes of behavior of all creatures." That is, Shabbat symbolizes our ability to not fall into habitual or instinctual patterns but rather to actively choose modes of acting and living that are liberating. Most basically, these verses come to teach that although our egos and our desire for wealth, success, and power might have us continue to force those under our power to work continuously and perhaps even in perpetuity (as well as potentially to enslave ourselves to continual labor), the Torah clearly tells us that we are obligated—through Shabbat and the Sabbatical year—to instead choose liberation for both ourselves and others.[5] We are commanded to liberate ourselves from consumerism, from acquisitiveness, and from the constant striving for wealth, security, and power.

In a broader sense, our ability—through Shabbat—to break with our habitual tendencies, to let go of that next project or bit of work which needs to be done, or some other thing (whatever it is) that we want to acquire—is liberating and it is what enables us to choose life, to fully engage with life. Indeed, the Sefat Emet continues by making this very connection, claiming that our offering thanksgiving each day in the Modim prayer, as well as our surrender of self and giving ourselves to God daily by singing the Adon Olam hymn and taking its lessons to heart, is what it means to choose life. In the presence of deep gratitude or awe, is not everything more fully alive, more fully vibrant, even evanescent with some extra presence or expansiveness? Gratitude and surrender, the Sefat Emet claims, is what it means for us to abandon our harmful habits and instead "be drawn after heavenly behavior." That is, our liberation and our choice of life is less a forceful assertion or conquering of harmful habitual patterns, and more a surrendering to a deeper and more profound truth of who we are, a depositing of ourselves into Divinity's hands. Trust and surrender are not the opposite of liberation, but rather its deepest meaning. Choice, especially the choosing of life, is not an assertion of will but is rather a letting go into that which is true.

The Sefat Emet then continues:

> The blessed Holy One "renews in His goodness the work of creation every day," as it says in the holy Zohar that this passes through us always, that for our sake something of the hidden light is revealed every day, so that Israel will merit to cleave to the inwardness of the creation. This is the illumination that spreads out from Shabbat to the six days of the week. For Shabbat is observed the whole week, but only in an enclothed form. But the Israelites were instructed: "*Akh*, keep My Sabbaths" (Exodus 31:13). The meaning of *akh* is: without being enclothed in garments. Rather, [one must keep] the essence of Shabbat. And in truth this depends on the spiritual practice of a person in one's ability to strip oneself of corporeality. And according to one's [level of] purification [one receives the essence of Shabbat], as it says: "Like water reflecting a face back to itself" (Proverbs 27:19). Therefore Shabbat is a remembrance of the exodus from Egypt, which is testimony that the Israelites are free and merit Shabbat. In the exodus from Egypt, God transformed nature for the Israelites. This testimony exists in every particular, for everything that merits heavenly aid is true testimony of a person's spiritual practice for God's sake.[6]

Choosing life is seeing the renewal of every moment, the newness of every moment, the vitality of every moment. As the Sefat Emet claims in the Zohar's name, this renewal is a constant aspect of our experience; it "passes through us always." But how often do we notice that it is there?

Choosing life is choosing to pay attention to this truth, choosing to live within that constant renewal rather than in the illusion of permanence and continuity, of habit and predictability, of never allowing oneself to be truly surprised. And why not allow ourselves to be surprised? Is our resistance to wonder not just some means of self-protection, for wonder feels exquisitely vulnerable? Being present to this wonder, to this renewal, to the constant possibility and reality of change, is the presence of Shabbat, the liberation of Shabbat—within the week and within every moment. Our task and practice, as the Sefat Emet describes it, is to learn how to taste liberation not only at peak moments and at moments of grace, but also to cultivate it as an intentional practice within our everyday life. This liberation from striving, the delight (*oneg*[7]) in life, is waiting for us—but it is hidden, enclothed in the seemingly mundane, predictable, fixed operation of the universe. But if we look, the Sefat Emet is telling us, that hidden light is there. We can observe the essence of Shabbat at all times, and not only in the twenty-five hours of formal Shabbat. To do this, to choose liberation and life, we must strip ourselves of corporeality—which, as we have noted above, means to loosen the bonds of our egos. It is to step away from the constant pursuit of our desires, from the constant attempt to protect ourselves and make ourselves safe, and to open to life as it actually presents itself right now. This life as it actually presents itself is never perfect. There is almost always something present that we would prefer to not be there, and there is almost always something lacking that we would prefer to be present. Yet what we ultimately receive from this practice of opening to life as it is, just as in a reflection, is what we offer. To the extent that we are able to loosen our own chains, life opens up before us and liberation is present.

This liberation is the recognition that we are never trapped. The message of the plagues in Egypt, the Sefat Emet explains, is that nothing is fixed; nature, *our* nature, can be changed. Every time we "merit heavenly aid" by breaking our habitual patterns, by returning (if only for a moment) to presence and an embrace of life, we demonstrate that life can be chosen, that we do not have to be trapped in the many varieties of living death that we often play out in our lives. Moreover, we demonstrate that we can choose life, that we can be alive even in the midst of death—whether we are actually facing our own imminent demise or grappling with the approaching death of a loved one, or the many deaths, the many losses, that we all face every day. It is the ability to die into each moment, to place ourselves in God's hands, and so to surrender into death (which is, in fact, what it means to be fully alive). And we do this choosing by choosing service. Our spiritual practice, our choice of life, is not a selfish act. It is for God's sake, for the Shekhinah's sake, for the healing and repair of the world and ourselves. We are not excluded from this healing. Rather, as early hasidic teachings on prayer make clear, healing our own wounds and waking ourselves to joy is part of the process of healing the wounds of the world, the wounds of the Divine, and waking both the Divine and the world to the inherent joy of existence.[8]

We are commanded by our tradition to choose life, to live life fully, to be alive even in the midst of death, even in the midst of the pain, sorrow, and loss that visits every human life. I don't want to die having not lived fully. I don't want to die having not fully opened this life to who I am, to this gift of vibrancy and divinity.

What about you?

I want to bless the sun's rising and setting. I want to bless the gift of food. I want to feel the liberation of Shabbat in the midst of my everyday experience. I want to feel the peace and joy of opening to life just as it is. I want to know the liberation and excitement of letting go of unhealthy patterns. I want to trust deeply enough that I can offer myself in service to the healing of the Divine, of the world, and of myself. I want to open to the delight that is the very nature of life, of Shabbat, of rest—just as it is.

What about you?

I often don't remember to make this possible. I often get lost in habitual patterns of protection and fear. But sometimes I can remind myself of the taste of true liberation, the taste of Shabbat, and that helps me remember how to inhabit myself again. This is part of our task. A teaching of the Babylonian sage Rav is preserved in the Talmud of the Land of Israel, where we learn that "a person will one day have to give an accounting [before the heavenly court] for everything his eyes saw that he did not eat."[9] Rav wasn't just talking about food. He was talking about fully engaging with life. He was teaching us, as our verse does, that we have an obligation to fully engage with life. It is not some extra luxury; it is what this life is for. As our verse on choosing life says, "I call heaven and earth to witness against you this day: I have put before you life and death, blessing and curse. Choose life!" (Deuteronomy 30:19).

What day? This day. Every day is this day. Every day we have the opportunity to ask whether we are going to choose life today. Every day we have the opportunity to ask whether we are going to open to the wonder, the liberation, the rest, the awe, and the surrender that the Sefat Emet describes. I hope we each choose life this day.

NOTES

[1] YHVH is my rendering of the four-letter name of God (*yod-hei-vav-hei*) that appears throughout Scripture.

[2] B. Berakhot 18a–b.

[3] *Midrash Tanḥuma, V'zot Ha-b'rakhah* (end).

[4] *Sefat Emet* to *parashat Ki Tissa* 5654 (ed. Petrikow, 1905), p. 210.

[5] The full text of the commandment concerning Shabbat (as part of the Decalogue) in Deuteronomy 5:12–15 makes clear that rest is commanded both of the receiver of the commandment and of everyone else in that individual's household: "Observe the Sabbath day and keep it holy...you shall not do any work—you, your son or your daughter, your male or female slave, your ox or your ass, or any of your cattle, or the stranger in your settlements, so that your male and female slave may rest as you do."

[6] *Sefat Emet* to *parashat Ki Tissa* 5654, pp. 210–211. The phrase "renews in His goodness the work of creation every day" comes from the daily liturgy (morning service).

[7] As in the phrase *oneg Shabbat*, "the delight of the Sabbath." Colloquially, that delight is often translated into the pleasure of food, drink, and company; hence the use of the phrase *oneg Shabbat* as a way to refer to post-synagogue mingling, drinking, and eating.

[8] See R. Moshe Ḥayyim Ephraim of Sudkylkow, *Degel Maḥaneh Efrayim* (ed. Jerusalem 1963), p. 34 (to *parashat Toldot*), as translated in Louis Jacobs, *Hasidic Prayer* (New York: Schocken, 1972), pp. 28–29.

[9] Y. Kiddushin 4:12, 66b.

Choosing Life: A How-To Guide

Gidon Rothstein

In the two-word biblical command to "choose life" (*u-vaharta ba-hayyim*), each word calls for detailed discussion. Here I will take up the first of those words, focusing on the complications that come with choice. I aim to show that the command to choose life assumes a general capability to choose, but traditional sources see that capability as more fragile than we might at first realize. Reviewing the ways in which we might fail to choose as well as we could, I hope to suggest some ways that we might become more adept at being sure to choose, in all sorts of positive ways—including choosing life.

The Bible's Call for Choice

The commandment is found in Deuteronomy 30:19, where Moses reminds the people that he has placed before them "life and death… blessing and curse." Verse fifteen had linked life with "good" and death with "evil"; the choice in question is not of one particular act, but rather of an entire way of life which can then lead to bounty, as well as to long-term settlement on the land promised to the patriarchs.

"Life," in this context, is a general term for acting correctly and properly—that is, according to the norms spelled out in Scripture. That explains why the Torah does not speak of choice in regard to each individual commandment; all of them are included in this catch-all call to "choose life."

To understand this idea a bit better, let's recall that the rabbis spoke of 613 biblical obligations but did not enumerate them. Later authorities, starting as early as *Halakhot G'dolot* in the ninth century CE, and including Maimonides and Naḥmanides, also produced lists specifying the precise commandments to be found in various verses in the Torah. The commandment to "choose life" does not appear on any of the major lists of the 613 *mitzvot* I have consulted—that of *Halachot G'dolot*, Maimonides, Naḥmanides, or the twelfth-century *Sefer Mitzvot G'dolot* of Rabbi Moses Coucy. I think that is because these words constitute a general call for adherence to "life," and are therefore not considered a specific *mitzvah*. (Maimonides points out, in his rules for counting *mitzvot*, that any such general assertions by the Torah will not be included in his list—and Naḥmanides accepts this principle as well.)

To say more on what we're supposed to choose would mean delving into what the verse means by "life," but I leave that for another occasion—at least in part because such a discussion could not but lead to fruitless disagreement and debate over the nature of God, Torah, and the commandments. In this essay, I will focus more narrowly on the call to choose, because it implies a series of obligations that might not be immediately apparent. It to these that I now turn my attention.

Human Beings Can Choose

First, the phrase reminds us that people do have choice, which creates an obligation to make that choice well. As in many areas of Jewish thought and practice, Maimonides expressed this idea forcefully and felicitously in the following passage:

> Everyone has the freedom to turn him or herself to a good path, to become a righteous person, or vice versa....[When God reacted to Adam and Eve's eating of the Tree of Knowledge, He said that] humanity has become singular in the world...in that knowing what is good and what is evil, and being able to choose between them.
>
> Do not consider what the fools of the nations and most unsophisticated Jewish people say, that God decrees whether each person will be righteous or evil; not so, but every person can be as righteous as our master Moses or as evil as Jeroboam, and so with all the character traits, and nothing coerces or decrees one way or the other. Each person makes that determination for him or herself...
>
> This is a great principle, a pillar of the Torah and the commandments...[1]

Other Jewish thinkers have taken somewhat different positions on the question. Rabbi Ḥasdai Crescas (1340–1411) in his *Or Hashem*, for example, comes closest to a modern psychological view, writing that humans are wholly shaped by the inputs in their lives—mostly the threat of punishment and the promise of reward. It seems to me, however, that a broad mainstream of Jewish thinkers through the ages have adopted Maimonides' idea (or something close to it): namely, that human beings have free will and can therefore in fact choose life. When we choose wisely, we are rewarded; when we choose poorly, it is our own fault.

I stress this point at the outset because, as in Maimonides' time, there are many in our own age who do not accept it, even among Jews who put much time and effort into their observance. Much in our surrounding culture sends messages to the contrary, telling us that external factors mold us, to the extent that we cannot be held responsible for our choices or their outcomes. My teacher, Rabbi Yehudah Amital, of blessed memory, used to complain about psychologists who claimed that people's behavior is fully deterministic, purely a function of the pleasant and unpleasant reactions that have accrued to their actions in the past.

The call to "choose life," with all that implies, begs to differ, begs to remind us that we each choose our path; we each choose who we become.

Guarding It Carefully

Important as the ability to choose is to the Torah's picture of Jewish life, it is not inalienable. In the same work cited above, Maimonides writes:

> It is possible to sin so greatly, or to commit so many sins, that the punishment meted out by the Judge of Truth for these willing and deliberate sins is that the ability to repent will be taken away, so that one dies because of all the sins one has committed....So, too, Scripture says: "They insulted the messengers of God, reviling His words, and mocking His prophets, until the wrath of God at His nation could not be healed" (2 Chronicles 36:16)—that is, they sinned willfully to the point that their punishment was that repentance, the balm for what ailed them, was taken away from them. That's why the Torah says, "I will harden Pharaoh's heart"—at first he sinned himself, causing ill to the Jews living in his land… and so justice was that repentance would be withheld from him…[2]

Later in the passage, Maimonides explains that taking away people's free will turns them into abject lessons for the rest of humanity, a living warning about what can happen to those who consistently fail or refuse to choose well. Such people, says Maimonides, live out the rest of their lives as examples for others, living proof that free will can be lost. They may sometimes die right away or sometimes after a long time, but the loss of free will means that they are no longer being judged for their actions: they are in fact already being punished, insofar as they are no longer able to right their own ship and cannot redirect themselves to a better path.

Maimonides does not give us more exact guidance on the issue, but his examples of those who lost their free will offer two important ways to avoid that fate. We should listen to those who bear God's messages, and we should refrain from acting so evilly that God gives up on us, deciding to use the example of our own behavior as a warning to others.

Each of those strategies raises questions that moderns can debate vigorously and interminably. Who is God's messenger? Which messages of observance, practice, and character are from God and which are the ones humans have made up on their own? What counts as evil and what as ordinary weakness?

Step 1: Don't Let God Take It Away; Avoid Addiction

The above questions are not amenable to specific or exact answers, but the first item on our list for how to choose life is to realize that our right to choose is precious and it can be lost. We must therefore keep these questions in mind, as part of making sure we do not lose this ability. Aside from the worry that God might suspend our right to choose, Maimonides also discusses the possibility that in some cases we can even fail to realize that we have given up that right and ability, have thrown it away—and so we must be sure to preserve our *ability* to choose.

Maimonides' discussion of this aspect of free will appears in a context about forcing a man to give his wife a *get*, a bill of divorce. In certain cases, Jewish law obligates a man to divorce his wife, and a court will coerce him should he refuse. As a technical matter, it is not at all clear how such coercion could be legitimate, since Jewish law maintains that a *get* must be given of the husband's own free will. To alleviate this technical problem, the court applies pressure on the husband until he says "Yes, I want to give her the *get*." (There are other areas where *halakhah* allows courts to force action; in those, too, the court will force not only the action but the person saying that he or she wants to perform the action.)

Maimonides is troubled by the obvious fiction: how does twisting a man's arm until he *claims* to want to do this act help us, when we all know he is only responding to unbearable pressure? He explains:

> Why isn't the *get* invalid, since he's being coerced…because we only consider someone coerced when forced to do that which is not obligated by the Torah…
>
> But someone whose evil inclination was controlling them to neglect a commandment or to sin, and was hit (or flogged) until they did what they was obligated…that's not being coerced. Rather, *such a person coerced oneself* (emphasis added) with his own bad view (that he originally intended to follow).[3]

This explanation understands that we can, at times, blind ourselves to what we *really* want. We let ourselves be convinced that we should choose that which is, in fact, detrimental to us.

Any form of addiction fits this rubric. It seems especially true in the case of addicts who destroy their lives (and harm people, such as their families, whom they in fact love). In such cases, it makes perfect sense to apply Maimonides' idea: that they are not in full control of themselves. Sometimes, we restrain such people to prevent them from harming themselves; sometimes, they recognize that they need restraint and choose it themselves. But when they do not, we can assume they would have, had they only been in their right mind—and so we then choose it *for* them, as it were.

A court can only coerce a *get* when it has determined that the marriage is irretrievably broken and so the husband must bid farewell to his wife. Once that determination has been made, his resistance shows he is not thinking clearly about the issue—and so the court's coercion can be seen as only helping him find his way back to what he would have done independently had his mind been clearer.

The idea of "right mind" is a sliding scale, not an all-or-nothing question. There are those who have lost their free will almost completely, such as addicts of various kinds or those struggling with mental illness; but there are many lower levels of loss of free will as well, where we know how we want to act but somehow fail to live up to those standards nonetheless. This may be in how we speak to others, in the choices we make about what foods to eat, or in whether and how often we exercise, or study Torah. In such cases, when we cannot motivate ourselves to do what we know we should, or when we fail to resist doing what we know we should not, we are not in full possession of our free will in that area of our lives. To be able to choose life, we have to be able to choose, full stop.

Step 2: Use It So You Don't Lose It

There is no fail-safe, guaranteed prescription to avoiding the loss of free will. It's a matter of being aware of the danger, of seeing ourselves and others lose that free will (in ways both big and small), and rededicating ourselves to the self-control and wise decision-making that are the central components of choosing wisely.

The examples I have given until now took for granted that we know absolutely what we ought to choose. But even that is not always so simple. There are many areas of life—including some in the sphere of religion—where the "right" choice is far from clear. Part of being able to choose life is knowing which are the choices that actually are aligned with choosing life, putting ourselves in a position to know what's what. Sometimes that may be a binary question, where one choice takes us toward life and the opposite choice moves us in the opposite direction, and that itself becomes the reason we will be unable to choose life. On any yes/no issue—Does God exist? Are people obligated to act as traditional Judaism says? Is four drinks too many to then drive? May parents ever spank children?—choosing wrong makes it immediately impossible to choose life.

That's all the more true of the many issues where the answer lies on a continuum and we need to know where a red line has been crossed. Some of the examples in the previous paragraph are, on further inspection, less black-and-white than a yes/no presentation suggests. Spanking children, for example, might be a question of a blurry line between discipline and abuse. Even where there are clear lines, such as driving immediately after downing many drinks, where the line is crossed might be up for debate. Identifying red lines is part of preserving our ability to choose life, in the sense that part of the call to choose is a call to know which choices are which.

There are also cognitive barriers to choosing well. We know that the framing of questions affects the way people answer. Based on that, some have argued for presenting issues to the public in such a way as to help them find their way to a good decision. (This approach, called "libertarian paternalism," is found in *Nudge: Improving Decisions About Health, Wealth, and Happiness.*[4]) If we are honest with ourselves, we admit that these choices are not simple or necessarily intuitive; to maximize our confidence that we are ready and able to choose life, we must work at getting better at choosing.

Step 3: Cultivate Skill at Evaluating Choices; See the People Around Us

Knowing how easily we can make wrong choices—even as we're confident we're making the right ones—reminds us that to "choose life" takes training and practice. Aside from maximizing our confidence that we know what counts as "life," it means disciplining ourselves to do that which we come to believe is right, and to see it all as part of building up our skill at choosing.

Choosing poorly matters, even on insignificant issues—because it weakens the choosing muscle (as it were). Moreover, part of the ability to choose well includes the responsibility to learn what constitutes a good or bad choice. Failing to cultivate that which points toward the good, and allowing oneself to come to believe that that which is bad is actually good, makes the choosing muscle irrelevant. That, too, is a way to fail to choose life.

Society impacts our choices as well, shaping our understanding of what to choose. In the Book of 2 Kings, we read that Jehoram son of Jehoshaphat did evil in the eyes of God, for he had married into the house of Ahab, and walked in their ways (8:18). Despite his father's great righteousness, Jehoram forged enough of a connection with his in-laws that they, rather than his own father, became his frame of reference. I doubt that Jehoram saw himself as evil, that he awoke every day knowing he had chosen a path counter to what good sense would tell him to do. That's the deeper tragedy of failing to heed the command to choose life: many of us are certain that we *are* choosing life—even though Scripture might say of us, as it did of Jehoram, that we did evil in God's eyes.

This is true concerning family relationships, friendships, and the people whose views we come to accept—whether philosophers, authors, politicians, or other public figures. On some matters, we are sufficiently expert that we can decide our path on our own. But in many areas we follow others we deem wiser or more knowledgeable. Health and finance are two such examples; for most of us, it's also true of religion, where we are guided by rabbis or scholars. And it is in the realm of religion where we primarily choose life in the biblical sense.

We should follow the advice of others; we should be aware that we don't have all the answers, but this means that our choice of advisors reverberates throughout the rest of our choices. If we decide to follow medical advice that turns out to be wrong, we might damage our health. The same goes for what we decide God wants of us. Part of choosing life is being as sure as we can that we accept the determinations of only those who deserve to have their determinations accepted.

Troublingly, that is not as clear as we would like. Almost all ideas, including religious ones, are a matter of debate. Whose views we decide to accept might mean we entrench ourselves in a worldview, broad or specific, that itself hampers our ability to choose life.

Step 4: Choose the Right Influences

Our horizons of choice are shaped tremendously by those around us. For example, most of us would never think of flouting communal standards. And this reality makes the choices of leaders, mentors, communities, friends, and loved ones all germane to the seemingly simple idea of choosing life. As we make these choices, we are well advised to realize the broader impact they have.

Jewish tradition viewed Lot negatively for having chosen to live in a city as evil as Sodom. His wife clearly made poor choices, and his married daughters had selected or been given to husbands who thought Lot crazy when he warned them of their impending doom. Rashi thinks Lot got drunk a second time even after knowing he'd had relations with his daughter the first time.[5] Had he made choices better than these, gone elsewhere than Sodom when he left Abraham, married a woman other than one who eventually became a pillar of salt, raised his daughters differently (and/or chosen different husbands for them), Lot would have more effectively chosen life.

**

The many components that go into choosing life may seem daunting. I close with Maimonides' assertion with which I started, that freedom is given to each of us to choose the kinds of people we become. It can unnerve us, but I hope we all walk forward with the confidence that when the Torah tells us to choose life, it is calling on us to do that which is in our power, if only we handle it well.

Choose well, and wisely.

NOTES

[1] M.T. Hilkhot Teshuvah 5:1–3; my own loose translation.

[2] Ibid. 6:3.

[3] M.T. Hilkhot Gittin 2:20.

[4] Richard Thaler and Cass Sunstein, *Nudge: Improving Decisions About Health, Wealth, and Happiness* (New Haven: Yale University Press, 2008).

[5] Rashi to Genesis 19:33, s.v. *va-tishkav et aviha.*

Biblical Purity Laws as an Affirmation of Life

Elaine Goodfriend

In the Bible, the Eternal is the Creator of life and represents eternal life. Further, God is the repository and source of holiness—the mysterious and awe-inspiring quality that makes anything bearing the label "holy" unique, distinct, and removed from the ordinary. The Bible's association of Israel's God with both holiness and life establishes a correspondence between the two so that holiness, which is seen as an extension of the Divine, is associated with the affirmation of life. At the same time, the Torah associates the forces antithetical to holiness with *tumah* ("impurity") and, as one might expect, impurity is linked with death or diminution of the life-force. The commandment *u-vaḥarta ba-ḥayyim*, "choose life" (Deuteronomy 30:19), therefore expresses an appropriate theme for biblical legislation regarding purity issues.

Impurity is viewed by the Torah as an invisible pollution with a dynamic and airborne quality. It defiles from afar and is capable of penetrating the inner precincts of the sanctuary, known in the Torah also as the "Tent of Meeting"; its holiest component, the Ark, was later incorporated into King Solomon's Jerusalem Temple.[1] The sacred therefore serves as an unwilling magnet for impurity, which can accumulate to the extent that Israel's God will refuse to reside in the sanctuary. This is viewed as the cause of the national catastrophe that befell the nation of Judah in 586 BCE, when Jerusalem was conquered by the army of King Nebuchadnezzar of Babylon. The prophet Ezekiel explained this catastrophe by saying that the Divine Presence abandoned the city because the Temple was no longer fit for divine habitation (Ezekiel 8–11). Israel effectively evicts God from the sanctuary with their actions which pollute it, and through their neglect of the rituals, which maintain its habitability.

What are the forces that generate this mysterious and dangerous pollution? While the Torah makes no distinctions in terminology between the various sources of impurity, Jonathan Klawans makes a useful distinction between two categories: moral versus ritual impurity.[2]

Moral Impurity

Moral impurity is associated with the grave sins of murder, illicit sexual relationships, and illicit worship. We will now, in turn, examine each of these three categories.

The polluting nature of the blood of innocent homicide victims can be seen in both legal and narrative texts in the Bible, and reflects the Torah's sense of "moral ecology"—that is, how immoral actions defile the earth in general, and the Land of Israel in particular. In the story of Cain and Abel, Abel's blood "cries out" from the ground, which will "no longer yield its strength."[3] The Torah's legislation regarding homicide warns: "You shall not pollute the land in which you live; for blood pollutes the land, and the land can have no expiation for blood that is shed on it, except by the blood of he who shed it. You shall not defile the land in which you live, in which I Myself abide— for I, the Eternal, abide among the Israelite people" (Numbers 35:33–34). Deuteronomy's legislation concerning homicide reflects the same concern, that innocent blood not be shed in the Land of Israel, "so that it will go well with you" (Deuteronomy 19:10–13).[4]

In fact, Deuteronomy offers a ritual in case a body is found in the open country between cities and no information about the killer is attainable: in that case a heifer is killed in a kind of purification ritual, so that "thus [i.e., by means of this ritual] you will remove from your midst guilt for the blood of the innocent" (Deuteronomy 19:9). Thus, the Torah reflects a very dynamic view of innocent blood and its potential to pollute the earth, thus endangering its ability to sustain human population.

The Bible prohibits various categories of sexual behavior and considers them polluting not only for the parties themselves but also for the Land of Israel. Both Leviticus 18 and 20 enumerate these practices and conclude with a warning that engaging in them will result in the land "vomiting out its inhabitants" (Leviticus 18:24–30, 20:22–26). The lists assume that males are the active party in all sexual liaisons and they prohibit relations with female relatives, with the exception of cousins and nieces.[5] The Torah also prohibits marriage to two sisters, sex with a menstruating woman, bestiality, and adultery (which is defined in the Bible as a man having sexual relations with a married woman).[6] The text of Numbers 5:11–31, the ordeal for the suspected adulteress, repeatedly refers to such a woman as "defiled" if she is guilty. Intercourse between males, "lying with a male as one lies with a female," is prohibited in both Leviticus 18 and 20; but female homosexuality is not—probably because in the Bible sexual acts were defined from a male perspective as penetration.[7] Remarrying a woman who has been married to someone else in the meantime renders her impure (as far as her former husband is concerned), and "brings sin upon the land that the Eternal your God is giving you" (Leviticus 18:18–20)[8] Narrative and prophetic texts also assume the defiling nature of illicit sexual relations.[9] The Torah emphasizes that its strict sexual code is life-affirming: "You shall keep My laws and My rules, by the pursuit of which a person shall live" (Leviticus 18:5). This may be based on the idea that some of the prohibited sexual practices lack procreative potential, or perhaps that they create potentially violent conflict within the extended family. In any event, they were considered polluting for both participants, with grave consequences for both individuals and the larger community.[10]

Prohibited worship in ancient Israel takes many forms, including: the worship of other gods, the worship of the God of Israel with a graven image, using forbidden cultic objects, consulting necromancers and diviners, and offering one's children to Molech (a deity perhaps identified in some circles with the God of Israel).[11] Legal texts employ the language of impurity only for the latter two practices (Leviticus 19:31, 20:1–4), both of which share an association with death.[12] In their denunciation of the people, the prophets utilize the language of pollution for all forms of forbidden worship and they emphasize the extent of Israel's defilement, which inevitably results in destruction and exile.[13]

These three categories of serious transgressions were thought to generate a pollution that affected both the individual and the community. In post-biblical Judaism, these constitute the prohibitions that a Jew should die rather than transgress.[14] In the Bible, all these actions, if witnessed, constitute capital crimes. But beyond the punishment of the individual, how can the danger to the nation posed by the pollution of the land be removed? For murder, atonement can be accomplished only by the execution of the person who committed the homicide: "the land can have no expiation for the blood that is shed on it, except by the blood of the person who shed it" (Numbers 35:33).[15] The Torah affirms the possibility of atonement—that is, the removal of the impurity generated by willful sins—in the ritual of the Day of Atonement. Two goats are used, one of which functions as a "purgation offering" (Hebrew ḥattat) whose blood ritually cleanses the polluted inner sanctum of the sanctuary. The second goat, the "scapegoat," carries the sins of people into the wilderness, beyond the realm of settlement. Both goats deactivate the danger caused by "the impurities of the people of Israel and their transgressions, including all of their sins" (Leviticus 16:16, 21). The inclusiveness of the terms in this verse (*mi-tume'ot b'nei yisrael u-mi-pisheihem l'khol ḥattotam*) indicates that both moral and ritual transgressions, willful and inadvertent, are the focus of the ritual.[16] The people themselves play a role in the process through self-affliction and abstinence (Leviticus 16:29–30). Thus, Yom Kippur ensures God's continued presence among the people by restoring the equilibrium. However, in the worst-case scenario, Leviticus holds that atonement for Israel's persistent rebellion against God is made via punishment and exile (Leviticus 26:40–44).

Ritual Impurity

Klawans terms the second category of impurity "ritual" because it affects an individual's status regarding the sacred, so that those who contract impurity may have no contact with the realm of the Divine. On a practical level, this means that the person may not enter a sacred place—the Tabernacle, or its later incarnation as Jerusalem's Temple—and may not touch goods set aside for the Tabernacle and for its staff, the priests and Levites. While this form of impurity is indeed ritual, it is not sinful. In fact, the conditions that render a person ritually impure are natural and inevitable, and this kind of impurity generally terminates after a fixed period of time, after which the individual immerses in water. The conditions that cause this kind of impurity are menstruation, childbirth, scale disease, male genital discharge, and contact with a corpse.

Menstruation is discussed in Leviticus 15. A woman is impure for the seven-day period, beginning with the onset of her menses; later Jewish law will extend this period of time.[17] While in modern times menstruation is a frequent condition for women who marry many years after the onset of puberty and who utilize birth control, it was an uncommon state for ancient women—who married soon after puberty and spent most of their fertile years either pregnant or lactating.[18] Leviticus 15 also lays down restrictions on sexual activity occasioned by abnormal vaginal bleeding. A woman so afflicted is impure for an additional seven days after the cessation of bleeding, after which she offers a purgation sacrifice (*ḥattat*).[19]

Childbirth is discussed in Leviticus 12. The woman who bears a baby is rendered impure—for thirty-three days if she gives birth to a boy, and for sixty-six days if she gives birth to a girl; the reason for the distinction is unclear.[20] After the termination of her impurity, she immerses in water and offers a purgation sacrifice to rid the sanctuary of the impurity her condition generated.

Scale disease (once commonly referenced as leprosy) is discussed in Leviticus 13–14. The Hebrew *tzara·at* refers to a group of diseases that cause scaly or discolored skin. Not only can it appear on human skin, but also on houses, fabrics, and leather. The afflicted individual can be declared "pure" (*tahor*) by a priest after an examination, but then must participate in an elaborate purification ritual and present a purgation offering.

Male genital discharge is discussed in Leviticus 15. The Torah groups together normal male discharge (ejaculation) and prolonged discharge, the latter which may be caused by an infection of the urinary tract or other organs. Both make the individual impure, albeit for varying periods.[21] Even licit marital relations render a man and his wife impure until nightfall (Leviticus 15:18)—which highlights the idea that ritual pollution is generated even when the action producing it is socially desirable.

Contact with a corpse is discussed in Numbers 19. The Torah decrees that anyone who touches a corpse or grave, or is found in a house where a corpse has lain, is rendered impure and must undergo ritual cleansing with water and the ashes of a red cow. The period of impurity is seven days.

While to the modern reader this collection of conditions might seem random and haphazard, the biblical system of impurity is actually selective and schematic. There are certainly other body fluids just as repulsive as those indicated above—maybe feces, or mucus, or pus, or the blood from a wound—yet the uncontrolled discharge of those do not render an individual impure.[22] The Bible mentions diseases more loathsome than *tzara·at*, but only this transient skin-disease is a carrier of impurity.[23] Thus, these conditions that create pollution and thus limit an individual's access to the sancta are not designated as such simply because they are repugnant or dangerous.

Rather, the key to understanding the logic of the system is the inclusion of the corpse and carcass—which suggests that the common feature of all the conditions listed is an association with death. Indeed, when we look at the narrative preserved in Numbers 12, the link between scale-disease and death becomes clear. When Moses' sister Miriam is stricken with *tzara·at*, her other brother Aaron pleads with Moses to heal her, with the appeal: "Let her not be as one dead, who emerges from his mother's womb with half his flesh eaten away" (12:12). It is obvious here that the skin of a person afflicted with scaly-disease looked like decomposing flesh.[24]

Male and female genital discharges also fit into this schema. The Torah views blood as the substance of life. Genesis 9:6 forbids the consumption of animal blood with the following explanation: "But flesh with its life—that is, its blood—you shall not eat."[25] The association of vaginal blood and life may have been even stronger because it was perhaps thought to contain the "seed" that united with semen to produce a human being.[26] Further, menstrual blood meant the loss of potential life, the failure of a woman to fulfill her reproductive potential by creating life. The loss of vaginal blood, therefore, was linked with the process of death. Semen and male discharge in general seems to have a connotation similar to that of blood in Israelite thought; since semen (like blood) is the fluid of life, its loss is associated with death.[27] Genital discharge—whether male or female, both normal and prolonged—is therefore incorporated into Israel's system because of its symbolic association with death.[28]

The Torah thus imposes a system of taboos based on its theology that the Eternal is perfect life, the Creator of life, and Source of holiness; and that impurity, *tumah*, is thus antagonistic to the Divine. Those who are ritually unclean are those who "in some way have an aura of death about them in that they manifest less than physical wholeness."[29] Contact with the dead, having the appearance of the dead, or losing one's "life liquids" thus exclude the Israelite from approaching the sacred. Moral impurity too is connected with death, murder explicitly so, but those acts of illicit worship that the Torah considers polluting also have an association with death. Several of the sexual practices that the Torah considers defiling are non-procreative, while others may be inimical to the peaceful continuity of the community. The Torah explicitly connects the sexual prohibitions to the validation of life: "You shall keep My laws and My rules, by the pursuit of which humankind shall live: I am the Eternal" (Leviticus 18:5). Thus, the Torah offers a legal and ritual system that rejects death in all of its manifestations and affirms the inextricable connection between the Holy One and life.

NOTES

[1] For these ideas I am indebted to the many scholarly works of Jacob Milgrom, and particularly his commentaries on Leviticus and Numbers: *Leviticus 1–16* (New York: Doubleday, 1991) and *The JPS Torah Commentary: Numbers* (Philadelphia: Jewish Publication Society, 1990); in the latter work, see especially Excursus 49, "The Effect of the Sinner upon the Sanctuary," pp. 444–447.

[2] See Klawans's article "Concepts of Purity in the Bible," in *The Jewish Study Bible* (Philadelphia: Jewish Publication Society, 2004), pp. 2014–2047. See further his monograph, *Impurity and Sin in Ancient Judaism* (Oxford and New York: Oxford University Press, 2000). I am indebted to Klawans for much of the information that follows.

[3] See also Genesis 3:17–19, where the disobedience of Adam and Eve affects the fertility of the soil, and Lamech's explanation for naming his son Noah: "This one will provide us relief from our work and from the toil of our hand, out of the very soil with the Eternal placed under a curse" (Genesis 5:29). Ultimately, human rebellion, especially in the form of violence, brings about the flood (Genesis 6:5–12). In other narrative texts, 2 Samuel 21 sees drought as the consequence of unauthorized homicide.

[4] It is interesting to note that Deuteronomy's concern is for the life of the person who kills by accident, whose life is endangered by the "avenger of blood," the next of kin of the deceased who is authorized to avenge the life of his kin. Thus, refuge cities must be added to ensure the safety of the inadvertent homicide (Deuteronomy 19:8–10).

[5] A man's daughter is not obviously included in the list but is included by the prohibition of having sex with a woman and her daughter (Leviticus 18:17). It is prohibited to have relations with the following: one's mother, father's wife, half-sisters and step-sisters, granddaughter, father's sister and mother's sister, father's brother's wife, daughter-in-law, and brother's wife (Leviticus 18:7–16).

[6] In the Bible, whether or not a sexual act is considered adultery is determined by the marital status of the woman, as men could potentially take a second wife. By severely sanctioning the violation of a married woman, the Torah is attempting to limit mistaken paternity. One's inheritance and tribal status was based on one's father's line.

[7] For male homosexuality, see Leviticus 18:22; the wording refers to anal intercourse. For a discussion of the biblical and rabbinic views on female homosexuality, see Rachel Biale, *Women and Jewish Law* (New York: Schocken, 1984), pp. 192–196.

[8] Deuteronomy 24:1–4. The best explanation of this unparalleled law is offered by Reuven Yaron, "The Restoration of Marriage," *Journal of Jewish Studies* 17 (1966), pp. 1–11. Jeremiah 3:1–2 echoes the language of this law.

[9] After Shechem sexually violated Dinah, "Jacob heard that he had defiled his daughter" (Genesis 34:5). The prophet Ezekiel denounces the generation that witnessed the destruction of Jerusalem because they "have all defiled other men's wives" (33:24; see also 18:11 and 22:11). Jeremiah uses the verb *timmei* when he accuses Israel of metaphorical adultery, the worship of other gods (2:23)—as does Ezekiel (in 23:17).

[10] Incest taboos, such as we find in Leviticus 18, function in several ways. They prevent competition for the available women within an extended family and prevent intra-family conflict. They also protect women from potential predators within their own extended family since these men have authority over them and easy access to them. See Biale, *Women and Jewish Law*, p. 180.

[11] There is an extensive literature on Molech-worship, the nature of which is still unclear. See Jacob Milgrom, *Leviticus 17–22* (New York: Doubleday, 2000), pp. 1551–1568. George Heider writes: "The 'Molech question' remains a good candidate for what Adolf von Harnack once called it: 'the greatest question, without a doubt, of the comparative history of religion'"; see his entry "Molech" in *Anchor Bible Dictionary* (New York: Doubleday, 1992), vol. 4, pp.895–898.

[12] This is obvious regarding necromancy. Regarding Molech worship, the practice reflected in the text may be child sacrifice; see previous note.

[13] See Jeremiah 2:7, 7:30, 32:34; Ezekiel 5:11, 20:30, 22:3–4, 36:18; Hosea 5:3, 6:10; or Psalm 106:39.

[14] B. Sanhedrin 74a; see also Maimonides, M.T. Yesodei Hatorah 5:2.

[15] A concession is if the homicide was committed inadvertently, without prior intent: in that case the killer stays in an asylum city until the death of the High Priest (Numbers 35:25).

[16] Milgrom notes that "impurities" refers to the ritual impurities described in Leviticus 11-15, while "transgressions" (*pisheihem*) "is the term that characterizes the worst possible sin: open and wanton defiance of the Lord," which "not only attacks the sanctuary but penetrates into the adytum and pollutes the *kapporet*, the very seat of the godhead." The last term, *hattotam*, is a "catchall phrase that incorporates all of the wrongs except for the brazen sins." Milgrom notes that the importance of this phrase is that it emphasizes that all of Israel's sin, not only the physical impurities, pollute the sanctuary (*Leviticus 1-16*, pp.1033–1035.)

[17] Leviticus 15 distinguishes between normal seven-day bleeding and abnormal uterine bleeding that is longer than a woman's normal period or that begins unexpectedly (vv.19–31). For abnormal uterine bleeding, the Torah prescribes that her impurity lasts a seven additional "clean" days. Later Jewish law collapses the distinction so that all women who menstruate are impure for at least twelve days: five for menstruation, and then seven more. See B. Shabbat 31b and Niddah 66a ("Rabbi Zera stated: 'The daughters of Israel have imposed upon themselves the restriction that even if they observe a drop of blood of the size of

a mustard seed they wait on account of it seven clean days.'")

[18] Milgrom, *Leviticus 1-16*, p. 953.

[19] Israel was not unique in its distancing of menstruating and post-partum women from religious life. Many cultures did this, but also cut them off from normal domestic life. While Leviticus 12 and 15 indicate the separation of women with these conditions from the sancta, there is no textual evidence that they were banished from their homes or socially segregated in any way. The woman afflicted with genital bleeding had to be careful about where she sat and lay, had to avoid physical contact with those whom she did not wish to contaminate, and rinse her hands often lest she spread her impurity, but otherwise she could go about her normal domestic responsibilities (Milgrom, *Leviticus 1–16*, pp. 952–953).

[20] See the discussion in *The Torah: A Woman's Commentary* (New York: URJ Press, 2008), p. 641.

[21] The man who had an ejaculation retains his status until nightfall, while the man with the more severe condition is considered impure as long as his discharge continues in addition to seven "clean" days.

[22] Two biblical passages mention that human feces are incompatible with holy places and people. Deuteronomy 23:13 commands that feces be deposited outside the military camp, which had to be fit for God's presence; and Ezekiel 4:12 declares that the prophet's purity as a priest prevents him using human feces as a source of fuel to cook his food.

[23] It is transient as opposed to chronic, because Leviticus 13 does foresee that the priest will at some point in the future declare the afflicted individual pure. Other diseases are mentioned in the curses of Leviticus 26:16, Deuteronomy 28:35, 59; and pestilence or plague is mentioned in Exodus 9:15, 12:13, Numbers 25:9, 2 Kings 19:35, and other places. For more, see Max Sussman, "Sickness and Disease," *Anchor Bible Dictionary* (New York: Doubleday, 1992), vol. 6, pp. 6–15.

[24] Abraham ibn Ezra comments here, "Let not our sister be like a dead (miscarried) fetus whose flesh is half eaten, just as the flesh of a person with scale disease." Above, I mentioned that ritual impurity is non-culpable (i.e., not necessarily associated with wrong-doing). This is certainly true in Leviticus 13–14, which discusses the diagnosis and remedy of the condition. No guilt is imputed to the person with the illness nor to the individual whose home is afflicted. However, other texts in the Bible contradict this generalization, such as Numbers 12 (the case of Miriam), 2 Kings 5 (the case of Gehazi), and 2 Chronicles 26 (King Uzziah); see also Deuteronomy 28:15 and Job 1–2. In these latter cases, the Bible is reflecting the widespread ancient Near Eastern view of skin disease as a punishment from the gods; Milgrom offers many examples of this understanding (*Leviticus 1-16*, pp. 820–821).

[25] See also Leviticus 17:14 and Deuteronomy 12:23.

[26] So Jacob Milgrom, *Leviticus 1-16*, pp.743-744, regarding the word *tazri·a* in Leviticus 12:2. It means literally "produces seed." Milgrom writes: "The rabbis held that conception occurred when the woman's blood united with male sperm. Moreover, many of the ancients . . . assumed that menstrual blood contains seed (i.e., ovum) that unites with the male seed to produce the human being."

[27] The Amṛtasiddhi, an eleventh-century CE work, has a section on "the restraint of semen," which reads, "Death [arises] from the fall of semen, life from the restraint of semen" (James Mallinson and Mark Singleton, *Roots of Yoga* [London: Penguin Classics, 2017], pp. 220–222). Also, James Mallinson has privately shared with me that "this verse occurs in various subsequent yoga texts, all of which are 'Hindu,' but the Amṛtasiddhi, the earliest text to teach the practices and principles of haṭhayoga, was composed in a tantric Buddhist milieu."

[28] A different view is suggested by Jonathan Klawans: "Because God has no consort, God does not have sex. Therefore, by separting from sex and death... ancient Israelites separated themselves from what made them least God-like" ("Concepts of Purity in the Bible," p. 2044). He therefore attributes the impurity of genital discharges to their relationship to sexuality, which is the antithesis of Israel's divinity. This notion has merit, but there is little indication in the Hebrew Bible of the fear of a sexualized view of God. There are several extended allegories about God as husband and Israel as wife (Hosea 1–3, Jeremiah 2–3, Ezekiel 16 and 23). The canonization of the Song of Songs is another indication that Jews did not fear erotic language in religious discourse. Fear of sexuality in the realm of religion would have led to a celibate priesthood for Judaism, as it did for Catholicism.

[29] Gordon Wenham, "Why Does Sexual Intercourse Defile?" *in Zeitschrift für die alttestamentliche Wissenschaft* 95 (1983), pp. 432–434.

Choosing the Path of Life in Old Jerusalem and Today

Martin S. Cohen

The intimate relationship between the language of the Book of Jeremiah and that of Deuteronomy has been a topic of discussion and scholarly debate for a very long time.[1] In this essay, I would like to explore how Jeremiah interprets the famous passage from Deuteronomy 30:19 calling upon the Israelites to guarantee their own longevity and the longevity of their descendants by choosing life over death and blessing over curse. Moreover, I will suggest what that interpretation might mean to moderns eager to obey the injunction to choose life but unsure how precisely the Torah imagines them actually doing so.[2]

Among the best-known passages in the Book of Jeremiah is the so-called "Temple Sermon" preserved in chapters 7 and 8.[3] The notice at 26:1 that references the prophet's call to preach in the "Temple courtyard" is generally supposed to refer back to the material presented in chapters 7 and 8; that verse notes that the call came to him "in the beginning of King Jehoiakim's reign," which would date the material in chapters 7 and 8 to the fall of 609 BCE or the winter of 609–608.[4] But even if the material cannot be dated with absolute certainty, the sermon is nevertheless one of Jeremiah's cornerstone addresses, a speech so rich with allusive meaning—and with eloquence richly born of rage—that it holds a rightful place in the front ranks of all prophetic discourses recorded in Scripture.[5]

The entire sermon is stunning, both in terms of its literary power and its spiritual audacity. At its conclusion, the prophet—perhaps having exhausted himself excoriating the people for their arrogance and shortsightedness in the past and the present—turns to the future. And the image before his eyes is truly shocking. He imagines the priests, prophets, and regular citizens of Jerusalem finally understanding themselves to be doomed—or rather *finally* realizing that life as they have known it is coming rapidly to a violent, irrevocable end—and responding to the terror before their eyes. They do this *not*, as might have been expected, by finally returning to God and attempting, even at the very last moment, to repent their evil ways. Instead, they exhume the remains of the kings of Judah and their courtiers, and also of past prophets, priests, and citizens of prominence, and then spread out the bones like so many articulated skeletons as a way of inviting the dead to join the living in begging for salvation, not from the God of Israel, but from "the sun and the moon and the entire host of heaven, whom they have loved and served, and whom they have followed and sought out, and to whom they have fallen prostrate" (Jeremiah 8:1–2).[6] But, of course, nothing will come of it, the prophet notes acidulously—and the bones so desecrated shall never be reburied or even gathered up respectfully, but instead will be left on the ground to rot like the waste that animals deposit on the road.[7]

And so, the prophet concludes grimly, the citizenry will have chosen death over life…and not only for themselves, but also for the remnant of this "wicked family" in all the many lands of their dispersion.[8] From this passage, it seems that the prophet understood the commandment to choose life to entail only choosing to serve the God of Israel exclusively—who would eventually (in one of the Bible's latest books) be called the "Life of the Universe"—and wished to teach that doing so would ensure eternal life on the nation's land, continuing through generations of one's descendants.[9]

But an even more powerful passage is to be found later in the book in a passage set in the reign of King Zedekiah, the last king of Judah.[10] The setting there is quite dramatic. The Babylonian threat is palpable. The royal house has finally begun to understand the heat of the fire that is threatening to consume them and the nation they lead. Zedekiah, who was a mere twenty-one years of age when ascending to the throne and who is now only a decade or so older, is truly worried. And so he turns to, of all people, his family's old nemesis and asks him to do whatever it might take to provoke a *bona fide* oracle that will reveal what is about to happen. Jeremiah, who has certainly never held back from declaiming the oracles to which he as a prophet was made privy, accedes to the king's demand, but the news is not good at all: not only is God not going to fight *for* Judah in the coming showdown with Babylon, but the Almighty is instead planning to fight *against* Judah. And then, when the battle is done and the nation has been totally defeated, God will deliver the survivors into the hands of their foes who will treat them beyond harshly, "taking no pity on them at all and showing neither mercy nor compassion" (21:7).

And then the prophet continues with a second part of the oracle intended not for the king but for the people. "Tell the people," the prophet quotes God as saying, "that the Eternal has this to say to them: Behold I am placing before you the path of life and the path of death. Those who remain in this city shall die by the sword, by famine, and pestilence, but those who leave [the city] to fall [prostrate] before the Kasdim [the Chaldeans] who are besieging [their city] shall live, their lives theirs to salvage. For I have turned My face against this city to its own detriment and not for good—this is God's word—and so shall the city be given into the hands of the King of Babylon, who shall burn it with fire" (21:8–10).[11]

The prophet then reports an oracle containing very bad news

for the royal house, but a challenge to the people: that they choose between life and death *literally*, by deciding whether to surrender to the Babylonians (and in so doing to save their lives) or to remain in the doomed city (and vainly to participate in its futile defense). It sounds simple enough! But to understand those words fully requires reading (or hearing) them in light of two passages in Deuteronomy.

Toward the end of Deuteronomy (30:15–20), in the closing passage of Moses' final oration, Moses waxes poetic as he describes in distinctly admonitory terms the choices facing the Israelites whom he has led for four long decades:

> Behold, by commanding you today to love the Eternal, your God, and to walk in God's ways and to keep God's commandments and statutes and laws, I am placing before you today, on the one hand, life and goodness, and, on the other, death and evil. And so shall you live and flourish as the Eternal, your God, blesses you in the land that you are now on your way to possess. If, however, your heart should turn away and you stop obeying—such that you actually turn to apostasy and prostrate yourself before alien gods and worship them—then I am telling you clearly today that you shall surely perish, that you will not live for long on the land that you are about to cross the Jordan to enter and possess. I call heaven and earth on this day as my witnesses that I am placing before you life and death, blessing and curse. *Choose life, so that you live, you and your progeny.* And love the Eternal, your God, by obeying God's voice and by cleaving unto God—for it is God who grants you your life and who determines how long shall last the days you dwell on the land that the Eternal swore to grant to your ancestors Abraham, Isaac, and Jacob.[12]

The similarities between this passage and the one in Jeremiah are obvious: in both, a prophet informs the people that God has placed before them two paths and he labels them clearly with several different names—so that life, goodness, and blessing constitute one path, whereas death, evil, and curse constitute the other. Moses' point, however, is not merely that these paths exist, but that there is a specific way to embrace one or the other—to wit, by choosing either to worship God alone, or to turn away to alien gods and worship them instead. In the end, it all comes down to turning from idolatry and embracing the exclusive worship of the one true God.

Nor is this an entirely new idea, in that the passage clearly echoes and amplifies an earlier one in Deuteronomy (11:26–28) that reads:

> Behold, I am today placing before you a blessing or a curse: a blessing if you obey all the commandments of the Eternal, your God, that I am commanding you this day, but a curse if you do not obey the commandments of the Eternal, your God, and swerve off the path that I am commanding you today and follow after other gods heretofore unknown to you.

The two passages lay along the same metaphoric landscape and teach the same unsettling lesson: the freedom to choose a personal path in life is as much a burden as a blessing…and the consequences for making the "wrong" choice will be dire.

Did Jeremiah know these passages? Surely, he did—regardless of what precisely the scroll was to which the High Priest Ḥilkiah was referring when, in the eighteenth year of King Josiah's reign (i.e., in c. 623 BCE), the latter said, "I have found the *sefer torah* [or "book of the Torah" or, less portentously, "book of the teaching" or "of teaching"] in the Temple," it seems impossible to imagine that Deuteronomy was unknown to Jeremiah.[13] And it thus seems reasonable to imagine Jeremiah consciously riffing off Moses' last words as he prepared to speak to the people at the dawn of what he personally understood to be the death throes of the nation in his own time.

He has, in fact, had a lot to say about paths and ways forward.

In some, the prophet imagines these paths not metaphorically but literally, as actual roads for the nation to walk along (or not). In one undated oracle, for example, the prophet hears God speaking directly to the nation and saying: "Stand at the [cross]roads and, looking out, determine which is the path of olden times; [if it is] the path of goodness, then walk in it and thus find some rest for your souls" (6:16). But it is to no avail, as the continuation of the verse makes clear: "But they replied, 'We shall not walk [upon it].'" Then, shifting metaphors, the prophet offers a far more pathetic image, in which God personally makes a very generous offer to a very recalcitrant people: "I'll [even] provide some scouts [to guide you forward so your job will be simply to obey this one injunction]: 'Heed the sound of the [scouts'] *shofar*'" (6:17). But the people will not be moved by that offer either, as the prophet laconically notes in just a few words later in that same verse ("but they said, "we shall not heed [it]"). And thus is their doom sealed: "…for, behold, I am bringing doom to this people, the [bitter] fruits of their own attitudes, for they have declined to heed My words and have been revolted by My Torah" (6:19). Judging Jeremiah from his surviving work, the prophet returned again and again to this idea of the existence of a path forward upon which all may walk, but which failing to take will lead to dire consequences indeed. The words become so familiar, in fact, that readers eventually barely even notice them: the stock phrase "your path and your deeds," for example, appears in various permutations ten different times throughout the book.[14] And in all those passages, and in many others as well, the prophet's point is clear: the faithful Israelite must choose to walk on the path of blessing (alternately labeled the path of life, of God's Torah, or of goodness). And that *that* is what it means to choose life, as the Torah commands.

As a result, there is something familiar about the introduction to the oracle the prophet received in the first year of King Jehoiakim (c. 608 BCE), referenced in the opening paragraphs of this essay. In that oracle, Jeremiah heard God commanding him to speak in the courtyard of the Temple, but he *also* heard some divine instructions, presumably intended for the prophet's ears only: "Stand in the Temple courtyard and give forth about the cities of Judah, [whose citizens] have come to prostrate themselves in the Temple. [Say] all the words that I shall have commanded you to say, omitting nothing, and perhaps they will [actually] listen and then return from their evil way. If that happens, then I will [gladly] turn away from the evil that I am planning to bring against them [precisely] because of the wickedness of their deeds" (Jeremiah 26:1).[15] And how is it exactly that they should do that one thing that will avert the disaster almost upon them? That too is not to be kept secret: "Say to them, 'Thus says the Eternal, if you do not obey Me and [if you decline to] walk in [the way] of My Torah, the one that I [personally] have bestowed upon you, *and* if you [continue to] ignore My servants, the prophets…then I shall make this Temple like [the destroyed sanctuary at] Shiloh and this city shall I make into [one large] curse…[*and* I shall do so in full view] of all the other peoples of the land" (Jeremiah 26:4–6; emphasis added).[16]

Generally speaking, it is considered virtuous to be loyal to one's country and its legitimate ruler or rulers. That is the case today, obviously, but it was also the case in antiquity—and it is in the light of the presumed civil virtue of absolute national allegiance that the prophet's work must be evaluated. Indeed, the single overarching notion of which *all* of Jeremiah's work can be considered a kind of oratorical amplification is that precisely the opposite is true: that the truly good individual is *not* one who obeys the king, but one who obeys God. And, of course, this is not at all impossible…and precisely because the institution of prophecy exists in the first place precisely to bring God's directives directly to the people.

But that leads to a different kind of choice entirely. In ancient times, people who heard voices often imagined themselves—and were supposed by others—to be hearing the voice of God.[17] Automatically including these unfortunates in the general category of false prophets seems uncharitable: there were certainly charlatans in antiquity who claimed prophetic status as a means of egotistical self-aggrandizement, but there were surely others who truly did perceive themselves to have been vested with the charism of prophecy and who thus saw themselves as morally obliged to proclaim the oracles they understood God to be vouchsafing to them. But there is no way to distinguish between the two categories—the legitimate prophets to whom God speaks, and the individuals who erroneously perceive God to be speaking to them and calling them to proclaim God's word to the world—other than with reference to the success they either did or did not experience in their own day. Nor should it be necessary to state that the prophets recalled as legitimate *also* perceived God to be speaking to them directly and urging them forward to proclaim God's word to the public—and, we can assume, in more or less the same way as those whom history remembers as frauds.

Surely the fact that false prophets don't perceive themselves as false hardly means that they were legitimate. And, indeed, the Book of Jeremiah mentions several of these "false" prophets by name, but without offering any practical instructions about how to distinguish between the legitimate and the false prophet. Nor can we simply assume that Jeremiah was right in his estimation of the others, because those others—Ahab ben Kolaiah, Ḥananiah ben Azzur, and Zedekiah ben Maaseiah—are known to us solely through Jeremiah's own gimlet eye.[18] But to say that it should have been obvious to all that they were charlatans merely because that is how Jeremiah saw things seems wrong, and precisely because the people did not have the crucial information from which to draw that conclusion until much later.

To return to Deuteronomy, the Torah itself acknowledges the problem of identifying false prophets in two oft-cited passages that appear to offer contradictory solutions. The first one, Deuteronomy 13:2–6, is the longer and more detailed one:

> Should a prophet or a dreamer of dreams rise up in your midst and predict a coming sign or wonder, and should that sign or wonder of which that one spoke to you then actually come to pass—if such a one then goes on to say, "Come, let us go follow other gods that you have not known and worship them,"— do not obey the words of that prophet or dreamer of dreams, for the Eternal, your God, is merely testing you to see if you truly love the Eternal, your God, with all of your heart and with all of your soul. You must follow the Eternal, your God, and it is God whom you must revere and whose commandments you must obey and to whose voice you must listen and whom you must worship and unto whom you must cleave. That prophet or dreamer of dreams shall be put to death for having spoken seditiously with respect to the Eternal, your God, who brought you forth from the land of Egypt and who is your redeemer from the house of bondage; that person shall have done so merely to seduce you away from the path in which the Eternal, your God, has commanded that you walk. And in so doing, you shall have eliminated evil from your midst.

According to this estimation, the solution is specifically *not* to focus on the prophet's skill at predicting the future, not even if the prophet seems to have known about some remarkable "sign or wonder" yet to come, but instead to focus on that individual's piety—so that a false prophet is defined as one who suggests that the people abandon the God of Israel and turn instead to the worship of other gods. That reads well, but does not really address our situation in Jeremiah's time: there is no indication in the book that any of the prophets damned as phonies by Jeremiah ever suggested idol worship or apostasy to their audiences.

Perhaps to speak precisely to that problem, Deuteronomy (at 18:18–22) also offers an alternate approach, one offered in the context of a final, heartening promise made by God to Moses as the latter, approaching death, wonders what the future will bring in terms of prophetic leadership on his personal level:

> I shall [one day] raise up a prophet for them from the midst of their brethren, [someone] just like yourself, and I shall place My words in that prophet's mouth so that he [may] say to them all that I shall command him. Indeed, I shall personally look after the matter of the individual who does not listen to those of My words that that prophet shall speak in My name. The prophet, however, who dares speak words in My name that I have not commanded that one to speak or who speaks in the names of other gods—such a prophet shall die. And should you ask yourself, "How exactly am I to recognize the prophetic utterance that the Eternal did not speak?"—the answer is this: should a prophet predict in the name of God that something will happen—when that thing does not happen and shows no signs of happening, then [that utterance] is assuredly *not* something that the Eternal said would occur. Such a prophet was intentionally speaking falsely; to such a one you need show no reverence.[19]

This passage seems to contradict the first one, but it also speaks directly to it: in the earlier passage, the false prophet was the one who recommended apostasy but specifically *not* the one whose predictions failed to materialize, whereas here the message is precisely the opposite: "when that [predicted] thing does not happen…such a prophet was intentionally speaking falsely." In other words, the second passage promotes the view that successful prognostication is the ultimate determinant of legitimacy. Eventually, history was going to prove Jeremiah right and the others wrong, but how can that have been useful to the residents of Jerusalem who lived before the debacle in the days of Kings Jehoiachin and Zedekiah? They—those living through the last days of Judah—*they* needed to know which prophets were legitimate. But neither test proposed by Deuteronomy would have worked for them: none of the prophets vying for public support was proposing apostasy and no one's predictions had or had not come true as of yet.

And so the ancients were faced with the challenge of choosing life for themselves and their descendants…but no practical way to make such a choice other than by filtering the words of others, all of whom claimed to be speaking in the name of God, through the triple alembic of their own spiritual consciousnesses, their own discerning hearts, and their own native intelligence.

As the Babylonian hordes gathered in the distance, the Torah's command to choose the path of blessing, goodness, and life challenged the ancients as they stood at the crossroads and wondered which of the competing prophets in their midst, if any, were truly speaking in the name of God. Like us moderns who live long after the age of prophecy, they needed to know what God wished of them. But, in the end, the words *u-vaharta ba-ḥayyim* ("choose life") could only have meant to them what they have come to mean in our own prophet-less day to all possessed of true spiritual integrity: that the choice to live a life in harmony with God's wishes cannot really be made outside the chambers of a heart alive with the wish to live a life in and of God—and in so doing, at least in a certain sense, to be God's prophet to oneself. As Jeremiah taught, one chooses life by listening to the word of God…and by choosing to walk along the path of life and of blessing, a path that one must ultimately pave for oneself. In the end, the age of prophecy is not truly over: we've just scaled it all down to the level of the individual able to listen when God speaks…and then to make the choice either to obey or to turn away.

NOTES

[1] See most recently Nathan Mastnjak's *Deuteronomy and the Emergence of Textual Authority in Jeremiah* (Tübingen: Mohr Siebeck, 2016), particularly the subsection of the introduction entitled "History of Scholarship" (pp. 2–11).

[2] A basic rabbinic presupposition is that all of the Torah's commandments are doable physically and not merely by adopting some specific attitude or belief. And, indeed, a lesson attributed to Rabbi Yishmael appears three different times in the larger rabbinic corpus to the effect that the injunction to choose life is fulfilled by teaching one's children how to earn a living. (See Y. Pei·ah 1:1, 15c; Sotah 9:17, 24c; and Kiddushin 1:7, 61a; M. Kiddushin 1:7 specifically applies this obligation equally to mothers and fathers.)

[3] The precise boundaries of the sermon are unclear: it clearly begins at 7:1 with the prophet's account of being called by God to declaim what follows in the Temple's entry gate, but doesn't have as clear an ending point. The shift from prose to poetry at 8:4 probably marks the beginning of a new text. On other possible "Temple sermons" in Jeremiah, see Pearle Felicia Stone, "The Temple Sermons of Jeremiah," *The American Journal of Semitic Languages and Literatures* 50:2 (January 1934), pp. 73–92.

[4] The fact that 26:1 references the Temple courtyard, whereas 8:2 refers to the Temple gate, is not necessarily problematic. On the date mentioned here, see John Bright's Anchor Bible series volume, *Jeremiah* (Garden City, NY: Doubleday & Co., 1965), p. 58.

[5] See for example the incisive comments of Walter Brueggeman in his *A Commentary on Jeremiah: Exile and Homecoming* (Grand Rapids [MI] and Cambridge [U.K.]: William B. Eerdmans, 1998), pp. 77–85.

[6] The text only references "residents of Jerusalem," but my understanding is that it must be speaking specifically of the prominent ones. The details of how the bones are to be arrayed are likewise not explicit in the text, but represent my own imagined understanding of the event described in the passage.

[7] The text is specific here that the bones so arrayed will end up as just so much dung lying around on the ground. Cf. Rashi's comment *ad locum*, in which he merely brings the Targum Yonatan's gloss of *domen* as the more familiar *zevel* ("manure") to his readers' attention. The notion of unburied cadavers rotting into the earth appears elsewhere in Jeremiah as part of the larger concept of the dead in the coming siege being so numerous as to make it impossible for the survivors to bury them all (see 9:21, 16:4, and 25:33), so the concept here is meant to be particularly ironic: the dead here, whose unburied corpses will turn to fertilizer, will specifically *not* be victims of the siege or the capture of the city, but rather people whom the citizens themselves shall have exhumed for their own perverse reasons. Cf. 2 Kings 9:37, Nahum 3:6, and Psalm 83:11 for other

applications of the same basic idea that being left unburied *post mortem* is far worse than death itself.

[8] The phrase "wicked family" (*ha-mishpaḥah ha-ra·ah ha-zot*) is strange and appears only here in Jeremiah; cf. Micah 2:3 for a passage that might possibly have inspired Jeremiah's turn of phrase.

[9] The God of Israel is referenced as the "Life of the Universe" at Daniel 12:7.

[10] Zedekiah was the third and last of King Josiah's sons to reign. He came to the throne in 597 BCE after the disastrous three-month reign of his nephew Jeconiah ended with the latter's exile to Babylon. The most likely date for this passage is the early 580s as the Babylonians began to gather the troops necessary to seize Jerusalem; see Bright, *Jeremiah*, p. 216.

[11] The prophet regularly references the Babylonians as "Kasdim," sometimes translated as Chaldeans. For more about the original Kasdim, see Zénaïde A. Ragozin's still fascinating *Chaldea from the Earliest Times to the Rise of Assyria* (New York: G. P. Putnam's Sons and London: T. Fisher Unwin, 1893) or the comments of J. A. Brinkman in his *A Political History of Post-Kassite Babylonia 1158–722 B.C.* (Rome: Pontificum Institum Biblicum, 1968), pp. 260–266. The word "God" in the expression "God's word" denotes the four-letter name (*yod-hei-vav-hei*).

[12] Emphasis added.

[13] 2 Kings 22:8. The fact that Jeremiah's own father's name was also Ḥilkiyah (see Jeremiah 1:1, where his father is called by the long form of his name, Ḥilkiyahu) and that he too was a priest does not mean that his father was the High Priest of Israel, which seems an odd thing for him never to have found a place in his many orations to have mentioned. Like Josiah, Jeremiah would have been a young man in his twenties when the announcement was made that a scroll of "*torah*" had been found in the Temple. The literature about this incident is immense. For a general overview, see Richard Elliot Friedman, *Who Wrote the Bible?* (1987; rpt. New York: HarperCollins, 1997), pp. 101–116. For a more recent and far more detailed discussion, see Mark Leuchter, *Josiah's Reform and Jeremiah's Scroll: Historical Calamity and Prophetic Response* (Sheffield [UK]: Sheffield Phoenix Press, 2006).

[14] Jeremiah 4:18, 7:3 and 5, 17:10, 18:11, 23:22, 25:5, 26:13, 32:19, and 35:15.

[15] As noted, the precise relationship between this passage and the great, so-called "Temple sermon" of chapters 7 and 8 is a matter of scholarly debate. See above, notes 3, 4, and 5.

[16] Note that the visual image of the path is so familiar that the word itself is not even mentioned here. But when the prophet hears God speaking about people walking "in" the Torah, surely the image evoked is one of people walking along a specific path—and surely it is the path of Torah of which the prophet speaks in so many different ways. Regarding Shiloh, see most recently Donald

Schley's *Shiloh: A Biblical City in Tradition and History* (Sheffield, UK: Sheffield Academic Press, 1984), published as volume 63 in the Journal for the Study of the Old Testament Supplement Series.

[17] This was long before mental disorders were understood in the modern sense as diseases that can be addressed therapeutically. For an exhaustive overview of the state of research, see *Mental Disorders in the Classical World*, ed. William V. Harris (Leiden [Holland] and Boston: Brill, 2013).

[18] The references are as follow: Ahab ben Kolaiah (Jeremiah 29:21), Hananiah ben Azzur (Jeremiah 28:1 and 28:5), Zedekiah ben Maaseiah (Jeremiah 29:21). On the other side of the ledger, Uriah ben Shemaiah (Jeremiah 26:20-23) appears to have been respected by Jeremiah as authentic. Huldah, the prophet mentioned in 2 Kings 22 and 2 Chronicles 34 (and clearly acknowledged in both books as legitimate), was a contemporary of Jeremiah's but is not mentioned in any sermons or oracles presented in the latter's book.

[19] Emphasis added.

The God of Revelation and the God of Hiding

Zvi Grumet

The first-time reader of the Bible cannot but notice the ubiquity of God's interference with the natural order, after having so painstakingly created it in the first place: floods, explosion of language, post-menopausal pregnancy, fire raining down from the heavens, plagues, splitting of a sea, manna from heaven, water from rocks, Samson's superhuman strength, and much, much more. It seems that the Bible's portrayal of God is that of a deity intent on repeatedly displaying power to us humans. This, indeed, would seem to be the thrust of Moses' words:

> Just ask about the earlier days, ever since God created humanity on earth, from one end of heaven to the other: has anything as magnificent as this—or anything similar— ever happened? Has any people heard the voice of a god speaking out of a fire, as you have, and survived? Or has any god ventured to go and take for himself one nation from the midst of another by extraordinary acts, signs, and wonders, by war, by a mighty and outstretched arm and awesome power, as the Eternal your God did for you in Egypt before your very eyes? You have been shown that the Eternal alone is God; there is none beside Him. (Deuteronomy 4:32–25)

The revelation at Sinai and the preference of the Israelites over other peoples are demonstrations "that the Eternal alone is God; there is none beside Him."

Less than one generation later we hear from none other than a Canaanite woman, Rachab (a prostitute in Jericho), who indicates that God's miraculous demonstrations have, indeed, convinced the Canaanites of God's uniqueness:

> For we have heard how the Eternal dried up the waters of the Reed Sea for you when you left Egypt, and what you did to Sichon and Og, the two Amorite kings across the Jordan, whom you annihilated. When we heard about it we lost heart, and no person had any spirit left because of you, for the Eternal your God is the only God in heaven above and on earth below. (Joshua 2:10–11)

This same thread continues throughout the Bible. The Queen of Sheba is so awe-struck by Solomon's superhuman (read: miraculous) wisdom that she exalts the God who put Solomon onto his throne (1 Kings 10:9), and in one of the closing books of the Bible it is Nebuchadnezzar who is so moved by the miraculous salvation of Hananiah, Mishael, and Azariah from the fiery furnace that he proclaims, "Blessed be the God of Shadrach, Meshach, and Abed-Nego [the Babylonian names of Hananiah, Mishael, and Azariah], who sent His angel to save His servants who, trusting in Him, flouted the king's decree at the risk of their own lives rather than serve or worship any god but their own God" (Daniel 3:28).

A more nuanced read, however, suggests that the Bible is ambivalent about the value of divine intervention in the natural order—that is, what we would call miracles. True, the story of revelation stands out in all of its supernatural splendor, whether reading the description in Exodus (19–24) or in Deuteronomy (4–5). But the sequel to the story of revelation describes the golden calf, the first traumatic crisis of the young nation. One must wonder how a people who just experienced revelation could so quickly descend to dancing around a golden calf and proclaiming it to be the god who took them out of Egyptian slavery, yet that is precisely what is described.[1] It seems that the Bible is trying to convey a not-so-subtle message about the power of a singular, dramatic miraculous event: it is very impressive, but its impact is fleeting. Even a direct divine revelation has minimal long-term effects.

A similar message emerges from another narrative many years later. In 1 Kings 18 we read the dramatic story of Elijah's contest on Mount Carmel. Elijah stands alone as he confronts 450 prophets of the Baal. In a climactic moment, Elijah summons a fire from heaven to publicly consume his sacrifice, whereupon the assembled spontaneously fall on their faces overcome by religious ecstasy and exclaim, "Adonai is the Almighty, Adonai is the Almighty!" (1 Kings 18:39). The theatrical theophany Elijah choreographed is quite impressive, yet the next day Elijah finds himself fleeing for his life as Queen Jezebel (presumably with the support of the same masses who had earlier proclaimed Elijah's God as the true one) launches a major manhunt to capture Elijah. The religious frenzy of the previous day dissolves in the face of prosaic practicality.

As if to drive the point home, Elijah's flight drives him to Mount Horeb. In a scene whose details quite deliberately mirror Moses' own trip up to Mount Sinai (Sinai and Horeb are apparently synonyms),[2] Elijah has a private revelation:

> He arose and ate and drank; and with the strength from that meal he walked forty days and forty nights as far as the mountain of God at Horeb. There he went into a cave and slept. Then the word of the Eternal came to him and said, "What are you doing here, Elijah?" He replied, "I have been zealous on behalf of the Eternal, the God of Hosts, for the Israelites have abandoned Your covenant, destroyed Your

altars, and killed Your prophets by the sword. I, alone, am left, and they seek to take my life." "Come out," He called, "and stand on the mountain before the Eternal." Behold, as the Eternal passed by there was a great and mighty wind, splitting mountains and shattering rocks in advance of the arrival of the Eternal, but the Eternal was not in the wind. After the wind—an earthquake, but the Eternal was not in the earthquake. After the earthquake—fire, but the Eternal was not in the fire. And after the fire—a sound of gentle silence. When Elijah heard it, he wrapped his mantle about his face and went out and stood at the entrance of the cave. Then a voice addressed him: "What are you doing here, Elijah?" He answered, "I have been zealous on behalf of the Eternal, the God of Hosts; for the Israelites have abandoned Your covenant, destroyed Your altars, and killed Your prophets by the sword. I, alone, am left, and they seek to take my life." (1 Kings 19:9–14)

Elijah had self-styled himself as both Moses and Pinḥas, the great zealots defending God's honor, and imagined himself as their spiritual successor. God challenges Elijah's self-perception, and God's question essentially asks, "You are no Moses; why do you think that you belong here?"

The content of God's revelation here is no accident. God speaks of a great and mighty wind, an earthquake, and a fire, each of which had previously served in the Bible as a vehicle of divine revelation.[3] Yet God's message is unmistakable: Elijah is mistaken in believing that God can be found in dramatic, nature-defying displays. Rather, God is to be found in the still, soft sound of silence. Elijah's showy pageantry is no more effective than God's own terrifying revelation at Sinai. Elijah, however, doesn't get it—so that when God repeats the rebuking question of "What are you doing here?"[4] Elijah repeats his earlier answer verbatim. He has learned nothing from God's message to him, and so Elijah is the only prophet to be fired (literally and figuratively) from his position, replaced by the mild-mannered and personable Elisha.[5]

The message is unmistakable. Much as God used these methods to try to win the people's loyalty, God's attempt was unsuccessful. In the long-term, miracles accomplish nothing; it is only in quiet, soft, dedicated, patient, and persistent work that people's hearts can be won.

The biblical downplaying of miracles finds expression in later Jewish literature and thought as well. The Mishnah recounts the tale of Ḥoni, who during a drought drew a circle on the ground and repeatedly refused to leave it until God brought sufficient rain for the people.[6] While many celebrate Ḥoni and his special powers, Shimon ben Shetaḥ had harsh words for him. The Talmud sharpens Shimon ben Shetaḥ's critique, presenting Ḥoni as a spoiled child whose father lacks the ability to say "no":

> Shimon ben Shetaḥ sent to [Ḥoni]: "Were it not for the fact that you are Ḥoni, I would decree upon you the ban of excommunication. For if these years were like the years of Elijah, in which the [heavenly] keys to the rains were in Elijah's hands,[7] would you not have been the cause of a desecration of the divine name? But what can I do, as you plead before God and He does as you ask just like a child who pleads with his father who does whatever [the child] wants! He says, "Father, take me to the hot baths, rinse me in cold water, give me nuts and almonds, peaches, and pomegranates"—and he just gives it to him.[8]

Just as the biblical emphasis on miracles is moderated by the broader biblical contexts, the ever-popular tradition of miracles and miracle-makers was rejected on theological grounds by Shimon ben Shetaḥ and his colleagues.

Among medieval thinkers, Maimonides is most prominent in downplaying the theological significance of miracles. Maimonides forcefully argues that faith based on miracles is not faith, and that none of the miracles in the Bible served as the foundation of the faith of the Israelites:

> Moses, our teacher, was not believed in by the Jews because of the signs he performed. For one who believes [in anything] because of signs has a doubt in his heart, since it is possible that a sign was done through trickery and magic....Moses, our teacher, knew that one who believes because of a sign has doubt and is apprehensive and suspects in his heart.... We do not believe every prophet that arose after Moses, our teacher, solely because of the sign....Rather, it is because of the commandment that Moses commanded in the Torah and said, "If he gave a sign, to him you shall listen" (Deuteronomy 18:15)...Therefore, if a prophet arises and performs great signs and wonders and seeks to contradict the prophecy of Moses, our teacher, we do not heed him, and we know clearly that those signs [were performed with] trickery and magic.[9]

Maimonides has both a philosophical objection to miracles (that God created nature and miracles disturb that order) and a practical one (that miracles cannot serve as the foundation of faith).

Maimonides struggles to downplay the role of miracles in faith, while embracing their existence in the Bible. Indeed, in the primary historical section of the Bible, from Genesis through Kings, there is not a single book that does not include accounts of miraculous divine intervention in human affairs. Despite our attempt to demonstrate that the Bible itself uses context to moderate the value of miracles, and despite the various rabbinic and medieval distancing from the importance of miracles, they are nonetheless quite present in the biblical narrative.

Beyond the problem that faith based on miracles is shallow and fleeting, or as Maimonides says, "one who believes [in anything] because of signs has a doubt in his heart, since it is possible that a sign was done through trickery and magic,"[10] I would further argue that miracles present a theological obstacle to meaningful faith. The very witnessing of a miracle make the option of faith impossible. Let me explain.

God's Thwarted Plan

A statement such as "the sky is blue" or "there is gravity" is not a statement of faith but of fact. One need not *believe* in gravity; one needs simply to notice that, with rare exception, things on earth fall down. Statements of faith are ones in which there is a choice to be made, and in which one could just as easily choose either to believe or to not believe. If so, then any overt display by God renders faith impossible and meaningless. Faith is irrelevant where there is fact. The Israelite declaration of their faith in God upon witnessing the splitting of the Reed Sea is meaningless, for it is nothing more than a restatement of a readily observable, incontrovertible fact. Assuming that faith—that is, meaningful faith—is a desideratum, overt miracles thus hinder human ability to achieve that faith, as the undeniable reality of the miracle renders achieving faith an impossibility.

Looking at the Bible, and especially its opening books, it appears that the biblical story is about God who creates humanity so that humanity can have a meaningful relationship with God.[11] For that relationship to be meaningful, it must be optional—so that humans have the capacity (intellectual, spiritual, moral, and circumstantial) to *choose* to have that relationship, but also the ability to choose to *not* have that relationship. In contrast, a robot programmed to praise its developer speaks only to the programmer's skill but not to the meaningfulness of the robot's declarations. Indeed, it is the capacity for meaningful choice that defines our very humanity.

Genesis describes how the process of bringing God's plan to fruition is fraught with obstacles and pitfalls—so much so that by the time we reach the tenth generation, the world is filled with violence, corruption, injustice, and immorality, and God acknowledges the failure of the experiment:

> God saw that the evil of humanity was increasing, and that the products of the thoughts in its heart were only evil, all day. God regretted that He had made humanity in the land, and He became pained in His heart. God said, "I will erase humanity which I created from the face of the earth—from human to domesticated animal to crawling thing to the birds in the sky—for I regret that I created them." (Genesis 6:5–7)

Humans had failed; God's attempt had failed. There was a need to restart the process, albeit with minor changes that would increase the chances for success, but still without guarantee. After all, a guarantee of success would render the entire effort meaningless. And so God starts again, with the one individual thought to hold promise for success: Noah.

That second attempt did not end in disaster, but neither could it be deemed a success. After another ten generations God changes tactic yet again. Foregoing destruction, God chooses an individual with whom to build that relationship, and through whom God's message can be brought to the rest of the families of the earth. Painstakingly, God works with Abram (later to become Abraham) and Sarai (later to become Sarah), Isaac and Rebecca, Jacob (later to also become Israel) and his wives—and ultimately with the nation descended from these founding forebears.

The Changing Need of Humanity

Biblical heroes are not static figures—that is, they are not usually depicted as having been born as great, but rather as all-too-human people who become great as a result of grappling with the challenges that ultimately help to transform them. Further, the various stories are not meant to describe the many ways in which these people are great or are to be emulated, but rather they trace the development of those characters as they grow into greatness.[12] It is only after twenty-four years of contact with God that Abram eventually earns the name Abraham and Sarai becomes Sarah. Jacob eventually emerges as Israel but only after struggling with his brother, with his uncle, and maybe even with his own conscience.[13] Judah abandons his family and is nearly lost from the biblical narrative; it is only through Tamar's agency that he learns to take responsibility and emerges as a heroic figure. Joseph is a hyper-talented but self-absorbed and immature young man who must learn to stop looking in the mirror in his search for greatness. Moses is an Israelite-Egyptian-Midianite shepherd unwilling to take on a leadership role who, only after a series of profound encounters, learns to become the transformational Israelite leader. If the great heroes of the Bible, the ones whom God identified as key figures in the drive to establish meaningful relationships with humans, need to undergo transformational growth, then it is even truer for the rest of humanity.

A parent-child model would be helpful in exploring this further. A newborn is completely dependent upon its parents. It is the way we are designed, and without the ever-vigilant watchfulness of parents none of us would survive those first few months—so much so that often the very presence of a parent itself becomes a source of comfort. As the child begins to grow and develop, it develops limited autonomy—the ability to reach for a toy, cover itself with a blanket, bury its head in a pillow, suck its thumb. These are tiny steps, not even baby steps yet, but they are the very earliest stages of autonomy. The child does not need the parent (or adult caregiver) all the time, but is still mostly dependent. As the child continues to grow he or she eventually begins to develop greater autonomy—in locomotion, feeding itself, entertainment, and more—and at every stage the presence of the parent becomes less necessary. It is, in fact, the way that children eventually grow into healthy adulthood.

For the child to seek out the parent in the early stages of life is self-understood, as is the need for the parent to assert his or her presence. As the child reaches adulthood, it would be improper and inappropriate for the parent to assert his or her presence and impinge on the autonomy of the now-adult child, just as it would be inappropriate for the adult-child to sever all ties with the parent. And even though the adult child may not necessarily need anything of a practical nature from the parent, in a healthy relationship the adult child will nonetheless seek to maintain the parent's presence in his or her life.

Returning to our central topic: humanity in its infancy needed God's ubiquitous presence. We needed God to provide for and guide us. Mistakes needed to be corrected by a divine parent, sometimes severely but always with love, so that that we could learn from them. With the passage of time God's direct appearance became not only unnecessary, but unhelpful, as God's ubiquitous presence would not let humanity to grow and develop.[14] Just as biblical heroes need to mature, so do the rest of the biblical players, including those behind the scenes—that is, the entirety of humanity. Divine miracles are the equivalent of the overt presence of the parent, and a careful reading of the Bible reveals that God repeatedly and progressively recedes into the background of the historical stage while people are expected to increasingly take up the divine mission on earth.

The Disappearance of Miracles

There are two ways to view God's progressive retreat from the human stage. One is to investigate God's gradual disappearance from overt and public interference with the course of human history; the other is to examine the human reaction to God's fading from view. The very existence of the Israelites in the wilderness is supernatural: manna from heaven; the pillar of fire by night and cloud by day, which guided their travels and protected them; and of course the occasional dramatic miracles of splitting the sea, water from the rock, heavenly fires burning sinners, and the earth swallowing up rebels.

The Book of Joshua stands as a significant transition point. On the one hand the book opens with God stopping the flow of the Jordan, bringing down the walls of Jericho, and stopping the sun for Joshua. On the other hand we see a transition from the supernatural into a natural existence. The manna stops and the people eat from the produce of the land (Joshua 5:11). While God brought down the walls of Jericho, there was still a military battle to be fought (Joshua 6:21), and Joshua needed to learn a variety of military tactics to defeat the walled cities of Ai (Joshua 8) and of the southern coalition of kings (Joshua 10). Even when God stopped the sun for Joshua, it was to enable Joshua to continue the military battle and achieve its objective. By the time Joshua fought the northern coalition of kings (Joshua 11) there was no longer evidence of divine intervention. While the Book of Joshua starts with miracles, it represents the switch from a supernatural existence to a fundamentally natural one.[15]

Next in the canonical order of the Bible, the Book of Judges is marked primarily by people who, aided by divine inspiration, work without miracles to help the nation with challenging oppressors.[16] The same is true for the books of Samuel and Kings: God's intervention is the exception rather than the rule, and miracles are invoked by a prophet to demonstrate the veracity of his status as prophet rather than to demonstrate God's power. When we move to the latter prophets (Isaiah through Jeremiah), the absence of unambiguous divine intervention (read: miracles) forced the prophets to contend with competing narratives offered by false prophets. It was the compelling nature of their messages rather than some dramatic supernatural sign that would have to ultimately win the hearts of their listeners. By the time we reach the final historical book, Esther, not only is there no apparent divine intervention—but God's name is absent as well.

While some may interpret the disappearance of miracles as a sign of God's displeasure or our unworthiness, it seems that what we are witnessing is the biblical equivalent of the parent pulling back, allowing for the maturing child to find his or her own way in the world. God's fading into the background is what makes room for the maturing Israel to discover the quiet, behind-the-scenes role played by God. God's receding from the limelight is what opens the door for people to choose to see God in their lives, enabling the quest for genuine faith to emerge.

The search for God who is not apparent is one of the central themes of the prophetic books of the Bible. Israelite and Judean kings tended to view the events of the world around them through a geo-political lens: the rise of an enemy in the north necessitated an alliance with Egypt in the south, or a different ally in the north. The literary prophets—Isaiah, Jeremiah, and others—interpreted these events through a religious lens—that is, as acts of God. In Jeremiah's eyes, Nebuchadnezzar was a servant of God doing God's bidding; in Elijah's eyes, the fall of the house of Omri had nothing to do with political unrest or dissatisfaction with Ahab but was the result of divine punishment for Ahab's sins; and in the eyes of Ahijah of Shilo, the fall of the house of Solomon was unrelated to the incompetence of his son Rechoboam but rather divine retribution for Solomon's sins.[17]

Miracles were critical for early humanity as well as for early Israel, much as parental omnipresence and care is essential for infants. The disappearance of miracles allows for faith and is accompanied by the growing prophetic voice in the Bible. The prophets are driven to reveal God's role in our life, and in doing so, to begin the earliest genuine search for faith. In the Bible, God's role is played out on the national level, where it is prophets' role to reveal that activity to the national leader, the king. In the post-biblical era, there is a shift toward finding God's role in our personal lives, where it becomes the task of every individual to discover the role God plays. In the absence of God's overt presence, we are given the option to choose to see God or not. And it is that option which makes the choice meaningful.

NOTES

[1] Many classical Jewish thinkers struggled with this question. See, for example, Judah Halevi's *Kuzari* I 97, Maimonides' *Guide to the Perplexed* III 32, and Naḥmanides' commentary to Exodus 32:1, s.v. *asher yeil'khu l'faneinu*.

[2] For more on these parallels see Elḥanan Samet, *Pirkei Eliyahu* (Maaleh Adumim, Israel: Maalot, 2003), pp. 275–278.

[3] The wind was prominent at the splitting of the sea (Exodus 14:21), earthquake in the event of Koraḥ (Numbers 16:32) and at the Sinai theophany (Exodus 19:18), and fire at the destruction of Sodom and the other cities of the plain (Genesis 19:24) and again at Sinai (Deuteronomy 5:4). Contrasted especially with Sinai, marked by extremely loud sounds (Exodus 19:16–19), God's revelation here is distinguished by its quietude.

[4] In the Bible, rhetorical questions asked by a divine figure are rebuke. See, for example, Genesis 3:9, 4:9, 16:8, and Exodus 4:11.

[5] For an alternate reading of this story see Uriel Simon, *K'riah Sifrutit Ba-mikra* (Jerusalem: Mossad Bialik, 1997), pp. 189–278.

[6] M. Taanit 3:8.

[7] Elijah decreed a drought upon the land (1 Kings 17:1) and later decreed the end of the drought in the aftermath of the showdown on Mount Carmel (18:41).

[8] B. Taanit 23a. See the analysis in Binyamin Lau, *Ḥakhamim* (Jerusalem: Beit Morashah, 2006), vol. 1, pp. 62–83.

[9] M.T. Hilkhot Yesodei Hatorah 8:1–3. See also Maimonides, *Guide to the Perplexed*, II 29, II 35, and III 24.

[10] M.T. Hilkhot Yesodei Hatorah 8:1.

[11] See, for example, Martin Buber, *Darko Shel Mikra* (Jerusalem: Mossad Bialik, 1978), pp. 63–81.

[12] See my *Moses and the Path to Leadership* (Jerusalem: Urim, 2014) and my *From Creation to Covenant* (Jerusalem: Maggid, 2017).

[13] This is one way of reading the scene of Jacob's nocturnal wrestling match with his mysterious adversary (Genesis 32:24–25). See *From Creation to Covenant*, pp. 353–362.

[14] I refer repeatedly to miracles. The same pattern of the disappearing God, with the same underling goal, is evident in the slow disappearance of prophecy— another overt manifestation of God's presence in the world.

[15] See Eliyahu Assis, *Mi-moshe Lihoshua Umi-neis La-teva* (Jerusalem: Magnes, 2005), pp. 8–30, for a careful literary analysis that highlights the transformation from miraculous to natural living. Naftali Zvi Yehuda Berlin, in his introduction to his *Ha·amek Davar* commentary on Numbers (Israel, 1975; p. 5), suggests that the switch from supernatural to natural living is the central theme of Numbers.

[16] The notable exception is Samson with his supernatural strength. Even in his

case, however, his strength is never understood by either the Israelites or the Philistines as miraculous or a sign of divine intervention.

[17] This is sometimes called the Dual Causality Principle, in which the same event is described in the Bible from two different perspectives, one human and the other prophetic. See, for example, Yairah Amit, "The Dual Causality Principle and Its Effects on Biblical Literature," *Vetus Testamentum* 37 (1987), pp. 385–400; and Jonathan Grossman, "The Design of the 'Dual Causality' Principle in the Narrative of Absalom's Rebellion," *Biblica* 88 (2007), pp. 558–566.

Free Will and the Hardening of Pharaoh's Heart

Shira Weiss

One of the most enduring philosophical debates throughout history has been over the problem of free will. In contemporary philosophy, determinist philosophers argue that though human beings appear to be free to choose, their actions are in fact compelled by various causes, whether physical, psychological, biological, or theological.[1] Libertarian philosophers counter that human beings are able to choose between alternative possibilities, and through their choices they become the cause of their actions and can, therefore, be held morally responsible.[2] Compatibilist philosophers argue that free will is compatible with determinism.[3]

The contemporary philosophical debate and its implications for Judaism can be traced back to the Middle Ages. Medieval Jewish philosophers argued over whether or not human freedom is compatible with external causation and with divine foreknowledge. Questions of theological determinism were contested: If God is omnipotent, would it not follow that God is the direct cause of everything, including human actions? If God is omniscient and possesses immutable knowledge, how can human beings have free choice when God's foreknowledge seems to determine the outcome? If God is the cause, would it be just for human beings to be held morally responsible for their own actions and thus be subject to divine retribution? Further questions regarding the general nature of human freedom were also debated: Are alternative possibilities prerequisites for choice? Is it necessary for one's true self to identify with that which one chooses, in order for one's choice to be free?

Three general approaches to the philosophical problem of theological determinism emerged among medieval Jewish philosophers. Some philosophers, such as Gersonides (1288–1344), limited divine foreknowledge in order to maintain human free choice. A second theory, advocated by determinists such as Abner of Burgos (1260–1347) and Ḥasdai Crescas (1340–1410), sacrificed human free choice in an effort to retain divine omniscience. A third reconciliatory theory, espoused first by Maimonides (1138–1204) and then by later fifteenth-century Iberian Jewish philosophers including Joseph Albo (1380–1444), aimed to affirm both human free choice and God's knowledge of future contingents.

While the Bible does not explicitly assert the doctrine of free will, the concept seems implicit. For instance, in Moses' final speech to the Israelites, he states:

> See, I have set before you this day life and good, and death and evil, in that I command you this day to love the LORD your God, to walk in His ways, and to keep His commandments and His statutes and His ordinances; then you shall live and multiply, and the LORD your God shall bless you in the land where you go in to possess it...I call heaven and earth to witness against you this day, that I have set before you life and death, the blessing and the curse; therefore choose life, that you may live, you and your seed. (Deuteronomy 30:15–19)[4]

However, elsewhere in the Bible the concept of free will is challenged. In the biblical description of the plagues that God brought upon the Egyptians in the Exodus narrative, it is written that God "hardened Pharaoh's heart" so that he would not agree to allow the Israelites to leave his land. The narrative seems to imply that God literally restrained Pharaoh's free will; however, such an interpretation calls God's justice into question since Pharaoh is held morally responsible for this divinely coerced refusal to liberate the Israelites. The divine hardening also challenges another one of Judaism's doctrines, that of repentance, which acclaims the remittance of punishment for the penitent. Classical exegetes, medieval philosophers, and modern biblical scholars and philosophers have all debated whether or not God's hardening deprived Pharaoh of his free choice, as well as the nature of God's justice and Pharaoh's moral responsibility.

In the fourth chapter of Exodus, God instructs Moses: "When you return to Egypt, see that you perform before Pharaoh all the marvels that I have put within your power. I, however, will harden his heart, so that he will not let the people go" (Exodus 4:21).[5] After God's introductory statements to Moses, the narrative of the plagues unfolds. God instructs Moses to appear before Pharaoh prior to the onset of each of the first five plagues, requesting to take the Israelites out of Egypt on a three-day journey to worship, but Pharaoh obstinately refuses to heed Moses' request—despite the afflictions he and his people endure from the plagues. After each of the first five plagues, we read that "Pharaoh's heart was hardened" (va-yeḥezak leiv paroh)[6] or that "Pharaoh hardened his heart" (va-yakhbeid paroh et libbo).[7] Following the sixth plague, a literary shift appears in the text. Instead of Pharaoh hardening his own heart, God is explicitly mentioned as hardening Pharaoh's heart.[8] God continues to harden Pharaoh's heart in the later plagues.[9] During the final plague, Pharaoh finally relents and releases the Israelites. However, shortly thereafter, God hardens his heart again, and Pharaoh pursues the Israelites into the sea.

The progression of the narrative raises the following philosophical questions:
  • Can divine hardening coexist with free will and moral

responsibility? If God causes Pharaoh to will an evil act (namely: keeping the Israelites enslaved), why should Pharaoh be held responsible for this act? Would not God, therefore, be responsible for the moral failing, not Pharaoh? Or did Pharaoh lack free will and therefore did not incur moral responsibility for his actions under those circumstances?

- If God wants sinners to repent, as the Bible preaches, why would God prevent any individual from changing his or her ways for the better? Why would God deprive someone of free will and the opportunity to repent? Or is God's interference compatible with the agent being possessed of free will and having an opportunity to repent?

Maimonides asserts the doctrine of human free will and argues that people have the ability to act freely and choose to do good or evil. He argues that were human beings compelled to act in a certain way, the commandments and prohibitions would become null and void, since people would have no freedom of choice (b'hirah) in what they do, and reward and punishment would therefore be unjust:

> In reality, the undoubted truth of the matter is that human beings have full sway over all their actions. If they wish to do a thing, they do it; if they do not wish to do it, they need not—without any external compulsion controlling them. Therefore, God very properly commanded Israel, saying, "See I have set before you this day life and the good, death and evil... Therefore choose life" (u-vaharta ba-ḥayyim; Deuteronomy 30:15,19)—giving us, as regards these options, freedom of choice. [10]

Maimonides argues that just as one can choose freely to sin, so too can one choose freely to repent; punishment ensues only in cases when the sinner chooses not to repent. He continues, however, that there are limits to the opportunities for repentance:

> A person may commit a very big sin, or numerous sins, that justice requires of the True Judge, as the punishment to be exacted from the sinner for the sins he committed voluntarily and of his own mind is that repentance shall be withheld from him and freedom to return from his evil shall not be afforded him, so that he may die in the sins which he committed.[11]

In his legal code, the Mishneh Torah, Maimonides explains that there are certain situations in which God makes it impossible for a sinner to escape the well-deserved irrevocable punishment for a heinous sin that was committed freely. He distinguishes between a person's power to choose freely between sinning and not sinning, and one's power to choose freely between repenting from sin and not repenting from sin. In the case of the former (which is a matter of justice), God will never interfere; in the case of the latter (which is a matter of mercy), God may occasionally interfere. Maimonides identifies the situation in which God hardens Pharaoh's heart as an instance of repentance, not sin—and therefore justifies God's intervention in that situation. Maimonides writes:

> Therefore it is also written: "And I will harden Pharaoh's heart" (Exodus 4:21). Because Pharaoh sinned out of his own will and mistreated the Israelites who dwelled in his land, as it said, "Come let us deal cunningly with them, so that they will not increase" (Exodus 1:10), justice required that repentance should be withheld from him until retribution had been exacted upon him. God, accordingly, hardened his heart.[12]

Because Pharaoh had initially freely chosen to enslave the Israelites and subsequently refused to liberate them in the aftermath of each of the first five plagues (as Scripture says, "Pharaoh hardened his heart"), God then intervened and hardened Pharaoh's heart by depriving him of an opportunity to repent after each of the latter plagues. Maimonides explains that the purpose of the divine hardening was that God wanted to teach the entire world the power of divine punishment:

> In order to show the world that when God prevents a sinner from repenting, that person cannot repent, but rather dies in the wickedness that one initially did out of free will.[13]

As a result, the lesson taught to humanity from the example of Pharaoh and the Egyptians was not to continue sinning with the expectation of a future opportunity of repentance.

However, in light of other passages in Maimonides' philosophical writings, his interpretation of God's hardening of Pharaoh's heart can be understood in an alternative, more naturalistic manner, and not as a direct or supernatural divine intervention that resulted in the withholding of his free choice. In his *Guide for the Perplexed*, Maimonides describes his conceptions of God's prophecy, providence, and miracles from a naturalistic perspective.[14] According to Maimonides, God fixed nature, which reflects divine wisdom and providence and thus allows for minimal supernatural intervention. He explains that while human actions are, in fact, free, they are often attributed by the prophets to God, who is the First Cause of all things, including human actions. Nevertheless, such attribution does not denote divine intervention:

> It is very clear that everything that is produced in time must necessarily have a proximate cause which has produced it. In its turn, that cause has a cause and so forth until finally one

comes to the First Cause of all things, I mean God's will and free choice. For this reason, all those intermediate causes are sometimes omitted in the dicta of the prophets, and an individual act produced in time is ascribed to God, it being said that He, may He be exalted, has done it.[15]

Similarly, in his interpretation of God's hardening of Pharaoh's heart, the "punishment" alluded to in the Mishneh Torah (discussed above) may be referring to the natural consequence of Pharaoh's actions, and not to God's direct intervention in order to exact a deserved punishment upon Pharaoh (which deprived him of his free choice and ability to repent and thus forced him to do evil).

The noted twentieth-century Bible scholar, Nehama Leibowitz (1905–1997) conceives of Maimonides' theory of God's hardening of Pharaoh's heart in a naturalistic manner that reflects Pharaoh's self-choice. In a psychological explanation, she argues that human beings initially have complete freedom to choose to do good or evil. However, as soon as one makes a first choice, one's options are no longer as equal. Even though at first one's alternatives of good or evil were evenly balanced, if one chooses evil and persists on the evil path, it becomes progressively more difficult for one to revert back to choosing good. Technically, however, one's freedom of choice is not affected and no external force is coercing one's decisions.[16]

Leibowitz interprets Maimonides' reading of Pharaoh naturalistically, in light of Maimonides' assertion of human free will: "There is no one who compels him, sentences him, or leads him towards either of these two paths. Rather, he, on his own initiative and decision, tends to the path he chooses. Accordingly, it is the sinner, himself, who causes his own loss."[17] Leibowitz concludes:

God did not force Pharaoh to choose evil. It was Pharaoh's own doing. Once he persisted in his course of action it became

more and more irresistible. God had built this response, as it
were, into man's make-up. The more he sins, the more his sins
act as a barrier between him and repentance.[18]

Jerome Gellman similarly reads the narrative naturalistically,
"reinterpreting the *prima facie* divine intervention in Pharaoh's
freedom in the biblical story of the Exodus as Pharaoh's self-defeat.
Pharaoh himself chose to be so wicked that he could not repent
and change his ways."[19] Thus, Pharaoh's punishment was not caused
by direct divine intervention but was rather the natural result of
his earlier free choices. Pharaoh's initial free decision to afflict the
Israelites was exacerbated by his continuous self-willed refusals to
release the Israelites after each of the first five plagues. Pharaoh
is therefore morally responsible for his actions, which caused his
unavoidable predicament in the latter portion of the narrative.

Such a modern naturalistic reading reflects an ancient Aristotelian
influence. Aristotle argues in *Nicomachean Ethics* that individuals are
responsible for their own character and unavoidable bad actions that
result from previous choices:

> If it is manifest that a man is the author of his own actions,
> and if we are unable to trace our conduct back to any other
> origins than those within ourselves, then actions of which
> the origins are within us themselves depend upon us, and are
> voluntary...Men are themselves responsible...they acquire a
> particular quality by constantly acting in a particular way.[20]

Along these same lines, Pharaoh's free initial decisions cause his later
inability to repent, for which he is appropriately held accountable.
While Leibowitz does not address the scriptural language of divine
causality, she implies that since God does not intervene, the ascription
of the hardening of Pharaoh's heart in later plagues to God must refer

to God's creation of the psychology of human beings such that the more one sins, the more one's evil decisions seem irresistible—even though there is no external compulsion.

Also in line with this naturalistic approach, Nahum Sarna articulates God's role even more explicitly. Sarna explains that from the biblical perspective, the heart is considered the source of the intellectual, moral, and spiritual faculties that determine one's actions. The "hardening of the heart" reflects a state of "arrogant moral degeneracy, unresponsive to human reason."[21] In the aftermath of each of the first five plagues, the hardening of Pharaoh's heart is self-willed, and only thereafter ascribed to God. Similar to Leibowitz, Sarna argues that the attribution to divine causality does not imply divine intervention. Rather, he claims that this is the "biblical way of asserting that the king's intransigence has by then become habitual and irreversible; his character has become his destiny. He is deprived of the possibility of relenting and is irresistibly impelled to his self-wrought doom."[22]

This naturalistic interpretation can also explain the lesson that Egypt and Israel were to learn from God's hardening of Pharaoh's heart—namely, not to perpetuate sin with the expectation of a future opportunity to repent. According to this reading, Pharaoh's self-willed downward spiral could serve as a lesson for Egypt and Israel not to underestimate the powerful impact of sinful behavior upon future actions, even without external coercion. The Egyptians and Israelites needed to learn from Pharaoh's example that they might not have the ability to reform their wicked conduct in the future—not because God deprives sinners of free will or the ability to repent, but due to the irresistible pressure of their habitual corruptive actions.

In his commentary on Exodus 7:3, Naḥmanides (1194–1270) echoes Maimonides' (interventionist) theory that God deprived Pharaoh of free choice as a divine punishment. However, he then offers an alternative explanation that half of the plagues came upon Pharaoh due to his own sins (as reflected in the verses "Pharaoh's heart was hardened" and "Pharaoh hardened his heart"[23]), because he had refused to let the Israelites go for the sake of the glory of God. However, when the plagues began having an effect on him, his heart softened and he became willing to liberate them—but this was only in order to alleviate the suffering caused by the plagues, and not in order to obey God's will. Therefore, God hardened Pharaoh's heart in order to make the divine name known throughout the world.[24]

Elaborating on Naḥmanides' second interpretation, Joseph Albo (c. 1380–1444) in his *Sefer Ha-ikkarim* ("*The Book of Principles*") argues that God's hardening of Pharaoh's heart must not be understood as God's coercion of Pharaoh, but rather as God's preservation of Pharaoh's free will in order to allow him the opportunity to repent freely from his wrongdoing and not be forced into liberating the Israelites solely as a result of the suffering caused by the plagues.[25] God preserved Pharaoh's free will by giving him the fortitude to withstand his afflictions and suggesting to him alternative explanations for the cause of the plagues. Accordingly, Pharaoh was morally responsible for his ultimate free choice of attributing the plagues to natural causes and refusing to let the Israelites go, and he was therefore deserving of punishment.

Albo asserts that God *does* desire that sinners repent; God hardened Pharaoh's heart in order to give him a free opportunity to do so. Albo's interpretation of the hardening of Pharaoh's heart comes in the context of a discussion about the nature of repentance, in which he distinguishes between repentance from love and repentance from fear. Albo further subdivides the latter category into repentance from fear of punishment and repentance from fear of God. Repentance due to fear of punishment, he explains, is similar to a slave entreating his master while he is being beaten; as soon as his afflictions are relieved, he reverts back to his disobedience. A slave lacks fear when not being beaten; therefore, a slave's repentance is the result of an episodic fear and not an abiding fear. Albo argues that such was the attitude of Pharaoh, and this does not constitute true repentance. For Albo, those who are penitent out of fear must be in a certain abiding cognitive and affective state, which was not true of Pharaoh. So long as the plagues were upon him, Pharaoh returned to God from the fear of the punishment, as he exclaimed: "I have sinned this time, the LORD is righteous" (Exodus 9:27).[26] But as soon as God alleviated his suffering, he hardened his own heart as before, demonstrating that his repentance was compelled only by the fear of death and was not the result of a conscious and free act. Such an attitude should not be regarded as repentance at all.

The second type of repentance from fear is that of people who fear God even in time of respite. Such people are afraid of God's punishment because they recognize that all things come from God as reward and punishment, and do not ascribe events to nature and chance. This is unlike Pharaoh, who associated each plague with a chance occurrence and then reverted back to his original bad behavior. Even after the culmination of all of the plagues (which testified to the omnipotence of God), as soon as Pharaoh thought that the Israelites had lost their way, he ascribed all of the signs and wonders that he had witnessed to chance. He pursued the Israelites, thereby proving clearly that his initial repentance during the plagues was due only to compulsion on account of his suffering. It was not voluntary. The plagues thus had an enfeebling effect on Pharaoh; he agreed to liberate the Israelites under duress, out of cowardice and fear of punishment. Albo writes:

> In this way, we must explain the statements in the Bible that
> God hardens the heart of the wicked, or makes them stiff-

necked and prevents them from repenting. The wicked man, when misfortune comes upon him, pretends to become pious and returns to God due to the fear of the punishment which is upon him, as Pharaoh said: "I have sinned this time, the LORD is righteous." Now, since this act is like one that is forced and not free, God hardens his heart by suggesting to him other causes to which he can attribute the misfortune—accident, for example—rather than divine providence. This is done in order to remove from his heart the softening effect which came from the misfortune, so that he may return to his natural state and act freely without compulsion. Then it may be discovered whether his repentance was free or not. Now since, when the yoke of the plague was removed from Pharaoh, his choice was evil, God said: "I hardened his heart," i.e., I removed from his heart the softening effect which came from the plague and restored him to the natural state of freedom; while he, owing to his wicked attitude, when in a state of freedom, sought various causes and excuses to which he might ascribe the plagues so that they might seem accidental.[27]

Albo seems to reject Maimonides' understanding, the divine punishment approach, and makes free will the focal point of his analysis. He suggests that the plagues caused cowardice, whereas choice requires courage. God thus hardened, or emboldened, Pharaoh's heart in order to afford him courage, which would enable him to overcome the cowering effect of the plagues and arrive at a free decision of whether or not to repent. Therefore, Albo writes, after the suffering from the plagues was alleviated, Pharaoh took *courage* and pursued the Israelites—thereby proving that his initial repentance (via liberation of the Israelites) was due to the compulsion of his punishment and was *not* a result of free choice. Albo explains that God hardened Pharaoh's heart by allowing him to consider other possible sources for the plagues. In order for Pharaoh to achieve true repentance (that is, the second type of repentance, out of fear), he would have to recognize that his misfortunes were a punishment from God. Relieved of the suffering from the plagues, Pharaoh had the ability to repent freely. But instead, he sought various excuses in order to make the plagues seem accidental, refusing to acknowledge God's providence.[28]

The various interpretations of God's hardening of Pharaoh's heart reflect different conceptions of the nature of human free will. Can one be deprived of free choice, and thereby the ability to change one's behavior? To what extent can God control human freedom? Albo presents a dramatically different approach to the hardening of Pharaoh's heart than that suggested by Maimonides. Albo views God's hardening as an effort to preserve Pharaoh's free choice and opportunity to repent, whereas Maimonides interprets God's hardening as the elimination of Pharaoh's free choice and chance for repentance—either because he did not deserve such an opportunity (due to his previous free sins) or as a natural consequence (which resulted from his earlier free choices). Whereas Maimonides' explanation imposes limitations on free choice as a punishment for, or consequence of, free actions, Albo's explanation preserves universal human free choice and maintains God's desire for all of humanity to repent by affording them the opportunity to return freely from their sinful ways without any external compulsion.

According to all approaches, Pharaoh's initial free choices demonstrated his abuse of human freedom and his failure to take advantage of his opportunity to repent and recognize the omnipotence of God. He was, therefore, deserving of punishment. This challenging biblical episode raises enduring philosophical questions that continue to be debated today, and it encourages modern readers to reflect upon the nature of their own free will and moral responsibility.

NOTES

[1] For example, see Derk Pereboom, *Living Without Free Will* (Cambridge: Cambridge University Press, 2001).

[2] For example, see Robert Kane, *A Contemporary Introduction to Free Will* (Oxford: Oxford University Press, 2005).

[3] For examples, see Thomas Hobbes, *Leviathan*, ed. R.E. Flatman & D. Johnston (New York: W.W. Norton & Co., 1997); David Hume, *An Enquiry Concerning Human Understanding*, ed. P.H. Nidditch (Oxford: Clarendon Press, 1978); Harry Frankfurt, "Alternate Possibilities and Moral Responsibility," *Journal of Philosophy* 66:3 (1969), pp. 829–839; Galen Strawson, *Freedom and Belief* (Oxford: Clarendon Press, 1986); and Susan Wolf, *Freedom within Reason* (Oxford: Oxford University Press, 1990). Hobbes's book was first published in 1651; Hume's in 1748.

[4] NJPS translation.

[5] Based on the NJPS translation.

[6] Exodus 7:13, 14, 22; 8:15; 9:7, 35.

[7] Exodus 8:11, 28, 32; 9:34.

[8] Exodus 9:12 (boils), 10:20 (locusts), 10:27 (darkness). God is described as the agent of hardening a total of ten times: Exodus 4:21; 7:3; 9:12; 10:1, 20, 27; 11:10; 14:4, 8, and 17.

[9] With the exception of the seventh plague, hail (Exodus 9:34), when Pharaoh hardens his own heart after God hardens his heart in the sixth. For an explanation, see note 29.

[10] Maimonides, *Sh'monah P'rakim*, chap. 8.

[11] M.T. Hilkhot Teshuvah 6:3 (my translation).

[12] Ibid.

[13] Ibid.

[14] *The Guide for the Perplexed* II 32–48 (prophecy), III 17–23, 51 (providence), II 29 (miracles).

[15] *The Guide for the Perplexed* II 48, trans. Shlomo Pines (Chicago: University of Chicago Press, 1963), p. 409. Pines's translation gives the title as *The Guide of the Perplexed*.

[16] Nehama Leibowitz, *Studies in Shemot* (Jerusalem: World Zionist Organization, 1976), p. 157, quoting Maimonides' Hilkhot Teshuvah 6:4: "This is what is implied...as David pleaded [Psalms 86:11]: 'God, show me Your way that I may walk in Your truth'; i.e., do not let *my sins* prevent me from [reaching] the path of truth which will lead me to appreciate Your way and the ones of Your name. A similar intent [is conveyed] by the request [Psalms 51:14]: 'Support me with a spirit of magnanimity'; i.e., let my spirit [be willing] to do Your will and do not cause *my sins to prevent me from repenting*...Rather, let the choice remain

in my hand until I repent and comprehend and appreciate the path of truth. In a similar way, [one must interpret] all the [verses] which resemble these." Thus Maimonides implies that what prevents repentance is one's sins, not God's supernatural intervention.

[17] M.T. Hilkhot Teshuvah 5:2–3.

[18] Leibowitz, *Studies in Shemot*, p. 157.

[19] Jerome Gellman, "Radical Responsibility in Maimonides' Thought," in *The Thought of Moses Maimonides: Philosophical and Legal Studies* (New York: E. Mellen Press, 1990), p. 253. Gellman also supports his approach based on Maimonides' reference to King David since, like Leibowitz, Gellman understands David's requests of God to "show him the way" and to grant him "a willing soul" as expressing hope that his sins will not keep him from repentance. Gellman reads the rest of Maimonides' Hilkhot Teshuvah naturalistically as well. He describes chapter 5 as focusing upon the human freedom that makes *t'shuvah*, the turning of oneself in the direction of God, possible, and chapters 8 and 9 as naturalizing the concepts of the World to Come and divine retribution. Gellman concludes as follows (p. 254): "Divine aid, therefore, is not interventionist, but consists in once having provided the stable background that a person can choose to take advantage of. The 'aid' he receives pertains to the rational structure that was available to him all along. King David wishes to be allowed to operate freely within this background structure. *In fine*, a new self-understanding emerges from chapters 5–9 of [*Hilkhot*] *Teshuvah*: an understanding of oneself as responsible, in total freedom, for one's fate, in a world where God's intervention is minimized or does not exist."

[20] Aristotle, *The Nicomachean Ethics*, trans. H. Rackman (Cambridge: Harvard University Press, 1956), III 5, p. 149.

[21] Nahum Sarna, *JPS Torah Commentary: Exodus* (Philadelphia: Jewish Publication Society, 2004), p. 23.

[22] Ibid.

[23] "Pharaoh's heart was hardened," Exodus 7:13, 22 and 8:15; "Pharaoh hardened his heart," Exodus 8:28 and 9:7.

[24] Naḥmanides to Exodus 7:3, s.v. *va-ani aksheh et leiv paroh*.

[25] Joseph Albo, *Sefer Ha-ikkarim* 4:25. For a more extensive discussion, see Shira Weiss, *Joseph Albo on Free Choice: Exegetical Innovation in Medieval Jewish Philosophy* (New York: Oxford University Press), 2017.

[26] NJPS translation.

[27] Joseph Albo, *Sefer Ha-ikkarim* [*Book of Principles*] IV:25, trans. Isaac Husik (Philadelphia: The Jewish Publication Society of America, 1930), pp. 226–228. The volume transliterates the title as Sefer Ha-iqqarim.

[28] There is a clear distinction between the first five plagues, in which Pharaoh hardened his own heart, and the next five, in which God hardened Pharaoh's

heart—as reflected in the shift in language. According to both Albo and the naturalist reading of Maimonides, the debilitating effect of the progression of the first five plagues took a toll on Pharaoh. According to both opinions, after the first five plagues, Pharaoh hardened his own heart and was thereby responsible for his decisions. By the sixth, according to Albo, the debilitating effect of the plagues caused softening of his heart, which motivated God to suggest alternative sources of the plague in order to allow Pharaoh to make a non-coerced decision. According to (naturalist) Maimonides, Pharaoh's habitual decisions in the first five plagues determined his decision in the sixth. Note that in the following plague (the seventh), the language reverts back to Pharaoh hardening his own heart. Albo might explain this brief shift back to the language of self-hardening as an attempt to demonstrate that God did not supernaturally compel Pharaoh's decision in the sixth plague, and similarly did not do so in plagues eight and on. Rather, according to Albo, Pharaoh himself chose an alternative explanation for the plagues—even when the debilitating pressure of the plagues would have motivated him to acknowledge their divine source, and hence he acted freely. A parallel explanation of the seventh plague is available to Maimonides, whose naturalist interpretation sees Pharaoh's earlier free choices making his later decisions irresistible, without any external compulsion; his choices were his own responsibility, even though in the latter plagues he could not have chosen otherwise. The language of the seventh plague, then, enables the reader to realize that God did not (and would not) supernaturally remove Pharaoh's free choice, even when the Bible says that *God* hardened Pharaoh's heart. Having made Pharaoh's freedom and responsibility clear by its language in the seven plague, Scripture can simply say in the subsequent narrative that God hardened Pharaoh's heart—and the reader will understand that Pharaoh himself was responsible for those decisions. Obviously, this explanation of the language of the seventh plague is pure conjecture and speculation. Note, however, that no matter what interpretation one adheres to, plague seven is an anomaly; why would God, in this one case, not harden Pharaoh's heart? Thus, any theory of the hardening of Pharaoh's heart necessitates a conjecture about why the text attributes Pharaoh's resistance in the seventh plague to Pharaoh rather than to God. The interchangeability of actions caused by Pharaoh's hardening of his own heart and God's hardening of his heart is supported by Cassuto:

> In early Hebrew diction, it is customary to attribute every phenomenon onto the direct action of God. Every happening has a number of causes, and these causes, in turn, have other causes, and so on ad infinitum; according to the Israelite conception, the cause of all causes was the will of God, the Creator and Ruler of the world. Now the philosopher examines the long and complex chain of causation, whereas the ordinary person jumps instantly from the last effect to the first cause, and attributes the former directly to

God. This, now, is how the Torah, which employs human idioms, expresses itself. Consequently, the expression "but I will harden his heart" is, in the final analysis, the same as if it were worded, but his heart will be hard. In the continuation of the narrative, sentences like "And the Lord hardened the heart of Pharaoh" (9:12, et al.) alternate with others like "And Pharaoh's heart was hardened" (7:13, et al.); they can be interchanged because their essential meaning is identical. (Umberto Cassuto, *A Commentary on the Book of Exodus* [Jerusalem: Magnes Press, 1951], p. 56)

For a different explanation of how a Maimonidean might explain the anomaly of the seventh plague, see David Shatz, "Freedom, Repentance, and Hardening of Hearts: Albo vs. Maimonides," *Faith and Philosophy* 14:4 (1997), pp. 478–509.

Existentialist Ethics in Eden

Alex Maged

Near the end of the Torah, as Moses' days draws to a close, he turns to the people whom he has shepherded through forty years in the wilderness and enjoins them to "choose life" (Deuteronomy 30:19). This charge—which doubles as the title of the present volume—is a curious one, for it implies an alternative equally attractive. But what force could possibly exert the same claim upon the human psyche as the elemental will to life?

In Moses' valedictory sermon it is "death" and "curse" that are offered in substitute, and clearly for rhetorical effect. Had he wished to, however, Moses might well have placed in opposition to "life" a value that could have meaningfully competed. In order to do so, in fact, he would have needed only to return to the very beginning of that book whose finals chapters he was in the midst of writing— all the way back to the Garden of Eden. There God, on the eve of creation, famously plants two trees that are set apart from the rest: "And the Eternal, God, caused to sprout from the ground every tree pleasant to see and good to eat, and the Tree of Life in the midst of the garden, and the Tree of Knowledge of Good and Evil" (Genesis 3:9).

As readers, our focus typically centers upon the latter of these two trees: the Tree of Knowledge. It is this tree, after all, whose fruit God explicitly forbids Adam from consuming; it is from this tree that the serpent nevertheless tempts Eve, and thereby Adam, to eat;

and it is this tree, then, that is most naturally associated with the so-called "fall of humanity," and humanity's concomitant expulsion from paradise. Meanwhile, Eden's *other* tree—the Tree of Life—disappears almost entirely from the plot from the moment it is introduced.

Yet it cannot be that the Tree of Life functions merely as a "stage prop." Its special mention indicates that it must contribute something of significance to the narrative of humanity's pre-history—be it symbolic, thematic, or otherwise. Indeed, a careful reading of our verse would appear to yield that it is the Tree of *Life* that ought to have attracted the bulk of our attention: it is this tree that is listed first, and it is the one placed *in the midst of the garden*; the Tree of Knowledge, by contrast, is almost mentioned as an afterthought. Thus, it is the Tree of Life that is central in Eden, both literarily and spatially. In relative terms, the Tree of Knowledge is peripheral.

Consider, moreover, God's instructions to Adam vis-à-vis the trees of Eden: "And the Eternal, God, commanded Adam, saying: 'Of every tree of the garden you shall eat. But of the Tree of Knowledge of Good and Evil you shall not eat, for on the day that you eat thereof, you shall die'" (Genesis 3:16–17). Here is the well-known prohibition of eating the fruit of Eden. Remarkably, the Tree of Life is not included in the prohibition. Indeed, God explicitly encourages Adam to eat from every tree of the garden, except for the Tree of Knowledge. Moreover, the reason God provides for why Adam may not eat from the Tree of Knowledge—"on the day that you eat thereof, you shall die"—strongly suggests that Adam should search for a tree whose fruit bestows life. Altogether, then, the data points to a nearly inevitable conclusion: God did not want Adam to eat from the Tree of Knowledge, *but God did want Adam to eat from the Tree of Life*!

If this reading is correct, it emerges that the Torah's first account of human activity features a deliberate contrast between "knowledge" and "life"—a contrast much more compelling than the one Moses constructs for us centuries later. Surprisingly, though, God does not frame this choice as a toss-up; indeed, God actively directs Adam away from "knowledge" and toward "life." Still, it is not immediately clear why tension should exist between "knowledge" and "life"—nor, therefore, what it means for God to privilege the latter.

To decode this dichotomy, it may prove helpful to invoke the celebrated typology of Rabbi Joseph B. Soloveitchik (1903–1993), widely known in modern Orthodox circles simply as "the Rav." In an essay on the early chapters of Genesis entitled *The Lonely Man of Faith*, the Rav distinguishes between two fundamental modes of human interaction with the world—that of "Adam I" versus that of "Adam II":

> The most characteristic representative of Adam the first is the mathematical scientist who whisks us away from the array of tangible things, from color and sound, from hear, touch, and smell, which are the only phenomena accessible to our senses, into a formal relational world of thought constructs, the product of his "arbitrary" postulating and spontaneous positing and deducing. This world, woven out of human thought processes, functions with amazing precision and runs parallel to the workings of the real multifarious world of our senses. The modern scientist does not try to explain nature. He only duplicates it. In his full resplendent glory as a creative agent of God, he constructs his own world and in mysterious fashion succeeds in controlling his environment through manipulating his own mathematical constructs and creations….Adam the second does not apply the functional method invented by Adam the first. He does not create a world of his own. Instead, he wants to understand the living, "given" world into which he has been cast. Therefore, he does not mathematize phenomena or conceptualize things. He encounters the universe in all its colorfulness, splendor, and grandeur, and studies it with the naïveté, awe, and admiration

of the child who seeks the unusual and wonderful in every ordinary thing and event. While Adam the first is dynamic and creative, transforming sensory data into thought constructs, Adam the second is receptive and beholds the world in its original dimensions. He looks for the image of God not in the mathematical formula or the natural relational law but in every beam of light, in every bud and blossom, in the morning breeze and in the stillness of a starlit evening.[1]

For the Rav, a key difference between Adam I and Adam II is their degree of separation from God's creation. Adam II inhabits the *living world* whereas Adam I ensconces himself in the *world of thought*. The former interacts directly with natural phenomena while the latter preoccupies himself with abstractions thereof. Or, as I might put it: Adam II draws sustenance from the Tree of Life; Adam I, from the Tree of Knowledge.

Each of these modes, argues the Rav, is essential to the human condition. Yet both the Rav's essay and the text upon which it is based seem to subtly suggest that of the two modes, the one that is more spiritually vital is the one that places vitality itself (i.e., life) at its center. Part of this, as mentioned, has to do with the fact that to "know" a given reality, one is required to remove oneself from it, whereas to "live" is to encounter reality from within. In "the world of thought," then, some are subjects, and some objects, speaking to each other in the language that Martin Buber (1878–1965) referred to as "I–It"; but in the "world of life," all are equally subjects, speaking the language of "I–Thou."[2]

Thus we return to Genesis. God's call to humanity, at the dawn of creation, is to *choose life*—to embrace it, to experience it fully, to appreciate it on its own terms—before aspiring to analyze it from a distance; in this sense, it might be said, the imperative of Eden is positively "existentialist." At first humanity rejects this call, opting for "knowledge" instead. But there is no value to "knowledge" that is divorced from "life," and thus, in the aftermath of the sin, God restricts access to the Tree of Life (Genesis 3:24), and imposes a limit upon the span of human life (3:19), so that the only way humanity can continue is if humans choose to place their "knowledge" in the service of "life." Hence our narrative's resolution, "And Adam *knew* his wife, Eve, and she conceived, and bore a son" (4:1): the measure of true "knowledge," intimates the Torah, is the degree to which it results in the sharing and giving of "life."

How appropriate that this lesson is situated at the very beginning of the Torah, for us to review each year before studying the Torah anew. To approach the Torah in search of "knowledge" alone—be it moral, theological, legal, psychological, or historical—would be to miss the point. That is why King Solomon, the "wisest of all men" (1 Kings 5:11), referred to the Torah specifically as a "tree of life" (Proverbs 3:18): for Torah study, properly performed, does not climax in astute observations, clever interpretations, or profound insights, but rather in the conduct that animates and elevates "life," in its totality.

May it be the will of the God of Life that we achieve this lofty purpose.

NOTES

[1] Joseph B. Soloveitchik, *The Lonely Man of Faith* (1965; rpt. New York: Doubleday, 2006), pp. 17–22.

[2] See Martin Buber, *I and Thou*, trans. Walter Kaufmann (Edinburgh: T&T Clark, 1975). The original German-language work was first published in 1923.

"So Pray From the Mother":
Choosing Life Withdrawn from the Garden[1]

Aubrey Glazer

As human beings, every one of us is radically alone in the face of the one thing that marks existence in its singularity—death. One thing we certainly all share is the knowledge that each of us must die. This raises the deep existential question: What, then, does it mean to live and to choose life? If you are up for a full-frontal, art-house-style horror show strike at an unsuspecting audience, like director Daryl Arnofsky, you might create something like his recent film, "Mother!" The movie is about Mother Earth, played by Jennifer Lawrence, and God, portrayed by Javier Bardem. This secluded couple lives in a rambling Victorian house and they are continually interrupted by uninvited guests who never seem able to leave. God is stuck with writer's block after one major hit, while Mother is renovating their home and is forever tidying up. As a result, it seems that all the visitors are clamoring for a piece of the Divine. In Arnofsky's allegory the house represents our broken planet, being destroyed by climate change, and calls attention to humanity's role in environmental destruction.[2] As a Jewish director, Arnofsky's *cri de coeur* for redemption from the apocalypse already in our midst is informed but not limited to Jewish sources, and some cynics would say it is more inspired by a Sierra Club cult of environmentalist religion than by an integral vision of praying to the Mother. We shall return to this lack of an integral vision later, but for now it suffices to note that there is both a Mother Earth and a Great Mother, both of whom nest in the womb of eternal time. Both are necessarily integrated within a robust spiritual vision that encompasses the immanent and the transcendent, the natural and the supernatural. So while communities of spectators watching *Mother!* may awaken to a newfound responsibility as stewards of Mother Earth, as a director Arnofsky remains radically alone with his vision.

Yet more than just radical aloneness comes with the singular experience of being a lone human, even a singular artist. That *more than* is found in community. Philosophers realized early on that community is the counterbalance to the individual, analogous to how life is the counterbalance to death. Life in community transcends the limitations of singular death. The experience of being together— more than as just part of a couple, but as part of a collective—is a kind of immanent transcendence that can never be exhausted, whereas the individual quest eventually ends and thus is exhausted, at least on a certain level.[3]

One expression of the collective search for redemption is found through religion. It is the communal envelope of religion that seeks to provide a framework for that collective kind of immanent transcendence that can never be exhausted, yet too often may feel exhausted. Within the margins of many religious streams, there have been gnostics who remain committed to finding light in these darkened forms of calcifying religion. Gnostics are those who seek gnosis or illumination, and their quest—through the Abrahamic religions and beyond—remains a perennial search for luminosity amidst the darkness of existence. Some see the return of Gnosticism in the modern period as an embrace of a version of existentialism featuring a deeper kind of nihilism than any earlier iterations in the history of religion,[4] while others see the blind embrace of scientific materialism as the key to liberation of the mind as succumbing to the limited ideology that traps even Gnosticism.[5] Modernity presents every seeker and every system—even Gnosticism!—with unending challenges in recovering the sacred and salvaging the light.

And yet, in a landscape devoid of holy names that marks that deep absence of the presence of the Divine, community too feels abandoned.[6] Consciousness can bring light but it can also dwell deep in luminal darkness. If consciousness is seen as "not only a progressive and affirmative development toward light but also…as an expulsion from the nocturnal bliss of sleep in the unconscious and—as, for example, in all world views of gnostic coloration—as loss of the original home,"[7] then there is much to be learned from singer-songwriter Bob Dylan and his post-exilic wanderings to and from the Garden of Eden. An exhaustive study of this motif of wandering as a vagabond on a train as a metaphor for perpetual homelessness has already been undertaken;[8] I hope to further analyze the implications of choosing life withdrawn from the Garden. Amidst this exile, there is a hope for the continued possibility of praying to pray from the deeper awareness of the Mother nesting in the womb of community.

We will explore examples from Bob Dylan's songbook, in order to delve more deeply into this aforementioned notion that there is both a Mother Earth and a Great Mother, the latter nesting in the womb of eternal time, and that both Mothers necessarily integrate the immanent and the transcendent, the natural and the supernatural. Strolling through the mystic garden is a place to search for the Mother. Entry into this garden is both an ascent and a descent from this paradise (or *pardeis*), as described with dark and daring detail in Dylan's song "Ain't Talkin'."[9] The opening stanza sets up a visionary ascent, wherein the bard sings: "I was passing *yon* cool and crystal fountain / Someone hit me from behind"—thus coincidentally picking up on a theme known to scholars of ancient Jewish mysticism from the obscure work *Heikhalot Zutarti* ("The Lesser Palaces).[10] It was here, in the very mystic garden of *pardeis*, that visions of ascent led to descent and then into heresy for mystical rabbis like Elisha ben Abuya, who saw the "splendor of the marble plates" in the crystal fountain and, mistaking them for cascading water, called out: "Water! Water!"—thus ruining his mystic experience by mistaking outer reality for inner essence.[11] The danger in entering paradise is that one may misperceive aspects of the garden as somehow unique and disjointed elements, leading to the heretical vision that there is more than one power competing within the other contained within separate forces of the Godhead. Elisha is said to be "cutting at the roots" of the Godhead by separating the force of God, the Creator of the pristine garden, from the force of the Demiurge that rules over the forlorn garden. So within the same stanza of Dylan's lyrical portrayal of the mystic garden, we may also perceive a return of descent to the post-exilic Garden of Eden: "As I walked out tonight in the mystic garden / The wounded flowers were dangling from the vines." How this descent occurs is not entirely clear, but there is some indication that life as lived outside the garden cannot fully support the quest for mystical ascent: "They will tear your mind away from contemplation / They will jump on your misfortune when you're down." Yet the seeker continues wandering on, living and choosing life amidst this darkening, forlorn garden of life.

Amidst the unsettling surroundings of "wounded flowers… dangling from the vines" there is a deep darkness that pervades this lone seeker who is not seeking the demiurge Dylan alludes to earlier in a different song, "Father of Night."[12] By contrast, the song at hand ("Ain't Talkin'") opens with a surprise encounter, "Someone hit me from behind," and closes by identifying the mysterious other: "Excuse me Ma'am, I beg your pardon / There's no one here, the gardener is gone." The identity of this female interlocutor in "Ain't Talkin'" is further explicated as the song progresses: "They say prayer has the power to help / so pray from the Mother / In the human heart an evil spirit can dwell / I'm trying to love my neighbor and do good unto others / But O, Mother, things ain't going well." Here there is a clear shift from the "Father of Night" to the Mother of the Garden. I argue that it is this shift from the symbol of the Father to the Mother—namely, the Great Mother in the Garden of Eden—that allows the seeker to choose life. This symbol of the Great Mother presumes a nourishing and nurturing association with the maternal that wants to care for the child, despite the opposite lived experience in this forlorn garden. In "Ain't Talkin'," Dylan further raises the question as to what the difference is to "pray *from* the Mother" and not the expected "pray *to* the Mother." To appreciate this difference implied in praying *from* as different from praying *to* requires a further understanding of the Great Mother.

This symbol of the Great Mother (*imma tata·ah*) is associated in many streams of Jewish mysticism with the Shekhinah. What She brings to the one wandering, seeking to return to the post-exilic garden, is the intimacy of prayer that partakes in Her suffering. Dylan, as the perennial seeker, is singing at this late stage in his songbook, with many loves lost: "Ain't talkin', just walkin' / Through this weary world of use / Heart burnin', still yearnin' / No one on earth would ever know"—what then remains?

When Dylan sings elsewhere that "Soon as a man is born / you know the sparks begin to fly,"[13] he means that from the moment of being born, there is a shift from containment in the womb to the expulsion of birthing, which comes with beginning to live an independent life. As the seeker leaves that "old shell of existence" in the womb, exile from the garden necessarily begins.[14] Being thrown into existence—as "God cast Adam forth from the Garden of Eden to till the ground from whence he was taken" (Genesis 3:23)—evokes a deeper sense of "rejection by the mother."[15] Dylan envisions this process of birthing as being akin to the deprivation of love that comes as an individual is born and then withdraws from the mother. It is through this withdrawal as individuation—mirroring cosmogenesis—that "the sparks begin to fly." The sparks that fly are simultaneously both giving and shedding the light that is life. Moreover, being "born in time"[16] is a process of inevitable corruption, in growing more and more distant from the source of that illuminating fire. By coming into existence, it is the fire of one's pneumatic soul that diminishes until one is able to return to that mystic garden where the Shekhinah cries out, hovering alone in exile. The garden here is imagined through a looking glass darkly, the place from which Adam and Eve have already been banished—so, who and what then truly remains east of Eden?

The entrance to the garden east of Eden is no longer guarded by the cherubim with the "ever-turning fiery sword to guard the path to the Tree of Life" (Genesis 3:24). In Dylan's rendering, it is upon returning to this post-exilic garden, at once emptied and forlorn "dangling with wounded flowers"[17] where the question "Where are you?" (Genesis 3:9) is inverted. It is not God asking the whereabouts of Adam hiding in the garden, but now it is exilic Adam returning to the garden in search of the Divine. This is a return to the garden in Dylan's songbook through the lens of Baudelaire's spleen-filled womb, where only *fleurs du mal* will dangle in their decomposition. The concluding poem in *Les Fleurs du mal,*[18] entitled "Le Voyage," best exemplifies Baudelaire's spleen symbolizing as an elusive journey to true self that Dylan's songbook continually mirrors. In one of the aforementioned poetic cycles of "*Spleen et idéal*" included above, Baudelaire's poetic pontifications on the quest for art and beauty that seduce the artist are precisely what lead him to portray the artist alternately as "martyr, visionary, performer, pariah, and fool."[19] What is key to appreciating Dylan's lyrical return to the garden as a spleen-filled womb is this Baudelairean dialectic of sexual and romantic love that oscillates between ecstasy (*idéal*) and anguish (*spleen*). This oscillation of the Baudelairean dialectic finds its fleeting fulfillment through erotic cycles, leading from intoxication to conflict and revulsion, to an eventual ambivalent tranquility born of memory and the transmutation of suffering into art.[20] The attempt of the artist to be fulfilled through the fullness of love ends in utter emptiness, and so Baudelaire's "*Spleen et idéal*" culminates with an anguished poetic vision of the soul imprisoned within itself, a familiar gnostic theme. The only certainty before the artist here is a vision of suffering alone in the throes of death's erotic embrace.[21]

To continue crying out after all these years with this feeling of one's "heart burnin', still yearnin'" is precisely the desire for the Great Mother, but in Her stead existence is marked by withdrawal from the garden, as well as a withdrawal of Her love from the individual. Not only is She in exile, but so is Her love, which then "leads to pronounced feelings of loneliness, misery, and exile. Birth is experienced not only as a release into life but also a rejection of the uterine paradise."[22] Dylan's songbook grows and expands only to realize this tragic truth: that the sparks of life and love are already flying away.

Return to the garden is a witnessing of the rejection by the Great Mother, a distancing of fire by fire, for She is the source of illumination. Even if "the fire's gone," there is still the realization that "the light is never dying." While the immanent passion of the Shekhinah's fire may have diminished from the very birthing of the seeker's soul, the Limitless Light continues to shine on. This oscillation between the Great Mother and the Lower Mother is a recurring theme in Jewish mystical literature.

Let us briefly turn to one such mystical exemplar in the homily of the hasidic leader in the community of Tiberias in 1777, Rabbi Menachem Mendel of Vitebsk (c. 1733–1788). In a homily on

Deuteronomy 16:18, the Vitebsker addresses the Lower and Greater Mother. The verse reads: "**Judges** and **officers** shall you make for yourself in all your gates, which the Eternal your God gives to you, tribe by tribe; and they shall judge the people with righteous judgment." It is unclear what the difference is between "judges" and "officers," and that is the issue the Vitebsker is trying to resolve, through a mystical interpolation of the Lower and Great Mother. Here is an excerpt from this mystical homily (bracketed interpolations are my interpretation of his words, while bolded words come from Deuteronomy 16:18, quoted above in full):

> Or one can say "**judges**" is the place of Binah [which is the Great Mother on the side of judgment], whereas the "**officers**" is the development of a true realization of the fear [of the Lower Mother of Malkhut as a lower level of fear and executing judgment; the task is to elevate the lower level of fear to the level of the Great Mother]. This realization that even fear emerges from the divine totality, allowing one to see that there is also vitality there [insofar as it all emerges from its source in Love from the Great Mother].
>
> "And you shall choose life" (Deuteronomy 30:19)—that is, there is life within it [and be aware of the source of life drawn from the Great Mother in any circumstance, even in the place of fear whose source emanates from Great Mother on the side of Judgment but is manifest through the Lower Mother. So choose to perceive the life force within any circumstance, even the most terrifying].
>
> "Which the Eternal our God gives to you"—it is known that this is the origin of change and extension [in the sphere of the ground of being, the Lower Mother, called Malkhut] as the gates of entry into any human bonds of affiliation to the promised Land of Israel. [Out of this ground of being emerges a deeper appreciation of the diversity of all sentient beings.]

How, then, does the seeker walk through life knowing and living, even when confronting the fear of death intertwined within one's very source of life? For the mystic, this dialectic of life and death, fear and love, is intrinsically imbedded within the symbol of the Mother, drawing from the Great Mother on the side of judgment while manifest through the Lower Mother. What, then, does the seeker encounter by returning to this "mystic garden"? Which Mother then is that "someone who hit me from behind"? That mysterious opening encounter feels like it is a collision with the Great Mother, which then recurs at the conclusion of the song "Ain't Talkin'" as a reunion with the Lower Mother: "Excuse me Ma'am, I beg your pardon / There's no one else here, the gardener is gone." Rather than merely pointing to the cherubim standing guard at the gate of the garden, the gardener is nowhere to be found—for all intents and purposes, the garden has been abandoned.

This gardener who tends the garden and its precious flowers symbolizes, in Jewish mystical literature, the *tzaddik*—the masculine righteous one who serves as a shepherd dedicated to tending to the souls.[23] The Lower Mother is the Shekhinah, also symbolized as the field of holy apples, who must be stewarded by her gardener, the masculine *tzaddik*. Whereas flowers can be seen as composed of precious petals, like letters of words for prayer, in Dylan's dystopian gnosis flowers are wilted and evil. Whereas these flowers are gathered into bouquets that create the possibility of prayer for the *tzaddik* tending to these souls, for Dylan these flowers bring another kind of prayer—nothing but lament to the Lower Mother. Whereas each generation births a *tzaddik* tending to its souls, like a gardener tends to the garden and can redeem all the flowers of language, Dylan finds himself at the abyss of language "in the last outback, in the world's end."[24]

Coming full circle from this brief wandering to and from the abandoned Garden of Eden where the Lower Mother abided, I wonder: *Is this gnostic quest a Jewish one?* Scholem sought to redress the *gnostic quest* for the abandoned Garden of Eden in astonishment: "It is one of the marvels confronting the explorer in the field [of Jewish mysticism] that scholars who have been looking far and wide to establish the source from which [Gnosticism] has come have been remarkably reluctant, or rather, unwilling to allow the theory that Gnostics tendencies may have developed in the very midst of Judaism itself, whether in its classical forms or on its heterodox and sectarian fringes."[25] Scholem is courageous in seeking to prove that the quest for illumination (or the *gnosis* known as Gnosticism) emerged as an intrinsic part of Jewish mysticism, rather than as being something derived from or influenced by a later religion known as Christianity. For Dylan's quest this further complicates the claim that he was ever "born again"—a mistaken claim negated by both himself and by those heretics throughout history who remained Jewish despite their attempts at self-exile from Judaism. The garden was long ago abandoned by the Lower Mother, and it appears that even Arnofsky's heavy-handed surrealist horror film *Mother!* has yet to turn the tide of the human hand in this exile.[26] As a relentless martyr, visionary, performer, pariah, and fool, Dylan remains enraptured by the trace of the elusive Lower Mother from whom he draws the inspiration to plead to pray. Dylan's lyrical walk through the forlorn garden is a return to a spleen-filled womb that oscillates between ecstasy and anguish. This return finds its fleeting fulfillment through erotic cycles of intoxication to conflict and revulsion to tranquility, all nesting in the womb of the Great Mother. In walking through this forlorn garden of the earth, the seeking singer succeeds in transmuting suffering within Mother Earth's violated garden into great art. The attempt of the artist to be fulfilled through the fullness of love ends in utter emptiness, but Dylan's songbook never fully relinquishes the artist's soul imprisoned within itself. Rather, the seeker can return to witness this state and sing about it from a distance. This thoroughly modernist vision of the suffering artist alone in the throes of death's erotic embrace is precisely the inspiration of the very beloved servant that Dylan encounters that fateful night walking in the mystic garden long abandoned, where She remains forever young.[27]

NOTES

[1] I am grateful to Martin S. Cohen and David Birnbaum for the invitation to contribute to this volume in the Mesorah Matrix series. The present essay has inspired my forthcoming monograph on Bob Dylan's songbook *God Knows, Everything Is Broken*.

[2] Melena Ryzik, "Revealed (or Not), the Meaning of 'Mother'!" *New York Times* (September 24, 2017).

[3] For many decades now, since the failure of the May 1968 Revolution in Paris, two French philosophers have been debating the possibility of living redemptively in community. See Maurice Blanchot, *The Unavowable Community*, trans. Pierre Joris (Barrytown, NY: Station Hill Press, 1988), as well as the following three books by Jean-Luc Nancy: *The Inoperative Community* (=*The History of Literature*, vol. 76; Minnesota: University of Minnesota Press, 1991), *La Communauté Affrontée* (Paris: Galilée, 2001); and *The Disavowed Community*, trans. Philip Armstrong (New York: Fordham University Press, 2016).

[4] See, e.g., Hans Jonas in his *The Gnostic Religion: The Message of the Alien God and the Beginnings of Christianity* (Boston: Beacon Press, 2001).

[5] E.g., John Gray in his *The Soul of the Marionette: A Short Inquiry into Human Freedom* (New York: Farrar, Straus & Giroux, 2016).

[6] See Jean-Luc Nancy, "Divine Places," in *The Inoperative Community*, pp. 110–150.

[7] Erich Neumann, *The Great Mother: An Analysis of the Archetype* (Princeton, NJ: Princeton University Press, 2015), p. 68.

[8] Bryan Cheyette, "On the 'D' Train: Bob Dylan's Conversions," in *Do You Mr. Jones: Bob Dylan with the Poets and Professors*, ed. Neil Corcoran (London: Chatto and Windus, 2002).

[9] Bob Dylan, "Ain't Talkin'," *Modern Times* (2006).

[10] Gershom Scholem, *Jewish Gnosticism, Merkabah Mysticism, and Talmudic Tradition* (New York: Jewish Theological Seminary of America, 1965), pp. 14–19.

[11] Scholem, *Jewish Gnosticism*, p. 15.

[12] Bob Dylan, "Father of Night," *New Morning* (1970).

[13] Bob Dylan, "What Can I Do For You?" *Saved* (1980).

[14] Erich Neumann, *The Great Mother*, pp. 67–68.

[15] Ibid.

[16] Bob Dylan "Born in Time," *Under the Red Sky* (1990).

[17] Bob Dylan, "Ain't Talkin'."

[18] Charles Baudelaire, *Les Fleurs Du Mal* (1861 ; rpt. Paris: Gallimard, 1966).

[19] Richard D. E. Burton, "Charles Baudelaire," in *Encyclopedia Brittanica* (www.britanica.com/biography/Charles-Baudelaire).

[20] Maria C. Scott, *Baudelaire's Le spleen de Paris: Shifting Perspectives* (Aldershot, England, and Burlington, VT: Ashgate, 2005).

[21] Edward K. Kaplan, *Baudelaire's Prose Poems: The Esthetic, the Ethical, and the Religious in the Parisian Prowler* (Athens, GA, and London: University of Georgia Press, 2009).

[22] Erich Neumann, *The Great Mother*, p. 68.

[23] On the gnostic elements of souls in their journey to liberation, compare Reb Naḥman, *Likkutei MoHaRaN*, no. 65 to the "Prince of the World charged with souls" mentioned by Scholem in *Jewish Gnosticism, Merkabah Mysticism, and Talmudic Tradition*, p. 49.

[24] Bob Dylan, "Ain't Talkin'."

[25] Scholem, *Jewish Gnosticism*, p. 1.

[26] Ibid., pp. 41, 49.

[27] Clinton Heylin, *Bob Dylan: Behind the Shades* (New York: Viking, 2000), pp. 354 and 519–520.

"Choosing" and "Chosenness":
Missionary Co-option of Jewish Scripture

Michael J. Cook

Early Christians would likely have processed Deuteronomy's mandate to "choose life" (30:19) as signifying "choose *life-in-Jesus.*" This would be consistent with Christianity's similar interpretations—Jews would likely term these *re*-interpretations—of dozens of other Jewish scriptural texts. Of course, this process, best known by the umbrella term "proof-texting," has long been challenged by knowledgeable Jews as utterly removed from their Bible's genuine intent. While many Christians may believe that they are reading out of Jewish biblical texts the "Christian" meanings genuinely found there, Jews would like to know how they can effectively expose such Christian misrenderings as ahistorical corruptions.

Yet throughout the centuries, the substance and modes of Jewish counter-education have proven ineffective if not inept, both in terms of imparting content and psychological confidence. This is especially the case because missionary intrusions so often earmark unknowledgeable *lay* Jews, and particularly impressionable Jewish *youth.* Today's enlistment of the internet renders the problem even more acute since many ostensibly Jewish sites instead turn out to be deceptively packaged by Jews-for-Jesus, Messianic Jews, and other varieties of Hebrew-Christians.[1] It is no surprise, then, how a high percentage of modern Jewish converts to Christianity readily pinpoint re-interpretation of Jewish biblical material as having been *the* determinative factor in their shift to a Jesus movement. This intensifies the problem of why indeed there still has not been devised—let alone widely implemented—overarching and effective Jewish counter-conceptualizations and counter-articulations, realistically comprehensible and manageable, to help Jews impede what strike them as distortions of the Jewish Bible's intent.

This essay lays out a centuries-old Christian approach to the Hebrew Scriptures and analyzes why traditional Jewish responses have never genuinely succeeded. At the end, I present my own quite different means of warding off this encroachment, a method now proving increasingly effective for many lay Jews—especially those away at college.

Early Christians' Choice of "Life-in-Jesus," as Culled from Jewish Scripture

Not until the mid-second century CE did gospels, epistles, and other Christian writings begin to coalesce into a New Testament corpus. Originally, then, "Jewish-Christians" and "Gentile-Christians"[2] could have recourse only to *Jewish* Scripture (often in Greek rendition[3]) for passages they insisted predicted Jesus' conception, birth, ministry and teachings, entry to Jerusalem, last supper and betrayal, arrest and Sanhedrin trial, as well as his suffering, crucifixion, burial, and claimed resurrection. Still other texts were held to prefigure persons ancillary to Jesus: Mary and Joseph, John the Baptist and his parents, Herod and the Magi, Judas Iscariot, and even the nameless young man who escaped naked from the Garden of Gethsemane upon Jesus' arrest! Mindful of Paul's prediction that "all Israel will be saved" (Romans 11:26[4]), many Christians enlisted themselves as agents in bringing to fruition God's presumed plan, with skilled reprocessing of Jewish biblical texts always serving as the easiest and most effective means to that end.

Imagine displaying the full text of both "Testaments" on computer screens. Within Jewish Scripture, color-highlight each passage that Christian re-interpreters have deemed predictive of Jesus' story. Do the same with New Testament verses said to "fulfill" Jewish biblical antecedents. In now scrolling through, imagine how overwhelmed, if not mesmerized, impressionable Jewish observers might be to observe this vast mapping-out of "text-plots."[5]

Ponder the consequential inferences: God controls the continuum of both "Testaments," as per the adage ascribed to St. Augustine: "The New Testament is in the Old concealed; the Old is by the New revealed."[6] Also, since claims to "authenticity" were enhanced by "antiquity," early Christianity's alleged fulfillment of *Jewish* biblical texts effectively retrojected its own origins by centuries! Further, processing the Jewish Bible through Christian re-interpretation tacitly implied the displacement of the Jews by Christians as God's "chosen" people.

Early Christian Directives to Comb Jewish Scripture

In emergent Christian writings, three especially important passages directed Christians to predicate their faith on Jewish biblical texts:

1 Corinthians 15:3–4
Christ died for our sins in accordance with the [Jewish] scriptures...he was buried...was raised on the third day in accordance with the scriptures....

This citation, in its fuller form (15:3–7), is technically termed the *kerygma*—Greek for a creed-like litany of fundamentals that

Christians were to internalize and recite liturgically. This formulation probably arose within but a decade after Jesus' death (ca. 30 CE).[7] Here passed on by Paul during the 50s, it appears to be the earliest extant affirmation of the new faith's grounding "in accordance with" Jewish Scriptures.[8] Further:

> *Luke 24:44–45*
> "These are my words which I [the resurrected Jesus] spoke to you, while...still with you, that everything written about me in the law of Moses and the prophets and the psalms must be fulfilled." Then he opened their minds [of those he was accompanying] to understand the [Jewish] scriptures.

Here the last segment of the Hebrew Scriptures, the Writings, appears referenced by its most conspicuous component, the lengthy book of "Psalms."

> *John 5:39, 46*
> You [Jews] search the [Jewish] scriptures because you think that in them you have eternal life...it is they that bear witness to me....If you believed Moses, you would believe me; for he wrote of me.

In medieval church art, this indictment of Jews' obtuseness generated sculptures (and other art-forms) depicting a woman termed "Synagogue" *blindfolded* to show how impervious she was to Christianity's presumed truths.[9]

Different Search-Lenses

The three most basic lenses through which Christians may claim to find Jesus in Jewish Scripture comprise predictions through *proof-*

texting; also foreshadowing through *typology*; and even claims of the pre-incarnate Christ's *actual presence* (not merely prediction) within the Jewish corpus:

1. Through the lens of PROOF-TEXTING: usually individual verses from Jewish Scripture (irrespective of their context) were reprocessed as "fulfilled" by the New Testament.

Table 1: Examples of Proof-Texting		
HOSEA 11:1 When Israel was a child, then I loved him, and out of Egypt I called My son.	predicts? →	MATTHEW 2:15 (regarding the child Jesus' family returning from Egypt to the Holy Land) This was to fulfill what the Lord had spoken by the prophet [Hosea], "Out of Egypt have I called my son."
ISAIAH 7:14 Behold, the young woman shall conceive, and bear a son, and shall call his name Immanuel.	predicts? →	MATTHEW 1:23 Behold, a virgin shall conceive and bear a son, and his name shall be called Emmanuel (which means, God with us).
ZECHARIAH 9:9 Thy king cometh... lowly, and riding upon an ass, even upon a colt the foal of an ass.	predicts? →	MATTHEW 21:4–5 (describing Jesus entering Jerusalem on Palm Sunday) To fulfill what was spoken by the prophet [Zechariah], "...your king is coming to you, humble, and mounted on an ass, and on a colt, the foal of an ass."

AMOS 2:16 He that is courageous among the mighty shall flee away naked in that day.	predicts? →	MARK 14:51–52 And a young man followed [Jesus], with nothing but a linen cloth about his body; and they seized him, but he left the linen cloth and ran away naked.
ISAIAH 53:7 He...opened not his mouth; as a lamb that is led to the slaughter.	predicts? →	MARK 14:60–61 (recounting the story of Jesus' trial) The high priest...asked [Jesus], "Have you no answer to make...?" But he was silent....

2. Through the lens of TYPOLOGY: In Bible study,[11] typology focuses on what are termed Jewish scriptural "types" allegedly mirrored, and thereby fulfilled, by New Testament "anti-types." The types can appear as isolated verses but commonly also as extended swaths of narrative.[12] Necessarily, the theological importance that "Old Testament types" originally possessed in their own right now fades relative to the supposed New Testament analogues said to supersede them:

Table 2: Examples of Typology	
TYPE	ANTI-TYPE
THE *FIRST* ADAM DISOBEDIENT Disobeyed God in the Garden of Eden. Eve emerged from Adam's rib-cage as he was sleeping.	JESUS (= "THE *SECOND* ADAM") OBEDIENT Obeyed God in the Garden of Gethsemane. The *Church* (figuratively) emerged from his rib-cage (blood = Eucharist; water = Baptism)[13] as Jesus was dying; see also John 19:34.[14]

	Cf. Paul (Romans 5:14, 19): Adam "a type of the one [Christ]...to come....By one man's disobedience many were made sinners, so by one man's obedience many will be made righteous." Cf. 1 Corinthians 15:21–22.[15]
ISAAC, ABRAHAM'S BELOVED SON Miraculous conception / parents aged. Offered himself obediently on wooden altar until (near) death.	**JESUS, GOD'S BELOVED SON** Miraculous conception (virginal). Offered himself obediently on wooden cross until (actual) death.
JUDAH THE BETRAYER *Judas* (Greek[16] for Judah), one of twelve, during a meal plans to sell Joseph for pieces of silver (Genesis 37:25–28). Cf. Psalm 41:9: "my friend... whom I trusted, who did eat of my bread, hath lifted up his heel against me."[17]	**JUDAS THE BETRAYER** Judas, one of twelve,[18] after the Last Supper sets out to sell Jesus for pieces of silver.
MOSES' INFANCY His life was threatened by Pharaoh; but he was saved by disobedient midwives (Exodus 1:15–21).	**JESUS' INFANCY** His life was threatened by Herod; but was saved by disobedient Magi (Matthew 2:1–12).
MOSES' RETURN HOME Once the wicked king dies (Exodus 2:23): "for all the men are dead that sought thy life" (4:19).	**JESUS' RETURN HOME** Leaves for home once the wicked king dies: "for those who sought the child's life are dead" (Matthew 2:19–20).

MOSES ON MOUNT GIVES TORAH, ALSO TRANSFIGURED:[19] coming "down from mount Sinai... knew not...the skin of his face sent forth beams" (Exodus 34:29).	JESUS ON MOUNT gives "Sermon on the Mount."[20] Also TRANSFIGURED: atop a "high mountain...his face shone like the sun" (Matthew 17:1–2).[21]
BRAZEN SERPENT HEALS FROM ATOP POLE: Encircled below by the mortally snake-bitten, heals all who look toward it (Numbers 21:4–9).	JESUS SAVES FROM ATOP CROSS: Encircled by those mortally wounded by sin, saves all who look toward him: "As Moses lifted up the serpent in the wilderness, so must the Son of man be lifted up, that whoever believes in him may have eternal life" (John 3:14–15).
ELIJAH AS MESSIAH'S HERALD Wicked Ahab/Jezebel seek but fail to kill Elijah who (taken up alive by heavenly chariot) remains available to return to herald a Davidic descendant as Messiah (2 Kings 2:11).	JOHN THE BAPTIST AS ELIJAH Wicked Herod/Herodias take John's life but not before John heralds a Davidic descendant (Jesus) as Messiah: "Then the disciples understood that [Jesus] was speaking...of John the Baptist [as Elijah]" (Matthew 17:13).
JONAH: GOD'S EMISSARY TO GENTILES Told gentile shipmates they would be saved if they sacrificed him overboard. Three days in a whale until spat up onto dry land. Brought gentiles of Nineveh to repentance (Jonah 1–4).	JESUS: GOD'S EMISSARY TO GENTILES Underwent being sacrificed so gentiles would be saved. Three days in a tomb until resurrection. "This generation...seeks a sign, but no sign shall be given to it except the sign of Jonah" (Luke 11:29–32; cf. Matthew 12:38–41; 16:4).

Even more sophisticatedly worked through are typologies by the church fathers.[22] Consider Cyprian of Carthage.[23]

JOSHUA: MOSES' OUTSTRETCHED ARMS	JESUS: OUTSTRETCHED ARMS
When Moses' outstretched arms are raised ninety degrees, Joshua (Hebrew: Yehoshua) defeats the Amalekites, bringing the Hebrews closer to the Promised Land (Exodus 17:11–13).	When the arms of Jesus (Hebrew: Yehoshua[24]) are outstretched on the cross, he defeats Satan, bringing all humanity closer to the promised salvation.

3. Through the lens of the Christ's ACTUAL PRESENCE *within* Jewish Scripture:[25] Focus here is on the theological time-frame from well *before* God's creation of the world, on the one hand, to the emergence of Christianity centuries thereafter, on the other. Since the pre-incarnate (spiritual) Christ-figure was held to have existed along with the Father from the very beginning of time, this opened a wide window of opportunity for this figurative "Christ" to make actual visitations *within* Jewish Scripture itself (i.e., far surpassing simple prediction there).

Awareness of these intermediate centuries is evinced by New Testament chronologies such as "given us in Christ Jesus before the world began" (2 Timothy 1:9) and "in the beginning was the Word [Christ], and the Word was with God...[and only later] became flesh and lived among us" (John 1:1, 14). As for mentions of specific actualizations of the Christ's presence *within* Jewish Scripture, consider Paul's affirmation (1 Corinthians 10:1–4): "Our fathers [the wandering Israelites]...all drank...from a spiritual rock which followed them [in the wilderness]; and the rock was Christ" (cf. Numbers 20:7–11). Analogous, also in the wilderness, could be the

Christ's theoretical presence and directional guidance from within the pillars of cloud by day and fire by night (Exodus 13:21–22). Extending the fire-motif: Was it the Christ's voice emanating from the burning bush? What of the burning furnace in Daniel 3:24–27, where a mysterious being inside the furnace (accompanying Daniel's three friends) is identified by the astonished Babylonian king Nebuchadnezzar as "a son of the gods"?

Why Traditional Jewish Responses Prove of No Avail

Traditionally, Jews *au courant* with the Hebrew Bible, and seeking to shore up other Jews vulnerable to missionary encroachment, have offered unrealistic directives like: "Master our Bible so that you can say: You missionaries mistranslate *verse A's* original Hebrew, or translate it literally instead of idiomatically; or twist *verse B* out of context; *verse C* was never fulfilled by Jesus; your use of *verse D* is arbitrary because *verse E* conveys the exact opposite meaning," and so on. Such counter-arguments, even if compelling, transcend what most Jews can master—let alone muster, even had they the wherewithal to do so. Consider the first three proof-texts listed in Table 1 above: they are among the easiest "proof-texts" for lay Jews to countermand—yet results are invariably disappointing.

> *HOSEA 11:1*
> When Israel was a child, then I loved him, and out of Egypt I called My son.

> *GOSPEL APPLICATION: MATTHEW 2:13–15*
> An angel...appeared to [Mary's husband] Joseph in a dream..."Rise, take the child and his mother, and flee to Egypt, and remain there till I tell you; for Herod is about to

search for the child, to destroy him."...He...took the child and his mother...to Egypt, and remained there until the death of Herod...to fulfil what the Lord had spoken by the prophet [Hosea], "Out of Egypt have I called my son."

Matthew's citation is weak since it refers solely to a past event, and not also a future event. A common missionary rejoinder is that understanding "Old Testament" prophecy requires a *double layer* of interpretation: one past, the other future. Hosea does not yet know the future, so he refers only to the past. But *God*, certainly knowing the future, has Hosea convey it unawares. Hence Matthew reads Hosea's words as cryptically signaling Jesus' *future* universal exodus of humanity from enslavement-by-sin.

This imaginative logic leaves Jewish respondents stymied. Moreover, Jews are unlikely to know that Matthew opts to rely on Hosea's original Hebrew because the Greek ("out of Egypt have I called his children") cannot serve Matthew's arbitrary purpose. The decisive point, meanwhile, goes unnoticed: Matthew, wanting to cast Jesus as a second Moses, *invents* the bringing of the *infant* Jesus both into and later out from Egypt so as to parallel God's earlier bringing of Moses' people out from Egypt (at the time of the exodus). The historical Jesus was never in Egypt during infancy, let alone any other time,[26] so there can be no connection whatsoever between Hosea's "out of Egypt" passage and Jesus! But is struggling through this maze a realistic pedagogical aid for the Jewish community? Hardly. Further, would many Jews be able to articulate it? Most doubtful. And this is for but one passage out of scores of others!

ISAIAH 7:14–16 (FROM THE GREEK)

The Lord himself shall give you a sign; behold, a virgin shall conceive...and...bring forth a son, and thou shalt call his name Emmanuel...Before the child shall know good or evil, he refuses evil, to choose the good...the land shall be forsaken which thou art afraid of because of [its]...two kings.

GOSPEL APPLICATION: MATTHEW 1:23
Behold, a virgin shall conceive and bear a son, and his name shall be called Emmanuel (which means, God with us).

Here relatively conversant Jews will say: (1) The foreseen child cannot be Jesus since Isaiah names him "Emmanuel," and (2) Matthew's "virgin" (Greek *parthenos*) mistranslates the verse's prototype "young woman" (Hebrew *almah*); hence, we have no basis for knowing that Isaiah alluded to any "virgin"—the Hebrew "young woman" is correct!

But we must notice how, in advancing "Emmanuel" as the child's proposed name, Matthew adds "which means, God with us" to frame as the post-resurrection Jesus' last words: "I am *with you* always" (28:20). Thereby, at this Gospel's very close, Matthew neutralizes the problem of Isaiah's designating the coming child "Emmanuel" (instead of "Jesus"). As regards the word "virgin" we face a standoff: even had the Hebrew Isaiah used "virgin," it would not matter since in Isaiah's day there surely were "young women" virginal *before* marriage but only up to consummation (not thereafter—a consideration so obvious that Isaiah would never think to clarify it!). Since, therefore, Isaiah's alleged use of "virgin" counts for nothing—because no such virgin would here remain such—there should be no bravado on either side as to the original word!

The effective answer to Matthew, however, is spotting how he truncates Isaiah's prediction. In Isaiah's historical context (ca. 734 BCE), his focus is *not on any woman at all* but rather on a *measurement of time*: Jerusalem, Judah's capital, is under joint siege by two enemies, and Isaiah specifies how much time it will be before Jerusalem emerges as saved—namely, less than the time when the expected child "shall know to refuse the evil and choose the good" (following the Hebrew of Isaiah 7:16). So the question of the woman's virginal status is *irrelevant* because the woman herself is irrelevant—except to produce the child who in the future will learn good from evil! Yet is navigating this maze—and on a relatively "easy" text to argue— genuinely a realistic pedagogical tactic for the Jewish community? Hardly.

ZECHARIAH 9:9
Behold, thy king cometh unto thee, he is triumphant, and victorious, lowly, and riding upon an ass, even upon a colt the foal of an ass.

GOSPEL APPLICATION: MATTHEW 21:4–7
This took place to fulfill what was spoken by the prophet [Zechariah]: "...Behold, your king is coming to you, humble, and mounted on an ass, and on a colt, the foal of an ass." The disciples...did as Jesus had directed them; they brought the ass and the colt, and put their garments on them, and he sat thereon.

Jews may declare preposterous Matthew's depiction of Jesus riding into Jerusalem on *two* animals simultaneously, and chalk this up to Matthew's unfamiliarity with how Hebrew prophets —here Zechariah—framed their message in parallel clauses, with the second clause paraphrasing the first. Accordingly, Zechariah meant "riding on an ass, even[27] upon a colt, the foal of an ass" (universally true of all colts). The animal in clause #2 thus simply repeats that of clause #1, hardly doubling it.

A missionary rejoinder? Two animals were indeed needed since the young (easily frightened) colt, assigned to Jesus, depended on its mother's company to brave and navigate Palm Sunday's Jerusalem crowds; and the "thereon" where Jesus sat was not both animals simultaneously but rather the *garments* laid on each of them. And why were the garments laid on *both* animals (the designated rider sits on only one)? The animals' journey was so fatiguing and arduous that Jesus might have had to switch from one animal to the other.

To seriously commend this kind of activity to Jews would be to validate a useless game played on the wrong field and with elusive if not evasive ground-rules. Jews require home-field advantages. Why has this not been universally engineered?

Reframing the Problem: Transcending the "Text-Game"

When looking through a camera's viewfinder, if what we see is unsatisfying we can *reframe* the scene. I now present constructive alternatives that are readily available for Jews to "reframe" the text-citation game—by measures that they can assimilate with relative ease. While no missionaries need to be addressed, I myself have experienced some who, taking my considerations to heart, have admitted that Jews certainly wear no blindfold. The key is to place missionaries on the defensive by destabilizing the proselytizing venture at its very core, thereby discouraging missionaries from venturing onto the Jewish playing field with all its own home field advantages.

Reframing #1—Gauging the Impact of "Cognitive Dissonance" on the Missionary Psyche
Underlying and potentially undermining the missionary psyche are at least four theoretical tensions that can best be relieved solely by proselytizing, all falling under the rubric of "cognitive dissonance" (a term operative in other fields besides religion). One classic definition is in the 1964 pioneering sociological study *When Prophecy Fails*:

Two...items of knowledge [cognition] are *dissonant* with each other if...they do not fit together...or if...one does not follow from the other....Dissonance produces discomfort and, correspondingly, there will arise pressures to reduce... the dissonance. *Attempts to reduce dissonance* [in our case, the attempts are missionizing] *represent the observable manifestations that dissonance exists.*[28]

The pedagogy Jews need to follow begins by memorizing four kinds of such "dissonance," whose verbalization will bring to the missionaries' own awareness what fuels their endeavor and thereby put them on the defensive—even, in some cases, reducing their conversionary ardor due to notions they have never heard before or been called upon to finesse. More important, Jews need only internalize these considerations to immunize themselves, without any need to speak to missionaries per se:

- *Dissonance 1*: How can Jews have originated the Messiah concept yet refuse to confirm Jesus as such? Since Jews are uniquely qualified to identify the Messiah, their rejection of Jesus (in particular) generates intense "dissonance" for missionaries, best eased by "proving" to Jews that Jesus was indeed the genuine culmination of their long-cherished Jewish hope for messianic redemption. Jews in turn should expose that the operative missionary motive is less to enlighten Jews than to calm missionaries' own dissonance that what seems so terribly amiss resides on the missionary side of the ledger, not the Jewish side.

- *Dissonance 2*: Jews possess divinely inspired Scriptures, yet refuse to admit that their Bible predicts Jesus' coming. That Jews today do not understand their own Scripture's alleged meanings spawns another nagging and potent "dissonance" among missionary ranks. This is so severe that its alleviation

can only be achieved by bringing even a single Jew to see—
and thereby confirm—what Christian believers contend is
the genuine truth of the Jews' own scriptural message. The
driving process here is thus circular reasoning.

- *Dissonance 3*: Jews have survived efforts to destroy them
  (sometimes justified by others as the Jews' recompense for
  having rejected Jesus), yet for what possible reason then has
  God preserved them? This "dissonance" is tied up with the
  otherwise incomprehensible delay in the Second Coming.
  To bring themselves peace of mind, many missionaries
  have convinced themselves that God has preserved the
  Jews to render them *available* for conversion! To what
  end? To hasten Jesus' Second Coming. Since no one knows
  what number of Jewish converts will constitute the critical
  mass required for Jesus' return, the continued delay of the
  Second Coming serves as a clarion call for intensifying
  missionizing efforts! This dynamic should be forthrightly
  stated to missionaries at the door. It erodes their ardor, even
  wears them down, especially when *continually* repeated to
  them.

- *Dissonance 4*: While missionaries speak of Jesus as a savior,
  Jews have for centuries insisted that he was a *victim* of
  Rome (and hence not the Messiah). Given that for all
  time the most inexorably recalcitrant fomenters of this
  "dissonance" will be *Jewish*, it remains *Jews* above all who
  must be converted—all the more so given that there are no
  Romans left in the world, at least not in the scriptural sense
  of citizens of the Roman Empire.

The fundamental impact of incessantly reciting this litany of dissonance
will be to score a break-through: that while what fuels missionizing
may initially be misperceived by proselytizers as residing within the

resistant Jews, this actually could be driven by deficiencies within the *missionaries' own faith experience*. This *manageable* destabilizing of the missionaries' tactics buttresses Jews' confidence and constitutes an "off-putting" strategy conveying a sense that Jews are insightful, not blind: a different choice of playing field is key, since the game is not to convince via details but to articulate broad conceptualizations—by nature a particularly congenial activity for Jews.[29]

Reframing #2—The "Bull's-Eye" Approach

Imagine that a farmer once arrayed his barn wall with bull's-eyes, with an arrow piercing the center of each. But appearances suggested something different from reality: he had shot the arrows first and only thereafter painted a bull's-eye around each! The end result looked the same, but not to someone who knew the underlying process. The task for modern Jews is to realize (internally) and if need be reveal (externally) that so many *alleged* predictions about Jesus from Jewish Scripture correspond to "arrows shot first," with Jesus' Gospel-images bull's-eyes belatedly made to surround each one. The following two transparent examples should be conceptually mastered by Jews:

A. Jesus' Passion Was Largely Matched to Jeremiah's

I once introduced a course on Jeremiah as follows:

> Long ago, there lived a righteous Jew who spoke for God. Defying the religious establishment, he aroused enmity from Jewish priests. Demanding they amend their ways, he threatened destruction of the Temple ("a den of robbers")! The priests threatened him with death. He warned that they could bring innocent blood upon themselves. The vacillating civil authority summoned and pronounced him innocent, expressing reluctance to heed his accusers' demands. As the just man warned, the Temple was later destroyed.

Was this *Jesus'* Passion? No, it was originally *Jeremiah's*. Typologists, sobered to see this correspondence (further detailed below), could argue that this was all God's foreshadowing—that is, the components in the case of Jeremiah were simply predictive of what would materialize with Jesus. All Jews need to counter-pose is that here traditions about Jesus were tailored to match the Jewish Bible on Jeremiah, revealing that Jesus' followers themselves likely were not sufficiently aware of enough details of what happened to him. Hence the "reverse" direction of the arrows in the table below, pointing left—indicating that the bull's-eye target (the image of Jesus) has been painted around the arrows (the imagery from Jeremiah). Indeed, note how Mark 11:17 actually has Jesus quote Jeremiah in the first example below.

Table 3		
The Passion of JEREMIAH		**The Passion of JESUS**
JEREMIAH 7:11 Has the house...become a den of robbers ...?	←	MARK 11:17 (AND PARALLELS) Is it not written [Jeremiah 7:11], "My house...you have made...a den of robbers"?
JEREMIAH 7:14 (CF. 1 SAMUEL 4–6; A PRIESTLY HOUSE DESTROYED) I will "do to th[is] house [temple #1]...as I did to Shiloh."	←	MARK 14:58 (AND PARALLELS; CF. JOHN 2:19) We heard him say, "I will destroy this temple [#2]..."
JEREMIAH 26:8 All the people laid hold of him... "You shall die."	←	MATTHEW 27:25 "All the people" demanded his death

JEREMIAH 26:10 An inquiry convened for Jeremiah.	←	MARK 14:53 (AND PARALLELS) A Sanhedrin convened for Jesus
JEREMIAH 26:11 Priests (and others) said Jeremiah "deserves...death" for words that "you have heard."	←	MATTHEW 26:66 (CF. MARK 14:64 AND 26:65) Sanhedrin decided Jesus "deserves death" for words that "you have heard."
JEREMIAH 26:15 You will bring innocent blood upon yourselves.	←	MATTHEW 27:25 His blood be on us and on our children!
JEREMIAH 38:5 His captors took him for execution to the vacillating King Zedekiah, who replied: "He is in your hands..."	←	MATTHEW 27:24 His captors took him for execution to the vacillating prefect Pilate, who replied: "See to it yourselves."
JEREMIAH 38:19 Wanting private conversation, "Zedekiah sent for Jeremiah" (38:14). Zedekiah was "afraid."	←	JOHN 18:33, 19:8 Wanting private conversation, "Pilate...called Jesus" to him. Pilate was "the more afraid."

If Jesus' trial, priestly enemies, and other elements of his Passion did
have a basis in Jeremiah's story, then we have to reckon with the
possibility that the fate of Jews for centuries, murdered as "Christ-
killers," was sealed by some traditions bearing no or relatively less
original connection to Jesus at all!

B. Jesus' Dying Cry

Table 4	
← Which Way Do the Arrows Flow? →	
PSALM 22 (BCE)	**MARK 15 (ca. 71 CE)**
(1) My God...why hast thou forsaken me? (6) scorned by men...All...wag their heads (16) evildoers...pierced my hands and feet (18) dividing my garments...for my raiment they cast lots	(34) Jesus cried..."My God...why hast thou forsaken me?" (29) derided him, wagging their heads (24) They crucified him, dividing his garments...casting lots for them

It is plausible that Jesus quoted Psalm 22:1, but the other multiple motifs of his crucifixion were created to match the rest of this psalm. This yields a compelling proposal: even regarding actual events in Jesus' life (here, Jesus' last cry), recourse to the Jewish Bible influenced how narrators dramatized those capable of "echoing the scriptures".[30]

Reframing #3—Conceptualize the Logistic Impediments to Early Proof-Texting

I have found that some Jews benefit enormously, once helped to ponder the practical impediments that early Christian preachers must have confronted in summoning Jewish scriptural proof-texting and typology. (These basic considerations have likely never occurred to most missionaries either!) Such impediments include those signaled by these questions:

- How scarce (and costly) were papyrus scrolls of Jewish biblical writings from which to locate and cite needed proof-texts?
- How tedious was it to unroll Jewish scrolls to find desirable "predictions" of Jesus?

- How cumbersome would it be for traveling preachers (e.g., Paul) to bring such scrolls along for ready access in preparing public remarks for new venues?
- Was it not inevitable that proof-texts and typological imagery increasingly be committed to memory (even if thereby risking errors in recall)?
- Would not lists of proof-texts then be separately compiled (the likes of which we see produced still today)?[31]
- Would this not of necessity lead to the disregard for the context of such passages?
- Would not a favorite aid be the search for recurring Jewish scriptural phrases most conducive as devices in proof-texting and typology?

Consider the recurring Hebrew expression *ba-yom ha-hu*, "[it shall come to pass] *on that day*." Inviting to the missionary mind, such a "day" could well signal the "day *of Jesus*"—especially since future times of significance are so predominantly signaled in other appearances of this term.[32] Jews need to benefit from memorizing but this one example:

AMOS 2:16
He that is courageous among the mighty shall flee away naked *in that day*, saith the Lord.

GOSPEL APPLICATION: MARK 14:51–52 (JESUS' ARREST IN GETHSEMANE)
A young man followed [Jesus], with nothing but a linen cloth about his body; and they seized him, but he left the linen cloth and ran away naked.

Some, assuming the young man in Gethsemane is historical, will cite Amos' supposed *prediction* as verification, even sparking theories about who that young man in Mark actually was. (A favorite surmise, without basis, is Mark's author himself!) Another explanation more compelling: collecting all instances in the Hebrew Bible of "in that day" netted Amos 2:16 among them, thereby stimulating the invention of a counterpart fulfillment: the naked figure at Jesus' arrest!

This kind of practice led to errors, with the Amos text typical of what can go awry. For the "in that day" Amos envisioned was actually the time of God's disciplining of the nation of Israel so severely that an escapee of this collective and warranted punishment would have to shed any garment impeding flight—but that is hardly a profile matching Jesus' arrest scene, where Mark renders the young man not a target of punishment, as per Amos, but repeatedly heroic:

- First, in Mark, he serves as a foil for Jesus' disciples: *they* "forsook" Jesus (14:50), diametrically *opposite* the young man who "followed" him (14:51).
- Second, Mark makes the young man part of a category of bit players who come through for Jesus in ways in which Jesus' designated supporters failed him, a key Markan theological motif. The rest of this cast of bit players? The woman wasting costly ointment (14:3–9), Simon of Cyrene (15:21), the Roman centurion (15:39), Joseph of Arimathea (15:42–46), and the women keeping vigil at the tomb (15:40–41,47).[33]
- Third, Mark adroitly uses the young man (now wearing glorious replacement clothes) to reassure readers that the women went to the correct tomb (not another that happened to be empty): recall the specification that he "followed" Jesus.

It is helpful for Jews to recite this litany of how early Christian preachers must have taken convenient short-cuts and that this process could lead to errors undermining missionary presentations.

Summary

In its "choosing life-in-Jesus," early Christianity construed even minute details of Jewish Scripture as predicting or reflecting Jesus, transforming Jewish Scripture from fundamentally Jewish to Christ-centered instead. Christian interpretative devices such as "proof-texting" and "typology" continue to pose *the* most effective means of seducing vulnerable Jews to adopt Christianity, causing heartache to Jewish families losing members to these seductive operatives.

For Jews to secure *immunity* to missionary encroachment, they should jettison fruitless debates on a passage-by-passage basis in favor of reframing, absorbing, and expounding three *globalist* realizations:

- That missionizing to Jews actually aims to relieve primarily subconscious or even conscious pain that missionaries experience due to the several kinds of cognitive dissonance we noted—that is, the deficiencies in understanding, mistakenly assigned to Jews ("blindness"), actually characterize the missionaries themselves.
- The primary reason Jesus appears to fulfill Jewish Scripture is that his image was *conformed* to match descriptive or figurative language from that corpus (as per the "bull's-eye" analogy).
- Practical logistical impediments that must have faced early Christian preachers pinpoint and explain how Jewish passages they cited became readily detached from their respective contexts, yielding thereby bizarre revisionist misunderstandings.

Not detailed textual analyses, then, but only teaching and comprehending the three aforementioned broad fundamentals have already become sufficient to fortify with confidence Jews learning this approach (with the option, if helpful or necessary, of articulating these to missionaries directly)—whether on individual or family bases, or within religious schools, synagogue adult education, Jewish summer camp curricula, and university Hillel programming. Even a *single teaching session* with an effective take-home handout summary could well suffice.

Jews will thereby bypass the idiosyncratic techniques and rules of engagement typical of the missionaries' own playing field and instead finally deflect, even if minimally trained, a roughly two-millennial harassment—substituting the realization that Jews, hardly "blind," are indeed penetratingly insightful. In my experience, this *globalist* package of strategies (which I have taught to over 1,000 rabbinical students and ordained rabbis, and to synagogue religious school teachers and students, and at university Hillel and other presentations), has already become welcomed, as well as easily and successfully applied, in the current day in all sectors of our country.

NOTES

[1] For distinctions between these, see Michael J. Cook, *Modern Jews Engage the New Testament: Enhancing Jewish Well-Being in a Christian Environment* (Woodstock, VT: Jewish Lights, 2012), pp. 261–262.

[2] The term "Gentile-Christians" in this context denotes non-Jews entering directly into Christian affiliation without first accepting Judaism, while the parallel term "Jewish-Christians" denotes persons of Jewish extraction accepting Christianity while continuing to consider themselves Jews (and also gentiles becoming Jewish as an intermediate step before accepting Christianity).

[3] The Septuagint (abbreviated LXX), a Greek translation of the Hebrew Bible, was accomplished predominantly, if not entirely, in Alexandria, probably from the third through first centuries BCE.

[4] Translations cited in this essay are: for New Testament, the RSV: *The Holy Bible: Revised Standard Version of the Bible* (New York: Division of Christian Education of the National Council of the Churches of Christ in the United States of America, 1971); for Hebrew Bible, the JPS: *Jewish Scripture from The Hebrew Bible in English* (Philadelphia: Jewish Publication Society, 1917). Citations by permission.

[5] See especially C. H. Dodd, *The Old Testament in the New* (London: University of London, 1952).

[6] Augustine of Hippo, *The City of God*, in *St. Augustine's City of God and Christian Doctrine*, ed. P. Schaff, trans. M. Dods (Buffalo: Christian Literature Company, 1887), vol. 2, p. 326.

[7] Cf. Ryan Turner, "An Analysis of the Pre-Pauline Creed in 1 Corinthians 15:1-1l," available online at http://carm.org/analysis-pre-pauline-creed-1-corinthians-151-11.

[8] Possibly the earliest extant creed-like hymn is Philippians 2:6–11; see Michael J. Cook, "Philippians," *Jewish Annotated New Testament* (2nd ed.; Oxford: University Press), 2017, ad locum.

[9] Wolfgang Seiferth, *Synagogue and Church in the Middle Ages* (New York: Frederick Ungar, 1970); Gertrud Schiller, *Iconography of Christian Art*, trans. Janet Seligman, 2 vols. (Greenwich, CT: New York Graphic Society, 1972), vol. 2, plates 385, 424, 442, 446, 450–452, 527 (cf. 528), 529–530, 570; Ruth Mellinkoff, *Outcasts*, 2 vols. (Berkeley: University of California, 1994), vol 2: sections II, 34–37; III, 17, 18, 20, 57, 90–97; XI, 6–7.

[10] So rendered in the Septuagint (Greek).

[11] The term "typology" denotes a system for dividing things into types in science and social sciences; here, in biblical analysis.

[12] For more, see Leonard Goppelt, *Typos: The Typological Interpretation of the Old Testament in the New* (Grand Rapids: Eerdmans, 1982) or Friedbert Ninow,

Indicators of Typology within the Old Testament: The Exodus Motif (Frankfurt: Peter Lang, 2001).

[13] That is, the waters of baptism and blood of the Eucharist interpreted as core sacraments by which the church, springing from Christ's wounding, is born and sustained: Eve drawn from the first Adam's side during "deep sleep" (Genesis. 2:21); the church, bride of Christ, drawn from Jesus' side in his death.

[14] "But one of the soldiers pierced his side with a spear, and...there came out blood and water."

[15] "For as by a man [Adam] came death, by a man [Christ] has come also... resurrection....As in Adam all die, so...in Christ shall all be made alive."

[16] Judas is the Greek equivalent of the Hebrew name *Yehudah* (Judah); see earlier, note 3, explaining Christian biblical recourse to the Greek rendition.

[17] Matthew 27:5 devises Judas hanging himself as the "anti-type" to trusted Ahithophel (King David's advisor/betrayer) who hanged himself (2 Samuel 17:23)—suggesting David, putative author of Psalms, recalling *his* betrayer.

[18] In the Hebrew Bible, Joseph is one *of* twelve, not a leader (cf. Jesus) *outside* them; and Judah's intent is to keep Joseph alive! With typology, details that correlate may suffice irrespective of others that do not, meaning that even Jewish biblical motifs more divergent than parallel might still be applied to "substantiate" Gospel episodes.

[19] Transfiguration is defined in this context as shining physical alteration radiating from pivotal encounter with the Divine.

[20] This explains why Matthew, casting Jesus as the second (and greater) Moses, is the only Gospel to construct a Sermon on the Mount (chapters 5–7).

[21] For the entire sweep of correlations: see Dale Allison, *The New Moses: A Matthean Typology* (Eugene, OR: Wipf and Stock, 2013), passim.

[22] The authors called "the church fathers" were influential theologians (from the first five centuries CE) not including New Testament authors or heretical writers. Typology is often practiced by the *Epistle of Barnabas* (early second century), Justin Martyr (mid-second), Tertullian (early third), Origen (early–mid third). See Alonzo L. Gaskill, "Types, Shadows, and Symbols of Christ Seen by the Church Fathers," *The Gospel of Jesus Christ in the Old Testament* (Provo, UT: Brigham Young University, 2009), passim.

[23] Cyprian of Carthage was the leading bishop of the Church of Africa during the mid-third century. Here see "The Treatises of Cyprian," *The Ante-Nicene Fathers*, eds. Alexander Roberts and James Donaldson, revised and chronologically arranged with prefaces and notes by A. C. Coxe (Buffalo: C. L. Publishing Co., 1885), Vol. 5, Treatise 11:8, p. 501.

[24] On interrelating the names *Yehoshua* and *Yeshua*, see James Price, "The Names Yeshua and Yehoshua," online at: http://www.essene.com/Yeshua/yehoshua. htm. The English "Joshua" translates the Hebrew *Yehoshua*, or its later Hebrew/

Aramaic form *Yeshua*, both of which were common first-century CE names. We cannot determine which Jesus used since our earliest sources mentioning him were composed in Greek.

[25] See Anthony T. Hanson, *Jesus Christ in the Old Testament* (London: SPCK, 1965); David Limbaugh, *The Emmaus Code: Finding Jesus in the Old Testament* (Washington, DC: Regnery Publishing, 2015).

[26] On distinguishing details *true* of Jesus from those *invented*, see Cook, "The Jews' Paradigm for Problem-Solving: Why Make the Gospels an Exception?" (forthcoming in the Mesorah Matrix *V'shamru* volume in 2019).

[27] Here "even," in both Hebrew and Greek, is susceptible of being misrendered as "and," although cognizance of prophetic style would rule out that "and" is here meant.

[28] Leon Festinger, Harry Riecken, and Stanley Schachter, *When Prophecy Fails* (rpt.; New York: Harper & Row, 1964), p. 25; emphasis added.

[29] Ironically, Festinger erred in not accepting early Christianity as matching this paradigm because he assumed, as genuine, Jesus' ostensible predictions of his crucifixion (Mark 8:31, 9:31, 10:32–34), thereby rendering Jesus' death *consonant* with alleged predictions. Actually, these were editorial additions to help Jesus' followers better cope with the *dissonance* of their disappointment, so early Christianity belonged as perhaps the strongest of all illustrations confirming Festinger's theory.

[30] Raymond Brown, *The Death of the Messiah* (New York: Doubleday, 1994), p. 15.

[31] Perhaps first explored by J. Rendel Harris, assisted by Vacher Burch, *Testimonies* (Cambridge: University Press, 1916–1920; rpt. 2012); see also Alessandro Falcetta, "The Testimony Research of James Rendel Harris," *Novum Testamentum* 45 (2003), pp. 280–299.

[32] That is to say, to missionaries the expression "in that day" appears so often in the diversity of Hebrew prophetic writing so as to prompt the inference that it must allude to the "day" of Jesus' return. Also note the widely-different imagery embedded in such passages as Isaiah 4:2;Ezekiel 38:14; Joel 4:18; Amos 9:11; Micah 4:6–7; Zephaniah 3:11,16; Zechariah 9:16–17 and 14:20–21.

[33] For elaboration, see Cook, *Modern Jews Engage the New Testament*, pp. 152–154.

The Torah of Stuff

Nina Beth Cardin

Having things is essential to life. Managing them well, choosing what to possess, what to forego, what to hold onto and what to divest is all bound up in the biblical injunction to "choose life" (Deuteronomy 30:19). For it is not just any life that we should seek, but the good life. Living the Torah of stuff is essential to choosing the good life. Though some people have too much, and many have too little, we all need stuff to get by in this world. We learn that early in the narrative of creation.

Eden was a place apart from our world, a place with different rules and expectations. "Things" weren't necessary. "Having" was not the primary human enteprise; "being" was. Work was done to make and keep the earth verdant. Food was plentiful. The climate was temperate. Wanting stuff, storing stuff, being measured by one's stuff was not part of the social or emotional equation. In the biblical account, humanity's first transgression was not motivated by a desire for possession, or greed for things. It was driven by an appetite for knowledge. The first material possession, the first constructed (as opposed to created) object—that is, clothing—was not made by Adam or Eve, as we might have thought, but wrought by the hand of the Divine: "And God made garments of skins for Adam and his wife and clothed them" (Genesis 3:21). Humans had to be taught to take nature and transform it into material goods.

Before that, there was no need for things. No need for pots and pans, shoes and socks, keys and wallets. No need for pockets, shelves, chests, or closets.

But it is different in the aftermath of Eden. Life now demands encounters with things. To construct a life of sustenance and purpose, to thrive as individuals and society, we need to negotiate well the world of possessions.

And so we collect, buy, gather, receive, and arrange stuff—for all sorts of reasons, both material and spiritual. "Goods assembled together in ownership make physical, visible statements about the hierarchy of values to which their chooser subscribes."[1] Collecting all the stuff of our lives is a necessary human activity, an essential tool for the way we embrace and manage the work of being us. Through these constructed and gathered items, we become curators of our persona, managers of our personal identity. Dressing each morning, outfitting ourselves for the day's tasks, is a kind of performance art that we act out both for ourselves and for others. It is a display that reinforces both "who" we are and "whose" we are, and thus the kind of life we seek.

Many of us pursue this material enterprise with gusto. Modernity has afforded us the privilege—or imperative, or burden—of procuring a lot of stuff to arrange. It is estimated that the average American home possesses 300,000 items.[2] We have so much stuff that it constantly gets lost or misplaced or covered over by clutter. One British insurance company studied 3,000 people and discovered that they lost (or at least misplaced) approximately nine items a day, causing loss of time and unnecessary upset.[3] Though we need some stuff to anchor us to the bedrock of our lives, a profusion of stuff could speak of confusion, flailing, or desperation. As the Talmud warns us, *tafasta m'rubbeh lo tafasta* ("to over-reach is to lose it all").[4]

Once upon a time, households were simpler places. Inventories of personal affects could be listed in a page or two of an estate registry.

Things did not easily get lost or misplaced by carelessness or clutter because there were so few of them. Each carried meaning, worth, and significance. Often the history of each item was known—who made it, with what materials, using what tools. Many family items might also have been homespun. Where possible, they were handed down from generation to generation. The management, arrangement, and disposition of these relatively few household and personal possessions captured and expressed one's values and one's position in life.

During the time of the Second Temple, when personal and household possessions were few, losing something was cause for divine intervention. A rabbinic text relates:

> These are the ones who, when visiting the Temple in Jerusalem, enter by circling counter-clockwise [everyone else circled clockwise]: a mourner, an outcast, one whose loved one is ill, and one who has lost something. [In meeting someone walking toward them, those walking clockwise inquire:] "What has befallen you, so that walk this way?" If they answer "I am a mourner," the inquirer responds: "May the One who dwells in this house comfort you." If they answer "I am an outcast," the inquirer responds: "May the One who dwells in this house turn their hearts so they may take you back." To the one whose loved one is sick, they respond: "May the One who dwells in this house be merciful to your loved one." To the one who has lost something, they respond: "May the One who dwells in this house cause the one who found it to return it to you."[5]

Spiritual, social, physical and material loss here all partake of a unified sense of painful deprivation.

While death, illness and even ostracism are beyond the capacity of humans to fully rectify, the architects of Jerusalem facilitated the restoration of a lost object by crafting the Temple's *even ha-to·ein*, the "stone of claims" (a kind of lost-and-found):

> Our rabbis taught: There was a stone of claims in Jerusalem. Whoever lost an article went there to seek it, and whoever found an article did likewise to return it. The latter stood and proclaimed, and the former submitted its identification marks and received it back."[6]

When we lose things today, we also try to find them. But unless the object is of significant value (either monetary or emotional), we resign ourselves to its loss if it does not resurface readily. We would rarely imagine invoking the help of God to get our sunglasses back, or our umbrella (though we may go to the lost-and-found on the rare chance they might have turned up there). And yet if we don't value that particular version of the thing, believing it to be fungible and replaceable, we still value the habit and aggregation of things— knowing, or more precisely, sensing, that there is an art to the task of possession.

The question then becomes: How do we manage—or perhaps better, curate—our things so that they most reflect who we are, and so that they enhance our lives? What things do we absorb into our permanent collection of stuff? How do we manage or display them? Which do we discard, and when? The answers depend largely on which of life's enterprise most engages us at a given moment. Indeed, the meanings of things, and the roles they play, change throughout the stages of our lives. In the words of Kohelet, "There is a time for everything under heaven…a time to keep and a time to throw away" (3:1, 6).

When we are young, when our bodies and minds, networks and identity, are growing, we need stuff to mark, confirm, test, and advance our development. We present the face of our emerging selves to others (and to ourselves) through the varying elements of our things: our wardrobe, our devices, our music, our wheels. Our repertoire of stuff is volatile, turning over season by season, year by year—appropriately matching and serving the turbulent pursuit of self.

As we grow older and begin to settle in, and settle down, when we are newly married or creating households of our own, our stuff serves to signal our entry into adulthood. We may no longer assemble trousseaus or speak about hope chests, but we recapitulate these gestures and dreams of homemaking when we "register" for dinnerware, purchase pots and pans, outfit our linen closets, and buy queen-sized beds and dining sets.

After this early, toughest part of constructing self is largely (but never fully) complete, our accumulation of things may slow down a bit. And this is fortunate, for as we become more rooted in our sense of self, we may be called upon to make room for a baby or two. Their material needs may overwhelm ours. Their stuff may define the interior of our home. And this is appropriate, for a while at least. For what is central to our heart becomes central in, and to, our home. I know of a marriage that foundered on the shoals of the allotment of space. He (first marriage) moved in to her (second marriage) parental homestead. She banished his stuff to a study reserved for him, and displayed only her stuff in the public rooms. Both his stuff, and he, were marginal in the space—and apparently the soul—of that home. The marriage did not last.

It is when we are older that our relationship to stuff truly begins to change. We no longer need as many things to remind us of who we are. Our deeds, our memories, and a few essential possessions can do that. And while we always (hopefully) have aspirations that drive us forward, we also come to realize that it might be time to compile what a friend of mine calls a "reverse bucket list." That is: we must begin to divest of some expectations of future adventures and unattainable accomplishments. Becoming a musical virtuoso when we have never played before, indulging in extreme sports, even pursuing an alternate professional career—all of these may demand more time to attain proficiency than we may have left. And so we can begin to divest of stuff…as well as of some of our dreams.

The Torah tells us that Moses was deprived of the privilege of entering the promised land because he struck the rock instead of speaking to it when coaxing water out of it (Numbers 20:12). Perhaps. But perhaps it was also because the task not just of leading hundreds of thousands of people across the Jordan but into their homeland demanded a younger man, and so that story was the Torah's way of saying that Moses did not have the time to complete the task. Either way, the story teaches that even the most worthy and accomplished of us will leave this life one day with dreams unfulfilled.

Hence the reverse bucket list. We should not rail against this anticipatory divestment, but honor it so that we can direct our later-in-life energies to those areas that are most promising, most achievable, and most rewarding. It does not mean that we should resign ourselves to a lesser life but rather, as the sustainable development market might say, to a "right-sized" life.

How, then, does our relationship to stuff change as we age? We often seek to occupy less space, not more…which often means that we need to rid ourselves of stuff. It is not easy to do but, like pruning, it is good. The right cuts yield more life. And we are positioned to do that. For after a lifetime of consumption, we are wiser to the true value of things and we need less of them to hold our identity. When young, when we were building self, we needed our things to bolster us. It was through our possessions' brands and function that we presented ourselves to the world and displayed the desired trajectory of our lives. In our later years, though, it is we who impart identity to our things.

A lifetime of consumption has taught us the limits and the

burdens of stuff. We know better what we need and what we don't. So discarding, recycling, and distributing are the tasks we are called to perform. This is not to say that older folks are ready to lie down and wait for the end. They (Does that include me as I cross into my seventh decade? When does one become "older"?) have not ceased growing, or being curious, or adventurous, or whimsical. It is just that the balance has shifted.

This is not our first act of divestment. We selectively discard stuff beginning early in life, as we grow from babies to toddlers, from toddlers to children, from children to teens, and so on. In addition to these stages, life may force upon us other moments of divestment, such as when we face the dislocations of divorce, or exile, or war. But this last divestment, the one undertaken because of age, is for keeps. We will not be replacing the items we give away this time. That is not the point. Their absence will hopefully leave room for assessing what really matters, both materially and spiritually. (And it will ease the task, for those who survive us, of disassembling the house.) Gifting these items to loved ones, or those in need, during our lifetime will mean more to us than keeping them.

It is stunning that the Torah gives us so little guidance here. It speaks almost not at all about domestic material culture[7] or the disposition of personal things, even at the end of life. It is not *stuff* that the elders of the Bible (even those of substantial means, like Abraham) actively bequeathed to their survivors but *blessings*. Most often these blessings offer a vision (sometimes good, sometimes not) of one's future. If material "goods" were mentioned, they were in relation to nature and its gifts—as in Moses' blessing to Joseph before his death: "And to Joseph he said: May his land be blessed with the dew from heaven and with goodness of the deep that couches below; with the abundant yield of the sun, and the abundant crop of the moons" (Deuteronomy 33:13–1).

How different our possession-heavy world is, often distracting us, even diverting us, from such blessings. We are eager, appropriately, to prepare for the proper disposition of our goods upon our death. It is often a prerequisite for a peaceful end. Some of the most comforting work done at a bedside is by accountants and estate attorneys. They help the ill get their worldly affairs in order, assuring them as much as is humanly possible that the disposition of their worldly goods is taken care of.

But we also know that, in the end, the material world is ephemeral. It is the spiritual that truly endures. Our sages taught: "Know that what is yours is not really yours, and what isn't yours surely isn't yours."[8] Stuff is not our enduring legacy.

Yet we may dare to add a coda to the saying of the rabbis: "What is not yours may in the end be yours." For we have not created the distinction between right and wrong, and we can neither claim authorship of values and goodness nor hold onto the love we give to others or the encouragement we send their way. Yet by doing right and pursuing goodness, and by teaching the wisdom of our tradition and offering love and encouragement, we will possess all that we give away. It is the accolades, the distinction, and the love that these acts bring us that will in the end forever belong to us.

Our task throughout the years is to choose life by taking the precious moments bequeathed to us, by making of our lives a monument to the values we cherish, and being intentional about how our stuff can aid us in that enterprise. Then, as we age, we can discern which of these objects that have populated our life we should keep as our years decline (for our own ongoing sense of identity, health, and joy) and which to give away...and how.

In each life, in each household, there are special objects that contain and carry forward the memories of who we are, what we love, and what we value. These are the objects that we seek most, as we grow older, to give our children—for memory often needs a goad, a holder, to keep it from slipping away. These objects are the keepers of our family heritage, our beliefs, our struggles, and our values. They might be a silver serving spoon that our ancestors brought from Europe, or the fountain pen our father used to build his business, or the *tallis* clips of a grandfather, or the cookie-cutters of a grandmother. The worth of these objects is far above their utilitarian, production, or monetary value. Yet they grow more precious with time. And in this ritual transfer from generation to generation, they become the guardians, the protectors, and the enduring physical presence of our memories and values.

NOTES

[1] Mary Douglas and Baron Isherwood, *The World of Goods: An Anthropology of Consumption* (New York: Routledge, 1996) p. ix.

[2] Mary MacVean, "For many people, gathering possessions is just the stuff of life," in the *Los Angeles Times* of March 21, 2014, available online at http://articles.latimes.com/2014/mar/21/health/la-he-keeping-stuff-20140322.

[3] "Lost something already today? Misplaced items cost us ten minutes a day," in *Daily Mail* (March 20, 2012), available online at http://www.dailymail.co.uk/news/article-2117987/Lost-today-Misplaced-items-cost-minutes-day.html. The top items were: smartphone, house keys, car keys, paperwork, glasses, purse/wallet, lip balm, hair brush, gloves, clothing, and books.

[4] B. Hagigah 17a.

[5] Tractate Semaḥot 6:11. Semaḥot is one of the minor tractates of the Talmud, of the same era but not the same authority as the major sixty-three tractates. It deals with matters of death and mourning.

[6] B. Bava Metzia 28b. A possible candidate for this even *ha-to·ein* has been discovered; see Richard Gray, "Was This the First 'Lost Property' Office?" (September 1, 2015), online at http://www.dailymail.co.uk/sciencetech/article-3218236/Is-lost-property-office-2-000-year-old-stone-podium-Jerusalem-s-Stone-Claims-unearthed.html.

[7] The greatest view of "domestic" items comes in relationship to the Temple cult. For example, 1 Kings 7:48–50 lists the Temple furnishings, all of gold: the altar, the table for the bread, the lampstands (ten in all), the petals, lamps, tongs, the basins, snuffers, sprinkling bowls, ladles and fire-pans, hinge-sockets for the doors of the holy of holies, and the doors themselves. No comparable view of a home—or the packing, unpacking, or bequeathing of stuff of home—is found anywhere in the Bible.

[8] Tractate Derekh Eretz 1:24. This minor tractate teaches appropriate behavior for a rabbinic scholar.

The Limits of Choosing Life, Theologically and Medically[1]

Elliot N. Dorff

See, I set before you this day life and prosperity, death and adversity. For I command you this day, to love the Eternal, your God, to walk in His ways, and to keep His commandments, His laws, and His rules, that you may thrive and increase, and that the Eternal, your God, may bless you in the land that you are about to enter and possess. But if your heart turns away and you give no heed, and you are lured into the worship and service of other gods, I declare to you this day that you shall certainly perish; you shall not long endure on the soil that you are crossing the Jordan to enter and possess. I call heaven and earth to witness against you this day: I have put before you life and death, blessing and curse. Choose life—if you and your offspring would live—by loving the Eternal your God, heeding His commands, and holding fast to Him, for thereby you shall have life and shall long endure upon the soil that the Eternal swore to your ancestors, Abraham, Isaac, and Jacob, to give to them.

—Deuteronomy 30:15–20[2]

"Choose Life" Theologically

In context, this passage bids us to follow God's commandments so that we may live in the land God promised to us. This is just one expression of a tenet that appears often in Deuteronomy: that obeying God's commandments will bring reward and that disobeying them will bring punishment. That doctrine, however, was already challenged in the biblical books of Job and Kohelet (Ecclesiastes).[3] Later the rabbis explicitly deny Deuteronomy's doctrine by asserting that *tzaddik v'ra lo, rasha v'tov lo*, "The righteous suffer, and the evil prosper,"[4] and they therefore create multiple justifications of God's justice ("theodicies") despite this.[5] The need for such justifications is even more evident to Jews of today, who can look back at the Crusades, the Inquisition, the pogroms of the Middle Ages and modern times, and the Holocaust to cast doubt on the Torah's assurances of just, divine enforcement of the law.

Contemporary thinkers have created a number of "post-Holocaust theologies" precisely to respond to the challenges the Holocaust poses for this traditional tenet that God will reward the good and punish the bad. Some theologians deny the connection between faithfulness and flourishing outright, by repudiating a God who acts in history and affirming only the God of nature (e.g., Richard Rubenstein).[6] Others go in the opposite direction, trying to justify God's role in the Holocaust either as just punishment for those who sinned (e.g., Menachem Mendel Schneerson, the seventh Lubavitcher Rebbe, 1902–1994)[7] or as vicarious punishment of the innocent to atone for the sins of the blameworthy, along the lines of Isaiah 53 (e.g., Ignaz Maybaum).[8] Most formulate a response somewhere in between, struggling in various ways to define how Jews can have faith after the Holocaust, the God in whom one can have faith, and the proper terms of our relationship with God in light of the Holocaust (e.g., Michael Wyschogrod, Eliezer Berkovits, David Blumenthal, Emil Fackenheim, Irving Greenberg, Harold Kushner, Harold Schulweis).[9]

I myself have written about this issue in my book *Knowing God*.[10]

Suffice it to say here that, like Job, Kohelet, and the rabbis of classical antiquity, on some level I believe that we cannot expect a tie between good actions and good results, certainly as individuals and even as communities; that we instead should be satisfied with the fact that, as the rabbis of the Mishnah said, "The reward of fulfilling a commandment is that you are prepared to fulfill another one, and the result of committing a sin is that you are more likely to commit another one, for fulfilling commandments leads to fulfilling other commandments, and committing sins leads to committing other sins" (M. Avot 4:2). At the same time, also like the Torah and the rabbis of old, I believe that our actions have consequences, even if we cannot always see them or understand them. Smoking makes lung cancer more probable; polluting our environment makes it unusable for our purposes. Beyond these pragmatic consequences, acts of unfaithfulness to our covenant with God through violating its terms, and even failure to attend to that relationship by neglecting the positive commandments that nurture it, will weaken our relationship with God and with other human beings, thus distancing ourselves from the goals of the covenant. Like all relationships, our covenantal ties to God and to other people become as deep or as shallow as we allow them to be through our actions, which variously undermine, neglect, or cultivate the relationship. It is in these senses that I understand traditional Jewish language of God as Judge and Enforcer of the Sinai covenant, the other laws that Moses announced in the Torah, and even subsequent Jewish law. Thus even if I have more qualms about these divine roles than some of my ancestors did, the traditional depictions of God as Judge and Enforcer are powerful metaphors for my understanding of Jewish law, and choosing life theologically still means for me nurturing my relationship with God through prayer and action in accordance with Jewish law, morality, and theology.[11]

"Choose Life" Biologically

A. The Basic Principles Governing Our Health

In this essay, however, I would like to take the phrase "choose life" to mean what it denotes literally when it is removed from its context—namely, that we must do what we can to preserve our lives. Even though this is not the contextual meaning of the phrase in Deuteronomy 30, this demand is deeply rooted in the Jewish tradition.

In part, the requirement that we do what we can to preserve our lives is based on some fundamental principles of Jewish theology. God, as Creator of the universe, is also the Owner of it: "Mark, the heavens to their uttermost reaches belong to the Eternal, your God, the earth and all that is on it!" (Deuteronomy 10:14); "The Eternal owns the earth and all that it holds, the world and its inhabitants" (Psalms 24:1). As such, our bodies are not our own vis-à-vis God; they are instead God's property, and we have a fiduciary relationship to God to take care of them.

This theological perspective on our bodies leads to legal demands in Judaism to preserve them. We must avoid danger even more than violating the other prohibitions of the Torah: *sakkanta ḥamira mei-issura* ("avoiding danger is more stringently required than avoiding the transgression of the Torah's prohibitions").[12] We must come to the rescue of people whose lives are at stake; in the Talmud, the examples of this are people who are drowning or being accosted by highway robbers.[13] Similarly, one of the cardinal demands that Jewish law makes of us is to redeem captives (this *mitzvah* is called *pidyon sh'vuyim* in Hebrew),[14] for captives are at risk not only of being molested, but also of being killed. Ultimately, saving a person's life (called *pikku·aḥ nefesh* in Hebrew) takes precedence over all the commandments except three,[15] and one is supposed to save one's own life before saving the lives of others,[16] just as one must give financial and other forms of support to those who need it in concentric circles—oneself first, then one's family, then the members of the local Jewish community, then the larger Jewish community, and then the general community.[17] Much less dramatically, but much more pervasively, one must live in a city with a physician, for only there can one get the expert help that one needs both to prevent disease and to cure it.[18]

In Western thought, the reasons why one should take care of one's body are pragmatic: one wants to live long, to be healthy, to look good, and to have friends and a good job, both of which are easier if one is in good shape. Maimonides, though, specifically rejects these pragmatic motivations to maintain one's health and suggests a very different Jewish reason to do so—namely, to be in a condition in which one can fulfill the commandments and worship God:

> One who regulates one's life in accordance with the laws of medicine with the sole motive of maintaining a sound and vigorous physique and begetting children to do one's work and labor for one's benefit is not following the right course. A person should aim to maintain physical health and vigor in order that one's soul may be upright, in a condition to know God....Whoever throughout one's life follows this course will be continually serving God, even while engaged in business and even during cohabitation, because one's purpose in all that one does will be to satisfy one's needs so as to have a sound body with which to serve God. Even when one sleeps and seeks repose to calm the mind and rest the body so as not to fall sick and be incapacitated from serving God, one's sleep is service of the Almighty.[19]

B. Applying These Principles to End-of-Life Care

Until recently in human history this clear principle of choosing life in the biological sense was almost self-evidently authoritative, and one was obliged to do this through both preventive measures like proper diet, exercise, hygiene, and sleep, and also through whatever curative methods were available. In recent decades, however, medicine has advanced so much that we often have to ask, with regard to other people and ultimately with regard to ourselves as well, whether to continue to intervene medically or instead to withhold or withdraw such interventions and let nature take its course, providing comfort care in the process.

This is a very new dilemma, for until recently in human history, when a person was dying, there was not much that doctors could do for him or her. Since Friedrich Sertürner (1783–1841) first isolated morphine from a poppy plant between 1803 and 1805, physicians could keep patients comfortable, and other opiates were also available in specific times and places.[20] Moreover, the psychological support that family and friends could offer a sick person was, frankly, better than what we do, for when you were sick, you were sick at home, in familiar surroundings, where those who knew and loved you were there for you emotionally as well as physically. Until 1938, however, when penicillin was discovered, there was very little curative care that worked. Now we have medicines and forms of surgery that can cure what was formerly incurable, as well as public health measures such as vaccines and public health education that help us avoid disease in the first place. These have combined to push life expectancy in the United States from approximately forty-five in 1900 to close to seventy-six just a century later, and it is still climbing.

This, though, raises the point made by the philosopher Immanuel Kant in the late eighteenth century. He pointed out that if you cannot do something, you never have to ask whether you *should* do that because you simply cannot. Once you can do something, though, you must ask whether you *should*, for there are many things that you *can* do that you *should* not. You can, for example, smoke, abuse drugs, or drink to excess, but you should not. So now that we can attach a person to a machine that will function in place of his or her heart or lungs or kidneys, we must determine the circumstances in which we should do that, and now that we can mitigate or even cure certain diseases with medications, we must define when we should and should not do that. Pneumonia, for example, used to be known as "the old man's friend" because a person would die of pneumonia earlier and less painfully than one would die of some other disease. This being the case, should we always seek to cure the pneumonia, only to subject the patient to pain for a longer period of time?

As you might imagine, because this dilemma is so new, rabbis who write about it disagree with each other across a broad spectrum. It is important to note that all rabbis who write about this are applying Jewish sources and values *as they read them*, as well as the advice of contemporary doctors, to arrive at their opinions. Because, though, our ancestors had little expectation that anyone could intervene in the natural process of dying, Jewish sources on such interventions are sparse, and they apply to contexts sometimes very different from a modern hospital setting. As a result, a large part of the decision-making process of each rabbi depends on how relevant he thinks the few sources on point are, how he interprets them, and what other parts of the Jewish tradition (theology, moral values, history, etc.) he brings to bear in determining how to guide Jews on these issues. (So far only male rabbis have written extensively about these issues.)

On one end, some rabbis (e.g., J. David Bleich) maintain that every moment of life is precious, regardless of its quality, and so we should always do whatever we can to sustain life and never withhold or withdraw life support, even if the person has no hope of recovery and is in excruciating pain or is comatose.[21] On the other end of the spectrum, some Reform rabbis (e.g., David Ellenson) maintain that, in line with Reform Judaism's emphasis on autonomy, each patient should decide what should and should not be done to keep him or her alive—either through directly asking the patient, if he or she is mentally competent, or through the patient's advance directive, or, in the absence of either of those, through the patient's surrogate decision-maker. The patient may consult doctors, family members, his or her rabbi, social workers, and others, but in the end it should be the patient's decision.[22]

In between those extremes, there is a range of opinions. To give just three stopping-points along the way, beginning on the right end of the spectrum (that is, the least permissive), some (especially Rabbi Moshe Tendler[23]) have argued that at least in some situations withholding machines and medications is acceptable, but withdrawing them is not. That is, even though we can intervene in a particular case, we may, and in some cases, should not do so because to so would only delay the natural dying process and not bring about healing. If we have already intervened through the use of machines or medications, however, we may not remove them because that would be the equivalent of murder. Most Orthodox rabbis follow Rabbi Tendler's position, as evidenced by the fact that it has been officially adopted by the Modern Orthodox rabbinical organization, the Rabbinical Council of America.[24]

Although I can appreciate the thinking that led to this distinction, insofar as he is trying to minimize the role of doctors in bringing about a person's death, from the perspective of the patient I think that his distinction does not make sense. At all other times in life, after all, if doctors tried something to cure a disease and it did not work, we would expect them to stop the intervention—because every intervention has bad side effects. So if the intervention in a dying patient is not effectively curing the patient, we should remove it so as to spare the patient the pain and other harms of its side effects. In an actively dying patient, removing life support is done just as much in the service of not delaying the dying process and letting nature take its course as is withholding such interventions in the first place.

Moving along the spectrum to the left (that is, toward the more permissive), Rabbi Avram Israel Reisner wrote one of the two positions endorsed by the Conservative Movement's Committee on Jewish Law and Standards.[25] He permits the withholding or withdrawing of machines and medications in a dying patient, but not the withholding of artificial nutrition or hydration when the patient cannot eat on his or her own. He reasons that living life normally does not require machines or medications, but everyone needs food and liquids, and that is exactly what artificial nutrition and hydration supply.

I wrote the other position adopted by the Conservative Movement's Committee on Jewish Law and Standards.[26] Rabbi Reisner and I agree on about 80% of the issues involved in end-of-life care, including the need to provide pain medication and the acceptability of hospice care. One of the things we disagree about, however, is artificial nutrition and hydration. He sees that as food because it functions in place of food. I, in contrast, see it as medicine because it lacks many of the qualities of food—it does not have differences in temperature or texture and lacks all taste—and it comes into the body through tubes, as some kinds of medicine do but food usually does not. So I would allow not only the withholding of interventions and the withdrawal of machines and medicines, as Rabbi Reisner would, but also the removal of artificial nutrition and hydration if it was used as part of an intervention designed to try to save the patient's life but ultimately failed to do so. So in the case of Terri Schiavo, a woman who was comatose for over fourteen years,[27] I maintain that they should have removed all life support, including artificial nutrition and hydration, after nine months or so, for that is the longest time that people have been in comas and awakened from them, but Rabbi Reisner would say that doctors never should have removed artificial nutrition and hydration, even after fourteen years.

C. Assisted Suicide

Every intervention discussed above amounts to standing aside and letting nature take its course in bringing an end to the patient's life. But what about hastening the dying process, usually through giving the patient an overdose of some medication?

It should be noted, first, that this is not murder in the usual sense of the term. When we say that someone committed murder, we mean that he or she took the life of a person against that person's will. In assisted suicide, by contrast, a person is helping the patient fulfill his or her wish to die, presumably because the patient cannot commit suicide on his or her own.

The second thing to note about this is that the usual cases that one thinks of when discussing assisted suicide are those in which the patient is in excruciating, uncontrollable pain despite all available interventions, medical, psychological, and social. That is what I will call "the pure case," and it is the one that most cogently calls out to us to alleviate pain. It is also that one that advocates for assisted suicide have in mind and most often describe when indicating why states and nations should allow assisted suicide. It is, in their words, "death with dignity," for it enables the patient to avoid a long period of suffering or dementia. People who are mentally competent but in severe pain, and people who are sinking into dementia due to Alzheimer's disease or some other malady, should be legally able, advocates say, to instruct their physicians and loved ones either directly, if competent, or through an advance directive, if not, that they want help to die sooner. It is precisely because of such pure cases that some American states and some other nations have legalized assisted suicide under specified conditions, thus freeing physicians and family members of any legal liability for providing such aid in dying.

Why, though, have not all states and countries adopted that stance? And why did I, who, as you read earlier, take a relatively liberal stance on withholding and removing life support at the end of life if the patient's welfare would be advanced by such measures, write the rabbinic ruling for the Conservative Movement's Committee on Jewish Law and Standards that prohibits assisted suicide?[28]

The answer is that most cases of assisted suicide are not pure. In some cases, the problem leading the patient to ask for assisted suicide is depression. Sometimes that is caused medically, in which case anti-depression medications should be used rather than helping the person die. In other cases, patients say that they want to die because they think that nobody cares if they live or die. I saw one such case when I was one of the authors contributing to a book on suicide. We interviewed a man suffering with AIDS. This was in the mid-1980s, before the cocktail of drugs that has helped many overcome the ravages of AIDS was discovered in 1996, and so the only future that this man saw for himself was a painful dying process. He bought a 22-caliber pistol to kill himself, but when he put it to his head and pulled the trigger, the gun jammed. Just then a friend of his stopped by, and when he saw what this man had intended to do, the friend set up 24/7 vigil in which at least one of this man's friends was with him at all times to prevent him from killing himself. Now, when we asked him whether he still wanted to commit suicide, he said "No, because my friends do not want me to die." So sometimes the proper remedy to depression is to provide interactions with other people, not assistance in dying.

Insufficient pain medication is another reason people ask to die. Doctors tend to prescribe less medication than what a patient needs, in part because they are not aware of the patient's level of pain, and in part because physicians do not want to risk revocation of their license to practice, a lawsuit, or a criminal charge for prescribing too many opiates. The remedy for this, however, is for family and friends to serve as stubborn advocates for their loved one, driving home with medical personnel just how much pain their loved one is suffering. Sometimes "the squeaky wheel gets the grease."

Money, though, is the major complicating factor in assisted suicide. In some cases, Mom or Dad does not want to "squander" the family's money on long-term, extensive care and therefore wants to die faster to avoid those expenses. In other cases, the children do not want Mom or Dad to squander their inheritance on long-term care for themselves. Insurance companies—including government programs of insurance—would surely prefer to pay for assistance in dying than for the much more expensive long-term care.

So while I recognize that there are pure cases where depression due to chemical imbalances in the brain or loneliness, pain control, and money are not issues, and while I am open to arguments to legalize assisted suicide in such cases, they are the small minority and probably should not be the basis for public policy. As the lawyers say, "Hard cases make bad law."[29] If a state or nation is going to legalize assisted suicide, the way Oregon first did that is still the best model, for Oregon built into the law protections against some of the factors described above that worry me, and they seem to have worked to make assisted suicide in that state both rare and humanely done. In June, 2016 a law permitting assisted suicide but with even more stringent requirements than the Oregon law demands went into effect in California, a state with a much larger and more diverse population, and it will be interesting to see how it will fare in avoiding the pitfalls of legalizing assisted suicide.

D. Advance Directives

Finally, everyone should fill out an advance directive for health care so that their wishes about their care can be known even when they are not mentally competent. I have long held that as soon as teenagers get their driver's license they should do this, for two reasons. First, filling out an advance directive will impress on these young drivers the responsibilities and risks that they are undertaking when driving and thus hopefully make them safer drivers. Second, all the hard cases about end-of-life treatment that ended in the courts were about young people who had never indicated what they would want if they were dying, for they presumed, as people that age do, that they will live forever, and therefore the farthest thing from their minds are decisions about dying. Granted that a directive filled out at that age is not legally binding, and granted that parents as well as teenagers resist doing this because they do not want to reinforce their current nervousness about letting their children drive, but this is at least a way to indicate what the teenagers would want if, God forbid, they are involved in a devastating accident.

In any case, people should fill out such forms well before they enter old age. California was the first state to legislate the authority of "living wills" in 1973, and now all fifty states have done so. The American reason for doing so is to preserve patient autonomy—the idea that all people should control their own way of dying. Advance directives sometimes work that way, but usually doctors will do what family members want whether that is what the patient indicated in an advance directive or not, because family members may sue the doctor while a dead patient cannot.

The Jewish reason for filling out such forms is much more cogent—namely, that you do not want disputes about your dying process to be a reason that your children are angry with each other after you die. I have seen cases like this: Mom is dying, and she has three adult children. Two of them want to remove life support from Mom because the doctors have assured them that there is nothing more that medicine can do to keep her alive, let alone enable her to recover. The third, usually the one who had the worst relationship with Mom during their lives together, refuses to allow removal of life support from Mom, largely as a result of guilt. One such person actually said while I was present, "Mom and I did not get along well, but in the end I was there for her, and you guys killed her." To avoid your dying process from being the reason your children do not talk to each other, you need to fill out an advance directive and give copies to your primary physician, your attorney, and all the members of your immediate family (and your surrogate decision-maker, if that is someone else). Then you should call a family meeting in which you distribute the copies and go over what you have written and why you wrote what you wrote. Nobody likes to talk about death, least of all one's own, but Jews know how to interpret a text, and so the process of going through the document will help to allay the discomfort of talking about the plans for a parent's death. Furthermore, even if your designated surrogate is one of your children, he or she can say to his or her siblings after you die, "Look, you all heard what Mom said. I may not want to die that way, but I was just carrying out her wishes." That may not guarantee good relationships among the siblings after you die, but at least it will avoid creating yet another reason for them not to like each other.

The Orthodox, Conservative, and Reform Movements have all produced advance directives for health care in accordance with their own understanding of Jewish law and values. In each case, the first part of the document is a Proxy Statement, in which the one filling out the directive names Person A as his or her surrogate decision-maker, together with that person's contact information, and then names Person B to act in that capacity if Person A either cannot or will not do so when the time comes (and some versions of the form also ask for Person C).

The Orthodox document then identifies the person's rabbi and asks that all decisions about the person's dying process be referred to him.[30] That accords with an Orthodox understanding of Jewish law being binding on us and seeing rabbis as the authorized interpreters of Jewish law. In the Reform document, the second part of the directive lists a whole variety of possible interventions and asks the person filling it out to indicate whether he or she wants those interventions always, most of the time, sometimes, rarely, or never.[31] Another document published by the Union of Reform Judaism analyzes the issue of assisted suicide.[32] In both these documents the Reform emphasis on individual autonomy is in evidence. The Conservative advance directive takes the reader through ten different situations in which decisions regarding end-of-life care must be made. In each case, decisions in accord with both the rulings by Rabbi Reisner and me are in bold print; those that only I would allow are in italics.[33] The document thus articulates in practice the Conservative view that Jewish law is binding but that it can have several different interpretations and applications as it evolves over time, especially in radically new circumstances such as those presented to us by modern medicine.

******

As an ever-greater proportion of the populations of Western countries ages, these issues of when to intervene to choose life and when not to do so have already become a major social, political, economic, and, at bottom, moral issue for an increasing percentage of us, whether as patients ourselves or as caregivers. Put broadly, we are facing the limits of when we should choose life medically, in the same way that the tragedies that Jews have endured historically have raised major questions about Deuteronomy's promise that we should choose life theologically so that we live long lives and prosper. On both the medical and theological planes, choosing life remains a deep Jewish value, even if sometimes we do so religiously for reasons other than the rewards and punishments the Torah describes, and even if we do so medically while recognizing the proper limits to preserving life using new medical facilities to help us do so. May the value of choosing life in both spheres, while aware of its limits, make our lives the meaningful, holy lives that the Torah intended them to be.

NOTES

[1] For further reading on choosing life theologically, see Elliot N. Dorff, *Knowing God: Jewish Journeys to the Unknowable* (New York: Jason Aronson [now Lanham, MD: Rowman and Littlefield], 1992). For further reading on choosing life medically, see Elliot N. Dorff, *Matters of Life and Death: A Jewish Approach to Modern Medical Ethics* (Philadelphia: Jewish Publication Society, 1998).

[2] This is the NJPS translation, altered slightly to follow the conventions of this series with respect to divine names.

[3] E.g., Job, 6:24–30; 9:1–35; Ecclesiastes 7:15–18; 8:9–14.

[4] B. Berakhot 7a.

[5] A good summary of the rabbis' attempts to do this can be found in Abraham Cohen, *Everyman's Talmud* (1949; rpt. New York: Schocken, 1975), pp. 110–120.

[6] Richard Rubenstein, *After Auschwitz: Radical Theology and Contemporary Judaism* (1966; 2nd ed., Baltimore: Johns Hopkins, 1992).

[7] Menachem Mendel Schneerson, *Madda Ve-emunah* (Kfar Chabad, Israel: Machon Lubavitch, 1980). On this see Yehuda Bauer, "God as Surgeon," Ha-aretz (June 1, 2007), accessible online at www.haaretz.com/print-edition/opinion/god-as-surgeon-1.221983. Menachem Mendel's father, the sixth Lubavitcher Rebbe, Yosef Yitzchak Schneersohn, also believed that the Holocaust was God's will to punish Reform Jews. See Bryan Mark Rigg, *Rescued from the Reich: How One of Hitler's Soldiers Saved the Lubavitcher Rebbe* (New Haven: Yale University Press, 2004).

[8] Ignaz Maybaum, *The Face of God After Auschwitz* (Amsterdam: Polak and Van Gennep, 1965).

[9] Michael Wyschograd, "Faith and the Holocaust," *Judaism* 20:3 (Summer 1971), pp. 286–294; Eliezer Berkovits, *Faith After the Holocaust* (New York: KTAV, 1973); idem, *Crisis and Faith* (New York: Sanhedrin Press, 1976); idem, *With God in Hell: Judaism in the Ghettos and Death Camps* (New York: Sanhedrin Press, 1979); David R. Blumenthal, *Facing the Abusing God: A Theology of Protest* (Louisville, KY: Westminster/John Knox, 1993); idem, *The Banality of Good and Evil: Moral Lessons from the Shoah and the Jewish Tradition* (Washington, DC: Georgetown University Press, 1999); Emil Fackenheim, *Quest for Past and Future* (Bloomington, IN: Indiana University Press, 1968); idem, *God's Presence in History* (New York: New York University Press, 1970); idem, *The Jewish Return Into History: Reflections in the Age of Auschwitz and the New Jerusalem* (New York: Schocken, 1978); idem, *To Mend the World: Foundations of Post-Holocaust Thought* (New York: Schocken, 1989); Irving Greenberg, "Cloud of Smoke, Pillar of Fire," in *Auschwitz: Beginning of a New Era? Reflections on*

the Holocaust, ed. Eva Fleischner (New York: KTAV, 1977), pp. 7–55 (and reprinted in large part in *Contemporary Jewish Theology: A Reader,* eds. Elliot N. Dorff and Louis E. Newman [New York: Oxford University Press, 1999], pp. 396–416); Harold Kushner, *When Bad Things Happen to Good People* (New York: Schocken, 1981); Harold Schulweis, *Evil and the Morality of God* (Cincinnati: Hebrew Union College Press and New York: KTAV, 1984); and idem, *For Those Who Can't Believe: Overcoming the Obstacles to Faith* (New York: HarperCollins, 1994). And see also Steven T. Katz, *Post-Holocaust Dialogues: Critical Studies in Modern Jewish Thought* (New York: New York University Press, 1985).

[10] Elliot N. Dorff, *Knowing God* (see note 1 above), pp. 129–148.

[11] I see Jewish law as embedded in the organic system that is Judaism and so, as in physical organisms, every part of the organism affects every other part. Thus we need to call on Jewish stories, maxims, history, theology, prayer, and study as well as Jewish social and economic conditions and contemporary science in order to know what God wants of us, and we must shape Jewish law accordingly. See Elliot N. Dorff, *For the Love of God and People: A Philosophy of Jewish Law* (Philadelphia: Jewish Publication Society, 2007), esp. chapters 2, 3, and 6. Roberta Kwall has argued for the same point from an anthropological point of view; see her book, *The Myth of the Cultural Jew* (New York: Oxford University Press, 2015).

[12] B. Ḥullin 10a.

[13] B. Sanhedrin 73a.

[14] M.T. Hilkhot Matnot Aniyim 8:10; S.A. Yoreh Dei·ah 252:1.

[15] B. Sanhedrin 74a. The three that one must observe even at the cost of death are the prohibitions against murder, idolatry, and incest/adultery. Even if someone has a knife or gun pointed at you, you must prefer to die rather than to murder someone else who is neither attacking you (in which case killing him or her would be an act of justified self–defense) nor part of an enemy at war with you (in which case killing him or her would be justified, assuming that the war is justified). Similarly, one must prefer to die rather than to commit idolatry in public, and one must also prefer to die rather than to commit adultery or incest, even if being directed to do either one by someone threatening your life. For more on the duty to rescue, see Elliot N. Dorff, *For the Love of God and People*, pp. 8, 38–39 (note 18); for more on the ethics of war, see Elliot N. Dorff, *To Do the Right and the Good: A Jewish Approach to Modern Social Ethics* (Philadelphia: Jewish Publication Society, 2002), chap. 7, and Elliot N. Dorff, "War and Peace: A Methodology to Formulate a Contemporary Jewish Approach," *Philosophia: Philosophical Quarterly of Israel* 40:4 (December, 2012), pp. 643–661, available online at https://link.springer.com/article/10.1007/s11406-012-9391-4.

[16] B. Bava Metzia 62a. See M.T. Hilkhot She'eilah U-fikadon 5:1 and S.A. Ḥoshen Mishpat 292:9.

[17] Sifrei Devarim 15:7; B. Bava Metzia 71a; B. Nedarim 80b; B. Gittin 61a (our duty to help non-Jews); M.T. Hilkhot Matnot Aniyim 7:13; S.A. Yoreh Dei·ah 251:3. On these topics generally, see Elliot N. Dorff, *The Way Into Tikkun Olam (Repairing the World)* (Woodstock, VT: Jewish Lights Publishing, 2005), chapters 5 ("Helping the Poor") and 6 ("Ransoming and Surrendering Captives").

[18] B. Sanhedrin 17b applies this to a student of Jewish law, but Y. Kiddushin 4:14, 66d, applies it to all Jews.

[19] M.T. Hilkhot Dei·ot 3:3.

[20] Cf. David T. Courtwright, *Forces of Habit Drugs and the Making of the Modern World* (Cambridge: Harvard University Press, 2009), pp. 36–37.

[21] J. David Bleich, *Judaism and Healing:Halakhic Perspectives* (New York: KTAV, 1981). Every moment of life is "of infinite and inestimable value": pp. 23 and 135. The implications of this principle for end-of-life care: chap. 24.

[22] David Ellenson, "How to Draw Guidance from a Heritage: Jewish Approaches to Moral Choices," in *A Time to Be Born, A Time to Die: The Ethics of Choice*, ed. Barry Kogan (New York: Aldine de Greuter, 1990), pp. 219–232; reprinted in *Contemporary Jewish Ethics and Morality: A Reader*, eds. Elliot N. Dorff and Louis E. Newman (New York: Oxford University Press, 1995), pp. 129–139.

[23] Fred Rosner and Moshe Tendler, *Practical Medical Halachah*, 3rd rev. ed. (Hoboken, NJ: KTAV, 1990), p. 54.

[24] "Halachic Guidelines to Assist Patients and their Families in Making 'End-of-Life' Medical Decisions (As of August 10, 2009)," available online at www.rabbis.org/pdfs/hcpi.pdf.

[25] Avram Israel Reisner, "A Halakhic Ethic of Care for the Terminally Ill," available at the website of the Rabbinical Assembly at www.rabbinicalassembly.org/sites/default/files/assets/public/halakhah/teshuvot/19861990/reisner_care.pdf.

[26] Elliot N. Dorff, "A Jewish Approach to End-Stage Medical Care," available online at the Rabbinical Assembly website at www.rabbinicalassembly.org/sites/default/files/assets/public/halakhah/teshuvot/19861990/dorff_care.pdf and reprinted in large measure in Dorff, *Matters of Life and Death* (see note 1 above), chap. 8.

[27] See *The Case of Terri Schiavo: Ethics at the End of Life*, eds. Arthur L. Caplan, James J. McCartney, and Dominic A. Sisti (Amherst, NY: Prometheus Books, 2006).

[28] Elliot N. Dorff, "Assisted Suicide," available online at the Rabbinical Assembly's website at www.rabbinicalassembly.org/sites/default/files/public/halakhah/teshuvot/19912000/dorff_suicide.pdf, and summarized in Dorff, *Matters of Life and Death* (see note 1 above), pp. 183–186.

[29] According to Neil MacCormick in his book *Rhetoric and the Rule of Law: A Theory of Legal Reasoning* (New York: Oxford University Press, 2005), p. 65,

Judge Robert Rolfe (1790–1868), although not the originator of the maxim, was the first to articulate it in print in the judgment of the 1842 English case *Winterbottom v Wright*, in which he said: "Hard cases, it has frequently been observed, are apt to introduce bad law." In 1904, Oliver Wendell Holmes, Jr. quoted it as well in his judgment of *Northern Securities Co. v. United States.*

[30] The Rabbinical Council of America, "Halachic Health Care Proxy," available online at www.rabbis.org/pdfs/FINAL_Revised_Halachic_Health_Care_Proxy.pdf.

[31] *A Time to Prepare*, ed. Richard Address (New York: Union of Reform Judaism, Commission on Jewish Family Concerns, 2002). The full set of documents that Rabbi Address created for preparing to die are available online at http://jewishsacredaging.com/wp-content/uploads/2016/05/Expanded-A-Time-To-Prepare-Jewish-Sacred-Aging.pdf and the advance directive alone is available at http://huc.edu/kalsman/articles/URJ,%20Jewish%20Family%20Concerns%20Advance%20Directive.pdf.

[32] Dr. Harvey L. Gordon, *When It Hurts Too Much to Live: Questions and Answers about Jewish Tradition and the Issues of Assisted Death* (New York: Union of Reform Judaism, 1998, reprinted and updated, 2005).

[33] Aaron L. Mackler, "Jewish Medical Directives for Health Care," available online at the Rabbinical Assembly website at www.rabbinicalassembly.org/sites/default/files/public/halakhah/teshuvot/19861990/mackler_care.pdf.

A Time to Heal and a Time to Cease from Healing: Reform *Halakhah* on End-Stage Medical Care

Mark Washofsky

The adjective "Reform"—as in "Reform Judaism"—might seem an unlikely modifier for the noun *halakhah*, generally translated as "traditional Jewish law." Yet it is a fact that over its two centuries of existence this supposedly "non-halakhic"[1] Jewish movement has produced a substantial halakhic literature, including manuals, guidebooks to religious practice, and responsa (*t'shuvot*), rabbinical-halakhic opinions written as answers to *she'eilot*, "questions" or queries submitted by individuals or communities. More than 1300 such *t'shuvot* have been published under the auspices of the Responsa Committee of the Central Conference of American Rabbis (CCAR), the Reform rabbinical association of North America, which makes them by far the largest genre of Reform writing on matters of Jewish religious practice. Although they speak from a liberal perspective and address themselves to a liberal audience, these responsa resemble those authored by rabbis in other movements in that they are explicitly halakhic documents, deriving their conclusions through engagement with the traditional halakhic literature by way of traditional halakhic argument. And like other responsa, those of the Reform variety not infrequently produce *hiddushim*, "new" ideas, that offer innovative approaches to long-standing halakhic problems.

This essay deals with one such *hiddush* in the field of bioethical *halakhah.*

As the title of this volume indicates, the Torah tells Jews to "choose life" (Deuteronomy 30:29). In no realm of human experience does that instruction figure more prominently than in the practice of medicine, or *r'fu·ah* (literally "healing"). Mainstream halakhic thought[2] declares practicing medicine to be a *mitzvah*, a commanded (as opposed to merely a "permitted"[3]) act, because it pertains to the *mitzvah* of *pikku·ah nefesh*, the duty to save human life—which in turn takes precedence over almost every other obligation imposed by the Torah.[4] As such, the practice of medicine stands at the summit of Jewish ethical responsibilities: "the one who is zealous in its performance is worthy of praise, but the one who refuses to provide it is considered a 'shedder of blood.'"[5] That the practice of medicine is defined as a *mitzvah* seems obvious to us, but it was not always so. The medieval *poskim* (halakhic authorities)[6] cite various biblical and talmudic passages that give the opposite impression. Thus, King Asa of Judah is criticized because "in his sickness he inquired not of God but of healers [i.e., physicians]" (2 Chronicles 16:12), while King Hezekiah wins praise for hiding away a medical book so that people would learn to pray for healing rather than seek out physicians.[7] A talmudic prayer, to be recited by a person treated by a blood-letter,[8] declares explicitly that God never intended for human beings to practice medicine; "rather, it became their custom."[9] Following a long struggle, the halakhic tradition ultimately overcame this ambivalence, deciding that the practice of medicine, far from frustrating God's will, is indeed a *mitzvah*, the proper human response to illness.

This definition, however, raises a painful question. If the Torah instructs us to practice medicine in order to preserve life, is it ever appropriate either *not* to turn to medical treatment, or to discontinue treatment once it has begun? This problem becomes particularly acute when the patient is judged to be terminally ill and unlikely to recover from his or her life-threatening condition. Although the sophisticated treatments developed by today's medical research may be able to keep such an individual alive for an extended period, they may offer no realistic possibility of reversing or controlling the illness. Many such patients and their families will wish to "let nature take its course," foregoing those treatments and accepting that death will come sooner rather than later. A powerful stream of halakhic thought denies them this option, holding that so long as the therapy is neither harmful to the patient nor experimental in nature it *must* be administered, no matter how "hopeless" the situation.[10] It is a view based firmly in the relentless logic of *pikku·aḥ nefesh*, and it holds that since all of life—every moment of it—is holy, we must work to preserve life until its very end and are thus forbidden to withdraw or cease medical treatment until death has occurred.[11] We are taught that a dying person—even a *goseis*, an individual whose death is regarded as imminent—is in all respects a *living* person, and we must do nothing, however well-intentioned, to hasten his or her death.[12] "Rabbi Meir likens the life of the *goseis* to a flickering flame, which is extinguished at the slightest touch. Should one even close the eyelids of the *goseis* [at the moment of death], it is as though one has killed that person."[13] Given that Torah places an inestimable value upon even the final moments of human life, we must do all we can to preserve and extend the life of the terminally ill. As one recent Orthodox authority puts it: "Everyone is obligated in every case to seek out medical treatment, even if one believes that the treatment will not heal but only prolong one's suffering, for we must wait hopefully for God's deliverance to the very last moment of our lives."[14]

The great exception to this rule is codified by Rabbi Moshe Isserles, the sixteenth-century Ashkenazic halakhist, in his gloss to the Shulḥan Arukh:

It is forbidden to hasten the death of the *goseis*. For example, it is forbidden to remove the pillow or mattress from beneath a person in a state of protracted dying, which one would do because it is said that the feathers of certain birds [retard the process of dying]. Similarly, it is forbidden to move him from his place or to put the keys to the synagogue under his head so that his soul will depart. But if there is a factor in the situation that impedes the departure of the soul—for example, if someone is chopping wood close to the house or if there is salt on the patient's tongue and these things are impeding his death—it is permissible to remove it, since this is not a positive act but merely the removal of an impediment.[15]

The medieval "technology" described by Isserles and his sources need not distract us from the central principle his words convey: the distinction between commission and omission, between active and passive measures to bring about the end of life, between killing and letting-die. The Isserles text is perhaps the best-known Jewish version of a distinction that is well known in the literature of contemporary bioethics[16] and is the subject of an ongoing debate between those who deny the substantive moral difference between "active" killing and "passive" letting-die,[17] and those who uphold that difference.[18] In medical *halakhah*, the distinction as embodied in the Isserles text plays a pivotal role in efforts to delineate the ethics of end-stage medical treatment. In particular, it is a major element in the reasoning of such twentieth-century Orthodox halakhic authorities as Rabbi Immanuel Jakobovits,[19] Rabbi Barukh Rabinovitz,[20] Rabbi Eliezer Yehudah Waldenberg,[21] Rabbi Hayim David Halevy,[22] and Rabbi Moshe Feinstein,[23] all of whom cite it by way of analogy in order to permit the discontinuation of medical treatment that can be characterized as an "impediment" to the imminent death of an end-stage patient.

For all its centrality, however, the relevance of the Isserles text to contemporary medicine is severely limited, and primarily for two reasons. The first concerns the analogy itself: are the "impediments" of which Isserles speaks truly comparable to modern therapies and technologies like the respirator and the heart-lung machine? The latter are unmistakably *medical* in nature, elements of a legitimate therapeutic response to the condition of a patient; by contrast, the woodchopper and salt on the tongue may have been thought to impede death but were never considered *r'fu·ah*. Can the warrant to remove such non-medical impediments to death be reasonably extended to the withdrawal or cessation of procedures that form an integral part of the practice—and *mitzvah*—of medicine?[24] The second difficulty is that, although the analogy can be defended,[25] in the end it doesn't prove very much. The passage explicitly addresses the situation of the *goseis* and not that of the patient diagnosed with terminal illness but who is not at this moment in the throes of death (*g'sisah*). Though clearly dying of an illness for which "medicine" as we know it offers no reasonable prospect of cure, reversal, or control, this individual is not yet a *goseis* and may have weeks, months, or longer to live. If so, the logic behind the concept of *pikku·ah nefesh*, as explained above, would dictate that the physicians continue to work to extend this person's life; "the terminal nature of an illness in no way mitigates the physician's responsibilities, because the physician is charged with prolonging life no less than with effecting a cure."[26]

It is here that the major Reform responsum (halakhic opinion) on the treatment of the terminally ill develops its *hiddush*. The opinion, issued by CCAR Responsa Committee in 1994, responds to a query (*she'eilah*) concerning two individuals: a 16-month-old girl with the progressive and fatal neurological disorder known as Canavan Disease and a 95-year-old woman suffering from Alzheimer's.[27] Though neither is a *goseset* (the feminine form of the Hebrew *goseis*), each is clearly dying; no known treatment can halt the disease that will eventually kill her and that at the moment severely compromises her quality of life. The responsum concludes that there is "no Jewish moral obligation to resort to any measures whose purpose it is to lengthen" the life of either patient.[28]

The responsum's reasoning begins by recognizing the intellectual difficulties that attach to the Isserles text, specifically the problem that the line distinguishing "active" killing from "passive" letting-die can be blurry indeed. The traditional halakhic commentators note that this very problem leads Isserles himself into an apparently fatal contradiction: if it is forbidden to remove the pillow and mattress from beneath the *goseis*, ostensibly because physical contact with and movement of the body may hasten the individual's death, why is it permitted to remove the salt from beneath the tongue, an act that also involves physical contact and movement? Why is the former considered an "active" measure to end life when the latter is merely the "passive" removal of an impediment? The difficulty leads one commentator to break with Isserles: we must choose one side or the other of this dilemma and, given that physical contact with the *goseis* is prohibited, it follows that we are forbidden to remove the salt.[29] But another, the *Shiltei Gibborim* of Rabbi Yehoshua Boaz ben Shimeon Barukh (d. 1557), justifies the salt's removal on the grounds that although it is forbidden to hasten the death of the *goseis*, it is also forbidden to take any action that would unnecessarily delay the person's death. Salt, which possesses no medicinal qualities and can serve only to hinder "the departure of the soul," should never have been placed on the person's tongue. "Whoever put it there has acted improperly; thus, its removal, even though it involves physical contact, is permitted as the restoration of the correct *status quo ante*."[30] The CCAR responsum suggests that the *Shiltei Gibborim* has redefined the issues at stake in the treatment of the *goseis*. The central question is not the distinction between "active" killing and "passive" letting-die, but rather the purpose or rationale behind the introduction of the particular factor into the situation. "Certain measures must never be applied to the *goseis* because they lack any trace of therapeutic value."[31] If such a measure merely delays the otherwise imminent death of the *goseis*, its presence is unwarranted and it may therefore be removed even at the risk of touching the patient's body.

This insight, the responsum argues, "helps to translate the medieval language of the texts into a usable contemporary vernacular. Does there not come a point in a patient's condition when, despite their obvious life-saving powers, the sophisticated technologies of modern medicine—the mechanical respirator, for example, or the heart-lung machine—become nothing more than mere 'salt on the tongue,' mechanisms which maintain the patient's vital signs long after all hope of recovery has vanished?"[32] The word "become" is critical. Unlike salt, these measures qualify as actual "medicine," and their use is legitimate as part of a therapeutic regimen. But when their therapeutic value is exhausted, when their continued use can no longer contribute to an acceptable medical outcome, they *become* "salt on the tongue" in that the only end they serve is to impede the patient's otherwise imminent death. Their presence, like that of the salt, has *become* "unwarranted," and they may be removed or discontinued.

But how effectively do these ideas address the situation of contemporary medicine? Even if we accept the controversial analogy between today's biomedical technology and the medieval woodchoppers and salt on the tongue, that analogy as embodied in the Isserles text applies only to the *goseis* and not to the patient whose diagnosis is "terminal" but whose death is not imminent. And since the patients described in the *she'eilah* have not yet deteriorated to that point, then "if we view their situation according to the criteria of [the Isserles text], we must conclude that we are not justified in withholding" the treatments that are keeping them alive."[33]

It is precisely here that the responsum seeks to develop the insight of the *Shiltei Gibborim*, making it the basis for a more general approach to the treatment of the dying. If Rabbi Yehoshua Boaz ben Shimon Barukh instructs us in the situation of the *goseis* to look past the issue of physical contact—does removal of the salt constitute an "active" or a "passive" measure?—and instead to evaluate the measure in question in terms of its medical rationale, we should do this is *all* cases: "we consider not only the patient's specific prognosis but also (and primarily) the nature of the practice of medicine itself."[34] That practice, as we have seen, is regarded as a *mitzvah*, part of the larger duty to save human life. It follows, then, that we apply the label "medicine" only to those drugs, technologies, and procedures that can reasonably be said to contribute to the therapeutic activity that the term purports to describe:

> The point and the essence of medicine is to heal. It is for this reason, and only for this reason, that we are permitted to administer harsh drugs and invasive surgical procedures which, under non-therapeutic conditions, would be strictly prohibited as *havalah*, the causing of unnecessary physical harm to the human body. This would imply that once a medical treatment ceases to be effective and beneficial it ceases to be "medicine" as that practice is conceived by Jewish tradition. A physician is obligated to administer those measures which in the judgment of the profession are therapeutic: i.e., they are regarded in medical opinion as contributing to the successful treatment of the disease. On the other hand, treatments which do not effect "healing" are not *medicine* and thus are not required.[35]

Medicine, in other words, remains a *mitzvah*, but the standard for determining the obligatory nature of treatment in any given situation is that of therapeutic effectiveness. A treatment that offers the prospect of medical "success"—defined as either a cure for a particular illness or an outcome that controls the illness and allows the patient a reasonable degree of function—is considered obligatory (*hovah*) under the terms of Jewish law. This standard explains the provision, mentioned above, that an individual is entitled to refuse a medical procedure that is experimental in nature, for unless the therapeutic powers of a particular treatment are "certain or and tested" they do not count as "lifesaving" and for that reason do not fall under the category of *medicine* that one is obliged to accept under the doctrine of *pikku·ah nefesh*.[36] By the same token, this standard of therapeutic effectiveness also helps to delineate the parameters of the *mitzvah* as it relates to those diagnosed as "terminal" but who have not arrived at the very last moments of life. On this view, a cancer patient would be obliged under *halakhah* to accept radiation and chemotherapy to the extent that these, according to informed medical judgment, offer a reasonable prospect for curing, arresting, or controlling the disease. But if—again, in the opinion of the physicians—those therapies offer at best a short extension of the patient's life, and especially if that extension is accompanied by continued suffering as the illness worsens, the patient is entitled to refuse them even if she or he is not yet a *goseis* whose death is imminent.

The most obvious difficulty with this line of reasoning is its lack of precise definition: what, exactly, do we mean by such inherently ambiguous terms as "therapeutically successful" or "reasonable prospect for curing, arresting, or controlling the disease"? The ambiguity, the responsum concedes, is real.[37] But then, ambiguity is the price we pay whenever we deal not with *rules*—definitive, hard-and-fast statements of law—but with *standards*, which are general and "open-textured"[38] and which require for their application an act of judgment.[39] "Therapeutic effectiveness" is such a standard, so that the determination that a therapy no longer meets that goal will require a judgment in each specific case. Patients and their families will have to make that decision within a context of uncertainty— when is medical prognosis ever 100% certain?—that they may never completely resolve. Many people are uncomfortable with uncertainty, and this discomfort lends support to those Orthodox halakhists who forbid the discontinuation of medical treatment for any patient, even one who is terminally ill, prior to the time of *g'sisah*. When even the most definitive prognosis is a matter of *safeik* (doubt), we can never be sure until the very end that there exists absolutely no possibility of recovery.[40] The responsum, again, acknowledges this doubt and discomfort but asks that we evaluate them against the very meaning of the word *r'fu·ah*:

> To this argument we would simply ask: is this truly "medicine" as we conceive it? Our answer, as liberal Jews who seek guidance from our tradition in facing the moral dilemmas of our age, is "no"…We cannot and do not believe that those texts, which bid us to heal the sick and to preserve life, demand that in fulfilling these duties we apply in indiscriminate fashion every available technological device to prolong the death of a dying person. Medical science has made immeasurable advances during recent times, and we are thankful for that fact….Yet there comes a point in time when all the technologies, the chemicals, the surgeries, and the machines that comprise the lifesaving arsenal of modern medicine become counterproductive, a point when all that medical science can effectively do for a patient is to indefinitely delay his inevitable death. This is not *pikku·ah nefesh*; this is not medicine; this is not what physicians, as agents of healing, are supposed to do….Yes, life is a precious thing, and every moment of it should be regarded as God's gift. But we are not required under any reading of the tradition that makes sense

to us to buy additional moments of life by undertaking useless and pointless medical treatment.[41]

To summarize: the modern practice of medicine is the way that most of us, on a day-to-day basis, fulfill the biblical exhortation *u-vaharta ba-hayyim,* "you shall choose life." And the *hiddush* of this Reform responsum on the treatment of the terminally ill proceeds from our understanding of what medical practice—*r'fu·ah*—is. Its approach abandons the classic but not always useful distinction between killing and letting-die, and proceeds rather from the very definition of the *mitzvah* of *r'fu·ah*: a therapy or treatment qualifies as obligatory to the extent—and *only* to the extent—that it contributes to a legitimate therapeutic outcome. Once the treatment loses that therapeutic rationale, it is no longer considered "medicine" and it may be discontinued. This theory, it is true, requires the individual or the family to make a specific judgment in each case, and such judgments by their nature are never entirely free of doubt. This uncertainty can be troubling to those called upon to make such life-and-death decisions, but in the spirit of Justice Holmes's observation that "certainty generally is illusion, and repose is not the destiny of man,"[42] the CCAR responsum concludes that it "is no reason to shrink from moral argument; it means rather that we have no choice but to enter the fray, to confront difficult cases, and to do the best we can."[43] In considering the treatment of the terminally ill, as with ethical and halakhic problems generally, we do well to accept doubt as our human condition. Our best response to it, in other words, is not to flee from it but to face it squarely, to resolve it in accordance with our best understanding of the underlying values of Torah and of Jewish law.

NOTES

[1] Shai Cherry, "Ethical Theories in the Conservative Movement," in *The Oxford Handbook of Jewish Ethics and Morality*, eds. Elliot N. Dorff and Jonathan K. Crane (New York: Oxford University Press, 2013), p. 227.

[2] Naḥmanides (Ramban), *Torat Ha-adam*, ed. H. D. Chavel (Jerusalem: Mossad Harav Kook, 1988), *sha·ar ha-miḥush, inyan ha-sakkanah*, pp. 41–42); A.T. Yoreh Dei·ah 336; S.A. Yoreh Dei·ah 336:1. Maimonides, meanwhile, derives this point by a *midrash* on Deuteronomy 22:2; see his commentary to M. Nedarim 4:4.

[3] See the statement in B. Bava Kama 85b to the effect that Exodus 21:19 grants permission or license (*r'shut*) to the physician to practice medicine.

[4] B. Yoma 85b and Sanhedrin 74a; M.T. Hilkhot Yesodei Hatorah 5:1.

[5] Naḥmanides (see note 2); the quotation is repeated in the Arba·ah Turim of Rabbi Jacob ben Asher and the Shulḥan Arukh (see note 2).

[6] On the following, see Naḥmanides and Arbaah Turim (see note 2).

[7] From an aggadic tradition derived from Isaiah 38:3. See B. Berakhot 10b (and Rashi *ad loc., s.v. she-ganaz sefer r'fu·ot*) and B. Pesaḥim 56a. Maimonides' commentary to M. Pesaḥim 4:9 seeks to blunt the anti-medical thrust of this passage.

[8] For a historical description of this practice, see Gerry Greenstone, "The History of Bloodletting," *British Columbia Medical Journal* 52:1 (January–February 2010), pp. 1–14, available online at www.bcmj.org/premise/history-bloodletting.

[9] B. Berakhot 60a. See, at some length, Naḥmanides to Leviticus 26:11, *s.v. v'hineih ha-b'rakhot ha-eilleh.*

[10] A position ably represented by Rabbi J. David Bleich in his prolific writings. See, for example, his "Treatment of the Terminally Ill" in *Jewish Ethics and the Care of End-of-Life Patients*, eds. P. J. Hurwitz, J. Picard, and A. Steinberg (Jersey City, NJ: KTAV, 2006), pp. 57–72. On "experimental" therapies, see below at note 36.

[11] For a powerful expression of this idea that holiness inheres in every moment of life, see Rabbi Menaḥem Hameiri, *Beit Ha-b'ḥirah* to B. Yoma 85a. See also Rabbi Yisrael Meir HaKohen, *Bei·ur Halakhah* to S.A. Oraḥ Ḥayyim 329, s.v. elka l'fi sha·ah; and Rabbi Eliezer Yehudah Waldenberg, *Responsa Tzitz Eliezer* (Jerusalem, 1985), vol. 5, "*Ramat Raḥel*," chap. 28.

[12] "Imminent" is understood as the likelihood of death within 72 hours. See *Hilkhot Ha-rosh* to B. Mo·eid Katan 3:97, S.A. Yoreh Dei·ah 339:2, and the *Beit Sh'muel* to S.A. Even Ha-eizer 17, note 94 (end).

[13] Tractate S'maḥot 1:1, 4. S.A. Yoreh Dei·ah 339:1 omits the metaphor of the flickering candle, but maintains the conclusion that one who closes the eyes of the *goseis* has shed that person's blood.

[14] Rabbi Natan Zvi Friedman, *Responsa Netzer Mata·i* (Tel Aviv: D'fus Tarbut, 1957), no. 30.

[15] Isserles to S.A. Yoreh Dei·ah 339:1.

[16] See *Killing and Letting Die*, eds. Bonnie Steinbock and Alastair Norcross (2nd ed.; New York: Fordham University Press, 1994).

[17] A sampling: James Rachels, "Active and Passive Euthanasia," *New England Journal of Medicine* 292 (1975), pp. 78–80; Dan W. Brock, "Voluntary Active Euthanasia," *Hastings Center Report* 22:2 (March–April, 1992), pp. 10–22; and Tom L. Beauchamp and James F. Childress, *Principles of Bioethics* (5th ed.; New York: Oxford University Press, 2001), p. 143.

[18] Again, a sampling: Thomas Fuchs, "'The Notion of 'Killing': Causality, Intention, and Motivation in Active and Passive Euthanasia," *Medicine, Healthcare, and Philosophy* 1 (1998), pp. 245–253; Daniel Callahan, "Vital Distinctions, Mortal Questions: Debating Euthanasia and Health Care Costs," in *Arguing Euthanasia,* ed. Jonathan D. Moreno (New York: Touchstone, 1995), pp. 173–195; and Helen Frowe, "Killing John to Save Mary: A Defense of the Moral Distinction Between Killing and Letting Die," in *Action, Ethics, and Responsibility,* eds. Joseph Keim Campbell, Michael O'Rourke, and Harry S. Silverstein (Cambridge, MA: MIT Press, 2010), pp. 47–66.

[19] Immanuel Jakobovits, "*Ba-din Im Mutar L'kareiv Mitato Shel Holeh No·ash Ha-soveil Yissurim Kashim,*" *Hapardes* 31:3 (1956), pp. 16–19.

[20] Barukh Rabinovitz, "Comments in a Symposium on Determining the Moment of Death," *Sefer Asya* (Jerusalem: Rubin Mass, 1979), vol. 1, pp. 190–198.

[21] See his *Responsa Tzitz Eliezer*, vol. 13, no. 89.

[22] Hayim David Halevy, "*Nittuk Holeh She-af'su Sikkuyav Mi-m'khonat Ha-han'shamah,*" *T'humin* 2 (1981), pp. 297–305.

[23] *Responsa Ig'rot Moshe* (New York, 1984) to S.A. Hoshen Mishpat vol. 2, no. 74.

[24] See especially Louis E. Newman, "Woodchoppers and Respirators: The Problem of Interpretation in Contemporary Jewish Ethics," *Modern Judaism* 10:1 (1990), pp. 17–42. For a similar challenge published in a halakhic journal, see Yaakov Levy, "*Davar Ha-m'akeiv Y'tzi·at Ha-nefesh,*" *No·am* 16 (1973), pp. 53–63.

[25] Mark Washofsky, "The Woodchopper Revisited: On Analogy, Halakhah, and Jewish Bioethics," in *Medical Frontiers and Jewish Law,* ed. Walter Jacob (Pittsburgh: Freehof Institute of Progressve Halakhah, 2012), pp. 1–62; available online at http://huc.edu/sites/default/files/people/washofsky/The%20 Woodchopper%20Revisited.pdf.

[26] Bleich, "Treatment of the Terminally Ill," p. 64.

[27] *Teshuvot for the Nineties,* eds. W. Gunther Plaut and Mark Washofsky (New York: Central Conference of American Rabbis, 1997), no. 5754.14, pp. 337–

363, available online at http://ccarnet.org/responsa/tfn-no-5754-14-337-364/.

[28] Ibid., p. 352.

[29] *Turei Zahav* to S.A. Yoreh Dei·ah, §339, no. 2.

[30] *Shiltei Gibborim* to Alfasi's comment to B. Mo·eid Katan 16a.

[31] Plaut and Washofsky, *Teshuvot for the Nineties*, p. 345.

[32] Ibid.

[33] Ibid., p. 346.

[34] Ibid.

[35] Ibid., p. 348.

[36] The terminology "certain and tested" (*y'di·ah vada·it v'hakkarah b'rurah*) is that of Rabbi Yaakov Emden (eighteenth-century Germany); see his *Sefer Mor U-k'tzia* to S.A. Oraḥ Ḥayyim 328.

[37] Plaut and Washofsky, *Teshuvot for the Nineties*, p. 350.

[38] See H.L.A. Hart, *The Concept of Law* (Oxford: Clarendon Press, 1961), p. 124: "The open texture of law means that there are, indeed, areas of conduct where much must be left to be developed by courts or officials seeking to strike a balance, in the light of circumstance, between competing interests which vary in weight from case to case."

[39] On the difference between rules and standards see Jack M. Balkin, *Living Originalism* (Cambridge, MA: Harvard/Belknap Press, 2011), p. 349: "Rules are distinguished from standards by how much practical or evaluative judgment they require to apply them to concrete situations….In comparison with rules, standards normally involve a greater degree of delegation to the future."

[40] See Rabbi Avraham Yitzhak Hakohen Kook, *Responsa Da·at Kohen* (Jerusalem, 1966), no. 142, where he argues that medical knowledge is always a matter of *safeik*; it never arrives at the level of certainty that would permit us to relax a Toraitic prohibition.

[41] Plaut and Washofsky, *Teshuvot for the Nineties*, pp. 350–351.

[42] Oliver Wendell Holmes, Jr., "The Path of the Law," *Harvard Law Review* 10 (1897), p. 466. Holmes, of course, was speaking of the uncertainty that attaches to every act of legal or judicial logic. The same would seem to be true of ethical and halakhic reasoning.

[43] Plaut and Washofsky, *Teshuvot for the Nineties*, p. 352.

Compassion That Never Fails[1]

Daniel Greyber

God's lovingkindness never ceases, God's compassion never fails.
They are new every morning; great is Your faithfulness."
                    —*Lamentations 3:22-23*

My teacher, Rabbi Mimi Feigelson, sang those words to me at my ordination as a rabbi. The melody was a playful and joyous waltz. So I was surprised when the Old Testament homily at my friend David's funeral was based upon those same words.

I woke up on a Tuesday morning in November 2009 and saw on Facebook that my old swim coach wanted to make sure I'd heard the news. David and I grew up together. We trained together eleven times per week, got drunk for the first time together, and made Senior Nationals our senior year of high school. I went to his wedding. He came to mine. He became a more serious Christian and got a Ph.D. in religion from Duke. I became a rabbi. David also became a long-distance runner until one day in November 2009, while he was on a long run with a friend, he had a heart attack and died. Just a few hundred feet from Emory University hospital, the doctors who rushed to his side never got a pulse.

I read the news, stunned. I decided to go to the funeral. I emailed two friends from swimming—Thomas Lee and Mike MacArthur—and I found a place for us all to stay within walking distance from both the First Presbyterian Church and the Beth El Synagogue. I do not drive on Shabbat, but I planned to go to the funeral late Friday afternoon and then walk to synagogue on Saturday morning.

Erudite people such as Walter Brueggemann, a famous Christian scholar and theologian, spoke. The service was longer than a Jewish funeral. After the Old Testament homily (whose words echoed my rabbinical ordination), I went outside the church and, as the sun was setting, I prayed the evening prayer to welcome Shabbat, even here on the doorstep of a church in Durham, North Carolina. I spoke to God, and cried. I spoke to David, and cried. Neither spoke back.

Thomas, Mike, and I were warmly welcomed to dinner after the funeral. People shared stories of David. We did too, but David had changed since our rowdy high school days. Most of the stories we could share felt inappropriate in such a religious setting, so we left after a while. Mike was the same old Mike, an atheist/agnostic filled with love and doubt and questions. Thomas had become a very religious Christian, a deacon at his church. He was very curious about my Judaism and he was respectful of my Shabbat observance. As we walked down Main Street on the way back to the hotel, Thomas turned to me and said, "Greyber, I know you can't buy a drink because of the Sabbath, but can we buy you one?"

"Yes, Thomas," I replied, "that would be great."

I love that moment. Thomas wanted me to be fully me. He respected my devotion to Jewish law. In a million years, Thomas would never have wanted me to violate my religious integrity, even if it was newly found since our youth. Knowing what I could not do, he was offering to do something for me. He and Mike wanted to create space for our friendship, to find for ourselves some comfort after David's death. His invitation was an act of spacious hospitality that said, "You've changed and we've changed, but we have a history and we've shared something special; let's find a way to toast what was, if only for a moment, before we each return to our separate lives."

We walked into the bar—the West End Wine Bar on Main Street—and sat at a table in the back to drink a toast to friendship, to David, to what we had growing up together. The next morning, I went to synagogue and loved it, and found out they were looking for a new rabbi. I gave notice at my job in Los Angeles, interviewed at the synagogue, got the job, and moved to Durham. And then, just a few weeks into the job, a woman in the community in her early forties named Bekah committed suicide. I co-officiated at the funeral with the rabbi emeritus, led condolence services for the family, and became close friends with Bekah's older brother, Jared. Jared, his wife Jennifer, my wife Jennifer, and I all went out for drinks one night at one of Jared's bars: the West End Wine Bar on Main Street in Durham. As we sat down at the table in the back, it all came back to me and I started to cry, wondering if I'd been led to that place, that moment, and whether my life's choices were really my own, or whether God really was looking over my shoulder all along.

Choose life, we are told. What do we really choose? What is chosen for us? David died. I did not *choose* to go to his funeral. I was called. I suppose I chose to listen, to respond…but is fulfilling a sacred promise *choosing*? I booked the tickets, put on a suit, and walked through the streets of Durham on a Friday afternoon. I do not remember if I touched David's coffin or if I merely sat in the church, but I made a pilgrimage to his funeral because that is what one does when a brother dies. I did not *choose* David's funeral—I want no "credit" for going. I want David back in the world, with his wife, Leigh, and their beautiful children.

But when Thomas Lee called me "Greyber" like he had done when were teens, and when he offered to buy me a drink even though I would not buy one for myself, I had a choice. I could say, "No thanks, that's not in the spirit of Shabbat." I could have played it safe according to Jewish law, falling back on the obviously wise thought that a rabbi probably shouldn't be seen at a bar on Shabbat. We could have walked back to the hotel, gone to sleep, and gone our separate ways in the morning. I could have said "No thanks" and continued on, walking side-by-side with Thomas and Mike with our feelings and grief and love unexpressed before going our separate ways. I could have returned alone to my family and my friends and my life in Los Angeles, grieving, and tried to muscle my way back into the world through the thick darkness that lingers when death comes too close, too soon. But I said "Yes." I chose, "Yes."

And in saying "yes," I danced on the borders of Jewish law—a rabbi in a bar on Friday night?—and I chose not to give death the final word. I chose not to be alone in my grief. I chose to cry with friends who loved me unconditionally and whom I love, even though we'd not spoken in years and have not spoken since. I chose to pause and remember David with people whose memories matched my own memories of childhood and adolescence, of carefree stupidity and invincibility, of brotherhood. I chose life—not in the sense of living for more days or months or years, but I chose to live my life fully, not to die, while alive. I chose to open myself to the possibilities that hid at a table in the back of a bar on Main Street in Durham on a Shabbat evening in the fall of 2009. I chose to return to Los Angeles and begin my life anew. Was that choice my own? Or was Adonai Tz'vaot, the Lord of Hosts (one of God's many names), my own "host" that night in the bar, showing me a seat that God had already chosen for me?

God commands us to choose life. The very idea presupposes human free will: If we are not free, how can we choose? If we have no choice, why would God speak to us at all? Yet the Ishbitzer Rebbe, Rabbi Mordechai Yosef of Isbitza, imagines that behind our choices is God's guiding hand.[2] Beyond our free will is God's.

In Exodus 30:1 God tells us, "You shall make an altar to burn the incense; make it of acacia wood." The Ishbitzer notices that the command to build the incense altar is out of place. The commandments regarding the vessels for the Tabernacle appear in chapters 25–27 of Exodus, but the command to build the altar occurs in chapter 30, among the commandments to make the various priestly garments. Why? The Ishbitzer says that to understand the reason, you first have to know a teaching about incense from the Zohar, the foundational book of Jewish mysticism. "What is incense? It is the connection of all."[3] "This hints that all that is done, even in this world, is all connected with the will of the blessed God, and without God's will nothing at all would be done."[4]

The incense—probably because it originates in the physical world but flows into the air and the spiritual world—represents the way in which everything is connected. Our will is not our own. Our decisions are not our own. Our lives are, in some fundamental way, not our own. That is the secret of the incense. But believing this could be dangerous. The Ishbitzer continues, "One who misunderstands this could come to irreverence, God forbid, since everything that happens is allowed to happen from Heaven."[5]

Since everything that happens is from God, I can do whatever I want. My free will is an illusion; my will is God's will and therefore, whatever I do has divine sanction. All is permitted. That's dangerous. "Therefore the incense altar, which represents this understanding, was not said in [the instructions about vessels], but only after the explanation of the priestly garments."[6]

How do the priestly garments guard against the dangerous implications of the meaning of the incense? Clothes form the barrier between our nakedness and the world. According to the rabbis, the symbolic meaning of the priestly garments is to

teach of the great fear of God and vigilant guarding from the vain pleasures of the world. As it is written in the Talmud, "the coat [of the priest] atones for the spilling of blood."[7] So it is with all the garments. By means of his priestly garments, the priest instills such fear in the heart of Israel so that they then have the ability to receive the joy and love that comes from the power of the incense.[8]

Before we can be tempted by the joyous (or horrific?) possibility that God wills everything, we must be instilled with fear not to sin. Before I play with the idea that God guided me from Los Angeles, to my friend's funeral, to the West End Wine Bar on Main Street in Durham, to the synagogue, to Bekah's suicide, to her brother Jared who owns the West End Wine Bar, to the gift of our friendship, I must be instilled with fear: I shouldn't believe that God's will is my own and, therefore, that everything is permitted. It is not. I may be part of God, but that doesn't make me God. And yet, as the incense teaches, everything is connected to the will of God.

A hundred fifty years after the Ishbitzer, the modern biblical scholar and theologian Michael Fishbane hints at a similar notion in his theology, *Sacred Attunement*. He describes a Torah that is not written, not oral, but something he calls "God's illimitable investiture of Being," a Torah that preceded the Oral and Written Torahs and that continues to pulse through all creation "pressing upon human consciousness on a daily basis." In the passage below, he develops these ideas more fully:

The Torah provides a rich record of the shaping of the divine thunder into a human voice and into viable human terms. This record, which includes traces of the ongoing revision of the norms, has been referred to since rabbinic antiquity as the *torah she-bikhtav*, the Written Torah, and has been revered as a canonical corpus. In it, the originary voice of covenant living has been inscribed; for it has become a scripture, fixed in form and sacred in character. Instructive in their own right, the letters of this Written Torah are infused with the spirit of ancient Israel.

But the words were also infused with the ongoing spirit of Jewish living, and founded upon its principles and formulations. The emergent record of this infusion (which includes traces of the vast revisions of the Written Torah as legal norms and theological teachings) has also been named since rabbinic antiquity, and referred to as the *torah she-be'al peh*, the Oral Torah. This is the multifaceted witness to ongoing covenant living and thinking, and characterized as something spoken through study and sustained by the ongoing articulations of tradition.

Why does the voice arise? One reason is surely the perceived need to understand and explain the Written Torah. But then the Oral Torah would only be a series of glosses and meager annotations. So something "more" must occasion this massive achievement. Put theologically, I would say that this "something more" is God's illimitable investiture of Being, the far-flung vastness of divine effectivity, pressing upon human consciousness on a daily basis.

This divine reality precedes the Written Torah, as said earlier, and may be designated as the *torah kelulah*, the Torah of All-in-All—an infinite enfoldment of all that could ever be in our world. Only this Torah truly comes from the mouth of God, forever and ever, as the kiss of divine truth upon the vastness of world-being...

Moses our master knew this when he first shaped the Torah of All-in-All for the specifics and values of earthly life; and he never forgot this theological truth in his lifetime, as he repeatedly reformulated his initial instructions, variously attuning the Torah of Sinai to this quintessential reality—as he grew in wisdom and experience, and as times and circumstances changed. Thus the *torah kelulah* preceded Sinai (it being an expression of the utmost divine promordiality); and it pulses throughout Being as a whole.[9]

Beyond the norms of a written and oral law is a Torah that "pulses throughout Being as a whole," within me and within you and within all that is. But the difference between this Torah and God is slippery; Fishbane says it is "the divine reality." Was it that Torah that I felt as I returned to that table at the back of the West End Wine Bar?

Choose life, we are told. Did I choose to go into the bar? Or did I merely (and inevitably) align my will with God's, with the secret of the incense, with the Torah of All-in-All? I do not know. I doubt I'll ever know. But to my grave I shall believe in the song that was sung to me at ordination and that returned to me at David's funeral: "God's lovingkindness never ceases, God's compassion never fails. They are new every morning; great is Your faithfulness" (Lamentations 3:22–23).

NOTES

[1] I would like to dedicate this essay to the memory of David Knauert.

[2] *Living Waters / The Mei HaShiloach: A Commentary of the Torah by Rabbi Mordechai Yosef of Isbitza*, trans. and ed. Betsalel Philip Edwards (Lanham, MD: Rowman and Littlefield, 2004), p. 163.

[3] Zohar III 151b.

[4] *Living Waters*, p. 163.

[5] Ibid.

[6] Ibid.

[7] B. Arakhim 16a. The connection is derived from how Joseph's coat was the means by which his brothers persuaded their father, Jacob, that Joseph had been killed.

[8] *Living Waters*, p. 163.

[9] Michael A. Fishbane, *Sacred Attunement: A Jewish Theology* (Chicago: University of Chicago Press, 2010), p. 61.

Choosing Life, Finding God:
A Theological Reading of a Hasidic Story about Rabbi Mordechai of Nesukhoyezhe

Admiel Kosman

Translated from the Hebrew by Martin S. Cohen

The precise relationship between human knowledge and freedom of will is among the most vexing of all issues for human beings.[1] Consider, for example, the following biblical verse: "I call heaven and earth on this day as My witnesses that I am placing before you life and death, blessing and curse; choose life, so that you may live, you and your progeny" (Deuteronomy 30:19). This text seems to suppose simply that the ability to choose between good and evil is entirely given over into the hands of any human being. Yet the question of precisely what kind of choice the text has in mind remains.

To suggest that Scripture here is simply speaking about people choosing to do good and then actualizing their intentions seems difficult to accept—because it is so often the case that human beings find themselves specifically *unable* to do good in the world; it thus seems that more than simply "choosing" to do good must be at play in this verse. Indeed, any thoughtful person understands that the desire to do good and success in translating that desire into reality are two separate things. There are many rabbinic texts that discuss the chasm that can exist between the desire to do some specific thing and the actual ability to do it. Indeed, the Mishnah even establishes the principle that the most important thing is not the ability to actually translate desire into reality, but rather the intentionality one brings to choosing to do the action. For example, we read in Tractate Menaḥot:

> Regarding cattle offered up as *olah* sacrifices, Scripture uses the words *isheh rei·aḥ niḥo·aḥ* ("a pleasant burnt aroma"). And regarding birds offered up as *olah* sacrifices, Scripture also uses the words *isheh rei·aḥ niḥo·aḥ*. And regarding grain sacrifices, we [again] find the same words: *isheh rei·aḥ niḥo·aḥ* [even though the latter is the choice of a poor person who does not have enough money to buy more than the grain sacrifice.] This [usage of the same expression in all three contexts] teaches that what matters is that individuals be possessed of the intention [to worship] Heaven, not the specific value [of their offerings].[2]

Furthermore, the rabbis of Yavneh used to repeat this very lesson so often that it was considered "a pearl in their mouths" (that is, a beloved aphorism that they considered a basic principle of their religious faith), of whose truth they felt called upon constantly to remind each other—and they certainly did not mean it solely as a principle of sacrificial law, but rather as a general principle to be applied to all aspects of worship.[3] Moreover, there are passages in rabbinic literature that suggest that there are times when, if an individual's intentionality is pure, even sin undertaken for the sake of Heaven can be considered a kind of worthy deed, and even a *mitzvah*.[4]

The question at the heart of the hasidic story I wish to present here is a simple one: How, given the tempestuous nature of human life, can an individual manage to undertake the kind of leap of faith necessary to attain the highest level of heartfelt submission to God (namely, a leap from infatuation with the world as one sees it all around to the far more exalted state in which one finds it possible truly to cleave unto God)? Indeed, references to this exalted state can be found even in the earliest rabbinic sources. For example, when the Mishnah talks about the "subjugation" of the heart to God, it presumably means to refer to a far more intense level of engagement with the Divine than the average Jew might normally attain.[5]

*

The following tale treats of the Vishnitzer rebbe,[6] Rabbi Israel Hager (1860–1936), who told his followers a story regarding Rabbi Mordechai of Nesukhoyezhe (c. 1752–1800). Rabbi Mordechai, one of the greatest pupils of Rabbi Yeḥiel Michel of Zolochiv (1721–1786), was in his course of life the master of the hasidic community in the small city of Nesukhoyezhe (today located in Ukraine) as well as several other communities.[7] The story is as follows:

> It happened once on the evening following a festival that the crowds that had celebrated the festival with the holy rebbe of Vishnitz…came in the traditional way to receive a final blessing before departing for home. Because there was such a crush of people, which led to a certain amount of shoving, eventually a huge glass window pane was broken. The rebbe, taking note, just laughed and said nothing at all. It is well-known that no one had ever seen the rebbe succumb to anger about anything. And, indeed, when he ought to have been angry, all that anyone could ever see was a moment of laughter cross his lips.
> That evening he told the crowd that the holy rebbe, Rabbi Mordechai of Nesukhoyezhe, once had the desire to have *tzitzit* from the Land of Israel.[8] He somehow managed, albeit with great difficulty, to acquire a piece of fabric from the Land of Israel that could serve as such a garment. One of his students then came forward to ask permission to fashion the fabric into *tzitzit* for his teacher. The rebbe assented to this request and handed over the fabric so that the student

could do with it as he had offered. The student then folded the fabric over in two so that he could cut an even neck aperture, but erred by folding it over twice instead of just once, thus ending up cutting not one but two neck apertures.

When the student saw what had happened, he was terrified—for he feared the wrath of the holy rebbe, who had gone to such extreme effort to acquire from the Land of Israel the fabric he wished to have fashioned into *tzitzit*, which the student had ruined entirely!

When the rebbe eventually asked the student if he had finished fashioning the fabric into *tzitzit*, the student, almost overcome with terror and worry, answered honestly: "What can I say to our holy rebbe other than the truth?" And then he told him what he had done. The holy rebbe responded, "Of what are you so afraid? Isn't it true that this particular *tzitzit*-garment actually needed two neck apertures—one for use in the normal way and the other to serve as a test to see if it awakens anger in Mordechai? But Mordechai will not succumb to anger, because it is also the will of God not to be in a state of anger [exactly as it is the will of God to wear *tzitzit*]![19]

At first blush, the story seems simple enough. The rebbe has a deep desire to wear *tzitzit* made from fabric from the Land of Israel and he manages to acquire such fabric, undoubtedly paying a fortune for it.[10] But the fabric needs to be tailored into an actual garment, and one of the rebbe's students willingly volunteers to do so. Since *tzitzit* is basically a piece of fabric worn over the torso with fringes hanging from its corners, the only real task involved is cutting the neck aperture. It all sounds simple enough…but is it?

We have here a story about two related desires, a kind of desire bred of desire. The first is the one that initiates the action in the story, the desire that motivates the rebbe who wishes for *tzitzit* made of fabric from the Land of Israel—which desire is prompted by a kind of mental image or fantasy that the rebbe has of himself garbed in such a wondrous garment, capable of inducing in him an exalted state of holiness.

The neck in the story is metaphorical: the rebbe imagined himself placing his head through the neck aperture of the garment, and this suggests that he was willing to submit himself to slaughter for the sake of God.[11] The idea seems to be that by pulling this especially holy *tzitzit* over his head and around his neck, he hopes to merit feeling himself attaining the spiritual level of those martyrs who willingly presented their necks for slaughter *al kiddush ha-sheim* ("for the sanctification of God's name"). The rebbe imagines that such a holy object, once it is readied for his use, will enable him to attain spiritual heights to which he has aspired but which he has not been able to attain.[12]

The student in the story displays deep yearning to prepare the *tzitzit* for his master and, in so doing, to share—albeit obliquely—in the spiritual exaltation that Rabbi Mordechai hopes to experience. In other words, the student sees himself as a *makh·shir mitzvah*, an "appurtenance" of the *mitzvah*—and he yearns for that role precisely because, through that specific act of service to his rebbe as the appurtenance to the *mitzvah*, he hopes to ride along on his rebbe's coattails and partake in some aspect of the anticipated holiness it will effect.[13] From the vantage point of the student, the rebbe and his entire environment are objectified as a focus of desire, as something the student wants to partake in to help on his personal journey toward spiritual fulfillment.

The two instances of desire in the story, then, both flow from the imaginative power of its two protagonists. And this power—and particularly the rebbe's ability to see himself wearing *tzitzit* made of fabric from the Land of Israel—is presented as an admirable instance of spiritualized imagining.[14] And isn't the basis for this imaginative yearning for something physical just the type of yearning with which we are all familiar from our own experience of yearning for material things? The rebbe, however, does not experience desire in the same key as his story's audience: he does not yearn to eat a meal in a five-star restaurant or to win a huge cash prize, or even to attain a new level of sexual satiety. Instead, his desire is for something exalted and spiritual: to envelop himself in a holy garment with fringes whose fabric came from the Holy Land. The central personality of the story is depicted heroically precisely because he is so different from us, the audience. Indeed, few of us will ever have the kind of libido that leads us to lust after spiritual attainment of the kind symbolized in the story by the desire to wear *tzitzit* from the Land of Israel.

Until this point, the story has unfolded in the traditional way of the kind of hagiographical stories that depict the lives of saints or religious leaders, intended to impress upon their audiences the spiritual grandeur of a lionized protagonist depicted as venerable because of living a holy and pure life. But now we come to a dramatic twist in the story. Not only does God fail to grant special powers to the rebbe (as so often happens in this sort of story, where the hero is a holy individual imbued with the kind of spiritual power that can alter the physical world through miracles and wonders), but just the opposite occurs: our hero's efforts to achieve spiritual greatness are ruined, as a disaster—albeit a simple and almost humorous one—is introduced into the narrative, as an inept student is incapable of correctly cutting a simple neck aperture in the fabric. The storyteller uses a play of images to subtly suggest a juxtaposition of the image of the student, whose human hand fails to **cut** properly, with the hand of God, which has ultimately enacted ("**cut**") the decree that led to the disaster in the first place. (The same Hebrew root, *gimel-zayin-resh*, is regularly used for both the verb "to cut" and "to enact.") The fabric intended to cover the rebbe's body and thus to provide him with holy warmth, symbolic of God's presence in his life, is mis-cut such that he will no longer be able to wear the garment, which will thus be unable to provide him with the sense of intimacy with the Divine for which he has longed.[15]

Interpreting the story along these lines, however, it is possible to interpret the accident as a kind of ringing slap by God in the face of Rabbi Mordechai, one intended (because God is, after all, the Author of accidents) to say to the rebbe something like: "You are not worthy to attain the holiness you seek, and I shall therefore not permit you to merit entering into My presence." Ruining the fabric that had been intended to usher the *tzaddik* into the presence of God would thus be seen as a decisive denial by God of the rebbe's request to be permitted to approach the divine realm—precisely because, in the rebbe's imagination, wrapping himself up in the holy garment was to be a means of wrapping himself up in the Holy One's own garment. Indeed, there are many sources that talk about a *beged kadosh* (holy garment) itself as possessing the ability to transform the one who wears it into a holy person.[16]

And now the rebbe faces a true test. Only now, once his ego has been tested by this disastrous turn of events certainly effected by God, does he truly understand that in order to prevail he must extend his neck as though for slaughter—because he now sees that his ability to not let the anger have any place in his inner state in this crucial moment is *itself* going to be the sacrifice he can offer to God: a sacrifice of his personal ego.

The story does not say this explicitly. But this reading is certainly in keeping with the general genre of this kind of hasidic story. For the storyteller, it is the rebbe's "sacrifice" that turns his *test* into the at*test*ation that his soul truly was worthy to be ushered into the Divine Presence (even without the *tzitzit* he had attempted to procure). It is only after the garment is ruined that the rebbe is able to sacrifice his own ego—by not giving in to the anger that anyone would naturally feel at the ruin of such an expensive undertaking, and by responding instead with the language of blessing, graciously accepting the "disaster" that has befallen him by casting aside the veil of illusion that his own spiritual imagination had provided.[17]

Moreover, the fact that the rebbe does not become enraged is likely not meant to suggest simply the physical subordination of any anger he might have felt toward his inept student (which would not be such a remarkable spiritual achievement at all), but rather a kind of interior disengagement from anger itself and interior silencing—which together point to the remarkable level of spiritual equanimity that the rebbe had managed to attain at the precise moment captured in the story.[18] And so, according to this interpretation, the end of the story indeed references the success of the rebbe in attaining the level of spiritual exaltation for which all followers of Hasidism naturally yearn: the level of supreme equanimity.

The Hidden Theological Lesson That Inheres in Failure

A second look at our story leads to a different, and far deeper, layer of meaning. The simple way to read the story is to take the rebbe's failure to attain closeness to the Divine through the chosen *mitzvah* as a simple accident, without any deeper meaning. It is also possible, however, that a more interesting theological statement is hiding behind the story of the student's ineptitude—one that practically asks to be taken like a *bat kol*, a heavenly voice issuing forth at precisely the moment the *tzitzit* is ruined, in order to chastise the *tzaddik* for thinking that one can "purchase" intimacy with the Divine through technical details such as the provenance of a bolt of fabric (or, for that matter, through any object understood to possess innate holiness).

According to this interpretation, we can imagine God saying to Rabbi Mordechai: "Intimacy with Me can be acquired solely through interior, never exterior state of mind—and certainly not by means of objects, even if they are very valuable and so suggest the great worth of coming into communion with the Divine…and this even includes objects like *tzitzit*, which the Torah says can cause an individual to remember all the commandments (and, by extension, God) by merely gazing at it."

How do we know that this sacred message was indeed transmitted to the rebbe at precisely that moment? The answer to this question derives from the plane of psychic reality, and we now turn to this interpretive level as we consider Rabbi Mordechai, who must have been deeply disappointed (as his terrified student must have been as well), and aghast at heaven's response nullifying the value of his own desire for spiritual advancement. We thus come to understand that it is the destruction of such a desire that is being described in our story, and so much more meaningfully than the destruction of the piece of cloth. Had the rebbe not planned to realize his desire to know God through the *tzitzit* made of fabric from the Land of Israel, he would never have dared hope for the kind of spiritual advancement that using such a garment might enable—and, consequently, he also would never have known the disappointment that surely came when his plan was ruined.

Most essentially, then, the story is about what it truly means to be a *tzaddik*. Does the test for such a status have to do with actions and deeds (for example, with an individual's willingness to cleave to the commandments)? If that were so, the story's ending would have to be considered, at best, dour: if the rebbe's goal had simply been to acquire a splendid *mitzvah*-appurtenance, then the story is one of ultimate religious failure, leaving a pessimistic and bitter taste in our mouths as we are left to wonder why God would behave so capriciously and harshly toward Rabbi Mordechai by denying him the opportunity to worship God by donning splendid *tzitzit* from the Land of Israel.

But that is not how we should ultimately understand the end of the story, which is not cast in a pessimistic light at all. Rather, its outlook is optimistic: the *tzaddik* does indeed attain his desired spiritual exaltation—by aligning his own inner will with the will of God, and thus achieving the level of submission in which the truth of God's ways becomes permanently embedded in his own being. And now we come to the real point of the story: that this success is attained because the rebbe's thought-patterns have been nudged away from a focus on ancillary appurtenances of worship intended merely to bring God to mind to the *actual* God who exists in reality in the heart. The story is touching *because* this happens *on account of* the disaster that ruins the fabric. The rebbe, of course, could have reacted to the disaster with the *tzitzit* with sadness, anger, and a deep sense of loss—in other words, just as most of us would respond to being denied something we had hoped for and anticipated. Or he could have allowed himself to sink into a state of melancholy reflecting a belief that God had turned away from him—again, just as many people facing unwarranted disappointment do.

And now we come to the whole point of the story hiding just beneath the surface of the narrative. The spiritual insight is this: the *tzaddik*'s greatness derives not from the fact that he yearns more ardently than others to sense God's presence in his personal ambit (and therefore experiences intense disappointment when God appears to be pushing him off), but rather from the fact that he knows where God is to be found, how to hear God's voice, and how to submit to God's will at any moment—even when he senses God not drawing close but pushing him off. At the precise moment that the *tzitzit* was ruined, the rebbe was able to understand that God was sending him a message, and that the ruining of the fabric was in fact a summons to a state of divine intimacy available to him not by wearing some specific piece of fabric but by transcending the experience of wearing it. And it was the trajectory of events, beginning with a plan fueled by the desire for God yet ending with the fabric's ruin, that allowed him to undertake a leap of faith forward, toward communion with God.[19]

At the end of the story, the rebbe understands (as do we, the readers, with him) that we cannot gain entry to the presence of God by acquiring material possessions, even if an item is formally designed as holy. And why is that so? Because all of those things are mere objects, and they are simply the means and never the end. Their function is only to prepare the way for the individual seeking communion with God. The reliance we all place on "sacred" things (in this, no different than symbols and identifications) is, usually, a kind of optical illusion, and precisely because God does exist in the here and now, fully present in every moment, and we therefore do not need to pile up objects of any sort to bring ourselves closer to God.[20]

On the Necessity of Distinguishing between Objects and Subjects

Now we can move to an even deeper level of meaning embedded in the story. Objects (such as the *tzitzit*, in our story) bear the responsibility of bringing us to God through stimulating the recall of earlier points of contact with God. But at a certain point, we must be ready to stop relating to the object sentimentally (because of its prior role in our lives) and instead undertake a leap of faith forward, *through* the object under consideration, into the mystery. This point is often forgotten entirely, given the degree to which we are used solely to looking at the world from the vantage point of the "It."[21] This encounter with the "Eternal Thou," to use Buber's timeless term, is invariably an encounter with the subjective. Indeed, the divine plain we hope to attain has no name (not *tzitzit*, not *mitzvah*, not even "Judaism")—because this "Eternal Thou" has no relationship to the concept of identity at all, which is inevitably some form of garment and, by its very nature, cannot bear relationship to the world of objects.

Nonetheless, the object in the story plays an important (albeit limited) role. As soon as someone hears the voice of God to leave and abandons a given vehicle (in our story, that would be the moment that God destroys the object, the *tzitzit*), it then becomes incumbent on that individual to take a leap of faith toward the plane on which the object rests, and from there to move forward to attempt a meeting with God, the divine "Thou"—that is, solely as a subject. But this is not as easy as it sounds. The stubborn attraction we feel for objects has the potential to drag us down much more than it has the parallel potential to assist us in seeking spiritual elevation.

In such a tragic situation, one in which the believer insists (and perhaps this is the correct way to understand the sinful people's "hardness of the neck" metaphor mentioned repeatedly in the Torah) not to recognize this—and instead to adhere to objects (no matter how worthwhile and precious such objects may be as tools)—at this moment, such a person turns such objects, falsely but from his or her own vantage point legitimately, into a deity; in such a case, the only reasonable name for what we are witnessing is *idolatry*, even if it is hiding behind the veil of legitimate divine worship via the observance of the commandments.

It should thus be clear that the desire we might have to possess holy objects—even if our goal is to use them to achieve spiritual growth—is merely an imagination-drive vehicle that can only bring us to feel that we ourselves can engage the will-driven motor and thus to arrive eventually at our desired destination. And thus is born in our hearts the fantasy that the choice to seek intimacy with the Divine is ours to make. But what happened to Rabbi Mordechai in our story teaches us that the correct path to follow in such situations is to desist from attempting to travel forward on the wings of desire-driven imagination entirely and, in so doing, to realize that God is present with us in every single moment, always.

The Naïve Departure on the Spiritual Journey and the Surrender to God That Corresponds to God's Command to Abraham: "Go Forth from Your Land!"

But the final sentence in the previous section isn't entirely correct, and now we must revisit and rework it slightly.

This hasidic tale teaches us that intimacy with the Divine occurs when we finally understand how to achieve it through the contemplation of our past failures, through the cultivation of despair and inadequacy, and through the embrace of our own spiritual impotence to do anything practical that might stimulate such intimacy. And despair indeed overwhelms us as we contemplate how we work incessantly and instinctually through objects to achieve whatever effect we wish on anything we encounter in our travels in the world.[22]

Still, it is worth noting that even as a desire for change awakens in Rabbi Mordechai, he begins his journey by yearning to approach God with the same naïveté that characterizes the efforts of all of us as we set forth on our lives' paths. And the same is true for anyone wishing to follow a spiritual path in order to leave "this world" as we know it, and to attain a more exalted level of spiritual reality that, by comparison, makes our mundane existence feel petty and bland.

This is not a bad thing. Indeed, for the seeker/wanderer in the first stages of the journey, there exists no viable option other than to set forth in exactly the same way that people set forth on all such journeys: by identifying methods of personal improvement and betterment in one's life and by mimicking similar achievements earlier in one's life or in the lives of other people. Nevertheless, the story tells us that one who seeks to set forth on the spiritual journey simply cannot remain on the same path as those whose journeys forward in life are focused on acquiring material goods. Spiritual travelers must be careful not to fall prey to their own human imaginations, and as a result they must only set forth on their pilgrimage after having cleansed themselves of arrogance and haughtiness. Both of these are qualities capable of causing anyone to err and to think that the journey itself—no matter how well planned or executed—is capable of bringing one to the goal that one so ardently seeks.

And why should that be? Because the essence of the spiritual journey lies in the fact that those who seek to know God must set forth possessed of a sense of humility accompanied by a willingness to submit to whatever happens to them along the way that will enable them to accept whatever befalls them as a blessing. Only in such a case is undertaking such a journey worthwhile—and that, in and of itself, constitutes the real meaning of God's command to Abraham (then still Abram): "Go forth from your land—from your homeland and your father's house—to the land that I shall show to you" (Genesis 12:1). This verse refers solely to the land that God promises to show to Abraham, and not to whatever land Abraham, possessed of desire of know God, might imagine as his future destination.

And so it should be clear that the place to which Rabbi Mordechai was brought was not the distant place symbolized in the story by the exotic fabric of distant Land of Israel, but rather to a place that was fully known to him, because he was already in that place—because his spiritual elevation occurs while he is still wearing the old *tzitzit* he had been wearing in the first place—and, at that, the very one he had wished to replace.

In another sense, though, the man's journey did indeed bring him to a new place—not the one that his desire for spiritual advancement drew him to seek out, but rather an inner destination, a "holy land" that he only became aware of upon accepting as a blessing, and without anger or bitter resignation, the destruction of the desire that had originally served as the setting-forth point on his journey. When his movement forward toward the fulfillment of his desire ended without leaving a trace of rage or bitterness—but rather bringing him to the state of silence and inner acquiescence which would henceforth characterize his inner world and make it a place of equanimity—it was then that the rebbe's eyes were finally opened to the fact that God had been present all along in his personal ambit, and that it would be possible for him to "find" God using the very same *mitzvah*-appurtenances that had served him up until that moment.

Rabbi Mordechai learned—as do we all—that an imaginary *tzitzit* cannot make perceptible our elusive God, but that in the ruination of fantasy lies the path forward to sensing the presence of God in the here and now, in real time, at the present moment in our lives.

NOTES

[1] Martin Buber's profound comment on this matter is: "it is senseless to ask how far my action reaches, and where God's grace begins; there is no common border-line. What concerns me alone, before I bring something about, is my action, and what concerns me alone, when the action is successfully done, is God's grace. The one is no less real than the other, and neither is a part-cause. God and man do not divide the government of the world between them; man's action is enclosed in God's action, but it is still real action" (Martin Buber, *Hasidism*, trans. Greta Hort et al. [New York: Philosophical Library, 1948, p. 109]). I have discussed this topic at length in my Hebrew-language essay "Notes and Explanations to Martin Buber's *I and Thou*," published in *Yahadut: Sugiyot, K'ta·im, Panim Z'huyyiyot—Sefer Rivkah*, eds. Ḥaviva Pedaya and Efraim Meir (Beersheva: Ben Gurion University, 2007), pp. 511–524, esp. pp. 519–524.

[2] M. Menaḥot 13:11.

[3] B. Berakhot 17a. Cf. the explanation of Rabbi Abraham Yitzḥak Hakohen Kook, who wrote that "the kind of wholeness that leads to finding favor in the eyes of God is a function solely of the wholeness of the human heart and its basic purity, a principle that no one can learn by inspecting the wellsprings of somebody else's faith"; see his *Ein Ayah al Aggadot Ḥazal She-b'ein Yaakov* (Jerusalem: Hamakhon al Shem Harav Tzvi Yehudah Kook z"l, 5747 [1986/1987]), vol. 1, p. 84. Regarding the emphasis on the intentionality of the pure heart as a core value in Judaism (and also in other faiths), see Bernhard Heller, "Gott wünscht das Herz: Legenden über einfältige Andacht und über den Gefährten im Paradies," *Hebrew Union College Annual* 4 (1927), pp. 365–404.

[4] The literature on this topic is immense. For a summary of the topic, see Yuval Blankovsky, "*Ḥeit L'sheim Shamayim: Aveirah Li-sh'mah B'olamam shel Ḥakhamim* (Jerusalem: Magnes Press, 2017). With reference to the expressions *aveirah li-sh'mah* ("sin for its own sake") and *mitzvah ha-ba·ah ba-aveirah* ("a *mitzvah* that is actualized through transgression"), see Gershom Scholem, "Redemption through Sin," in his *The Messianic Idea in Judaism* (New York: Schocken, 1971), pp. 78–141; and see also Tzipi Kaufman, *B'khol D'rakhekha Da·eihu: T'fisat Ha-elohut V'ha-avodah B'gashmiyut B'reishit Ha-ḥasidut* (Ramat Gan: Bar Ilan University Press, 2009), pp. 220–223 and 523–571. Regarding antinomianism in general, see the survey by Shaul Magid in *Vocabulary for the Study of Religion*, eds. Robert Alan Segal and Kocku von Stuckrad (Leiden: Brill, 2015), vol. 1, pp. 102–103.

[5] M. Rosh Hashanah 3:8. There are versions of the *mishnah* that speak merely of "focusing the heart" (*m'khav'nim et libbam*) instead of subjugating it (*m'shaab'din et libbam*), but it hardly matters which term is the original one in the present discussion—both refer to the same exalted spiritual state characterized by being

totally given over to the quest for communion with the Divine. Regarding the problems involved in translating the passage as referencing "surrender" to God, see Yonah Frankel's comments in his *Darkhei Ha-aggadah V'ha-midrash* (Givatayim: Hotza·at Yad La-talmud, 1991), vol. 2, pp. 484–485, and also the notes on those pages; and see also the 2001 Hebrew University doctoral dissertation of Avraham Walfish, *Shitat Ha-arikhah Ha-sifrutit Ba-mishnah Al Pi Massekhet Rosh Ha-shanah*, pp. 106–107.

[6] The word "rebbe" (rather than "rabbi") is used throughout this essay when referring to a hasidic teacher.

[7] Nesukhoyezhe, located twelve miles to the northeast of Kowel in the province of Volhynia, was called Nezkizh in Yiddish. Rabbi Yeḥiel Mikhel is widely referenced as the Maggid of Zolochiv, called Zlotshev in Yiddish, and was a direct pupil of the Baal Shem Tov (c. 1700–1760), the founder of Hasidism.

[8] The garment popularly called *tzitzit*, also called a *tallit katan*, is a kind of sideless undershirt worn under one's regular shirt, so as to fulfill the commandment of wearing ritual fringes all day long, as ordained at Numbers 15:37–40.

[9] *Sefer Sippurim Nifla·im,* ed. Ḥayyim Yitzḥak Malik (Satu Mare, Romania: M.L. Hirsch, 1940), pp. 57–58.

[10] The link between *tzitzit* and the Land of Israel that so motivates the rebbe has to do with the textual juxtaposition between the story of the spies (sent by Moses to reconnoiter the Land) and the passage ordaining the wearing of *tzitzit*. See, e.g. the typical hasidic sermon of Rabbi Avraham Mordechai Alter of Gur in his *Imrei Emet* (ed. Tel Aviv, 5750 [1989/1990]), vol. 1, p. 96. Yehudah Moriel points out that there is a specific turn of phrase that links the two passages: Numbers 15:39 says that by wearing *tzitzit* "you will not spy (*taturu*) after your heart and after your eyes," which recalls the Numbers 13:2, the beginning of the story of the spies, in which God instructs Moses to "send forth men who will spy out (*v'yaturu*) the Land of Canaan"; see his *Iyyunim Ba-mikra* (Tel Aviv: Tziuni, 5729 [1968/1969]), vol. 4, pp. 87–88. This connection was already hinted at by Rashi in his comment to Numbers 15:39, s.v. *v'lo taturu aḥarei l'vavkhem,* in which he noted that "the heart and the eyes are the body's spies."

[11] Any reference to the "neck" brings to mind the laws of kosher slaughter, which require that an animal be killed by having its neck slit (see B. Ḥullin 43b). Even beyond the laws of slaughter, the neck is connected in biblical texts to death: cf., e.g., Exodus 13:13 ("the firstborn of a donkey must be redeemed with a lamb, but if this is not done then its neck must be broken") and 1 Samuel 4:18 ("he fell off his chair backwards at the side of the gate and his neck was broken and he died," describing the death of the priest Eli). Furthermore, the image of the rebbe inserting his head into the neck opening also calls to mind the rabbinic idea of "extending one's neck for slaughter" (see, e.g., Eikhah Rabbah, *petiḥta* 24

[ed. S. Buber; Vilna, 5659 (1898/1899), p. 14a], where Isaac at the Akeidah is imagined to have said: "Master of the Universe, when my father said to me 'God will provide a lamb for the offering' (Genesis 22:8)…I willingly allowed myself to be bound atop the altar, sticking my neck out beneath the knife.") Also, the neck often metaphorically suggests submission—just as the rebbe, in our story, yearns (via his idealized observance of the *mitzvah* of *tzitzit*) to submit completely to God. Indeed, the story's ending is a surprise precisely because he manages to achieve this act of submission despite having failed to perform the *mitzvah* in the way he had anticipated. Regarding this metaphoric use of the neck to suggest submission, cf. Jeremiah 28:10–11 ("But the prophet Ḥananiah removed the bar from the neck of the prophet Jeremiah, and broke it, and said… 'Thus said the Eternal: So will I break the yoke of King Nebuchadnezzar of Babylon from off the necks of all the nations…'").

[12] Regarding the holiness that inheres in the appurtenances of observing *mitzvot*, Rabbi Norman Lamm explains that both preparing the animal skins for use in a Torah scroll and writing one of God's names in the scroll are commandments that must be done *li-sh'mah* ("for its own sake"): "[the action must be undertaken] for the sake of the holiness that will inhere in such scrolls when they are completed"; see Naḥum (Norman) Lamm, *Torah Li-sh'mah* (Jerusalem: Mossad Harav Kook, 5732 [1971/1972]), p. 136.

A brief explanation of this, from the vantage point of the *halakhah*. The question of whether the *mitzvot* require intentionality is left undecided in the Talmud (for example, see the differences between B. Pesaḥim 114b and Rosh Hashanah 28a–28b), which obliged the post-talmudic halakhists to determine what the law actually does require. Many halakhic decisors (cf., Rabbi Joseph Karo, at S.A. Oraḥ Ḥayyim 60:4) in fact determined that there is a legal requirement that "*mitzvot* be undertaken mindfully," and one must bring mindful intentionality to an action in order for it to be considered to have been undertaken solely sake of the performance of that specific *mitzvah*. On the other hand, this does not apply to the mere creation of the appurtenances of worship (for instance, building a *sukkah* before the holiday); since such an undertaking does not constitute the fulfillment of a commandment per se, but merely the creation of an object to be used in fulfilling a *mitzvah*, such efforts do not require mindful intentionality. Yet, there are some *mitzvah*-appurtenances that do require that they be undertaken intentionally for the sake of their subsequent use in the performance of a *mitzvah*. The preparation of the materials for *tzitzit* and *t'fillin* fall in this latter category, and Lamm writes that their manufacture must be undertaken *li-sh'mah*, with intentional regard for the holiness that will inhere in the objects once they are ready to be used in the performance of the *mitzvot* that require them.

[13] Regarding *mitzvah* "appurtenances," see the previous note. Note also that the

rebbe's original yearning could not be realized purely emotionally, but in fact requires both money to buy the fabric and the means to procure it. After this initial set of desires is fulfilled, when the fabric from the Land of Israel is finally in the rebbe's hands, a second wave of desire then seizes the rebbe, shifting his focus to a new object of desire: a *hasid* who knows how to sew, who will be able to fashion the fabric into *tzitzit* that the rebbe can finally wear.

[14] This calls to mind Numbers 15:39, the verse that links the *mitzvah* of *tzitzit* with the concept of remembering God ("when you see the *tzitzit*, you will remember all the commandments of the Eternal and thus fulfill them, rather than going astray after [the desires of] your heart and your eyes.") The verse mentions two different kinds of memory associations, one negative (those imaginative fantasies that can lead the human heart astray) and one positive (those that prompt the *tzitzit*-wearer to remember to fulfill the *mitzvot* and, in so doing, also to remember God).

[15] Regarding the midrashic conception of intimacy with the Divine, see Judith A. Kates, "Entering the Holy of Holies: Rabbinic Midrash and the Language of Intimacy," in *Scrolls of Love: Reading Ruth and the Song of Songs*, eds. Peter S. Hawkins and Lesleigh Cushing Stahlberg (New York: Fordham University Press, 2006), pp. 201–213. For a later rabbinic discussion about intimacy as the basic element of Jewish religious life, see Shlomo Wolbe's Hebrew-language essay "Psychiatry and Religion," *Bi-sh'vilei Ha-r'fu·ah* 5 (1982), pp. 57–90.

[16] Regarding the use of the term "holy garment" in biblical and rabbinic sources (where it sometimes serves to designate the priestly vestments and other times a regular *tallit*, and still other times any garment at all that one wears when ushered into God's presence), see the Hebrew essay co-authored by myself and Nissan Rubin, "Socks Inside and Socks Outside: Ultra-Orthodox Clothing and the Perception of Time in the Religious Society," *Akdamot* 20 (2008), pp. 131–153, and esp. pp. 142–149 regarding the concept of holy garments. That essay puts forth two important insights relevant to the story under discussion here: (1) the holy garment often serves as a stand-in for the self, in the effort to find both paths from the world below to the realm on high and from the past (e.g., the primeval age) into the future (e.g., the messianic age); and (2) wrapping oneself up in a holy garment can symbolize the suppression of the self and its willing self-negation as a way of seeking entry into God's presence (see in this regard particularly pp. 144–145).

[17] The wordplay between Hebrew *nes* (usually used to mean "miracle," but which can also denote a flagpole) and *nissayon* ("test") is difficult to capture in translation. The underlying idea is that the *nes* (pole) is to be imagined as standing straight up vertically, so that climbers can ascend as far as they can on their way toward spiritual perfection, just as an individual facing a divine *nissayon* (test) can also ascend toward heaven by such means. Cf. Bereshit Rabbah 55:1

(ed. Theodor-Albeck, p. 585): "Test after test, growth experience after growth experience—the whole point is to provide the context for those who pass the tests to grow in the world to be as tall as the mast (*nes*) of a ship." Regarding this midrash, see Menaḥem Kister, "*Aḥor Va-kedem: Aggadot V'darkhei Midrash B'sifrut Ha-ḥitzonit U-v'sifrut Ḥazal*, in *Higayon L'yonah: Hebeitim Ḥadashim B'ḥeiker Sifrut Ha-midrash, Ha-aggadah V'ha-piyyut – Kovetz Meḥkarim Li-kh'vodo shel Professor Yonah Frankel Bi-m'lot Lo Shivim V'ḥameish Shanim*, eds. Yehoshua Levinson et al. (Jerusalem: Magnes Press, 5767 [2006/2007], pp. 252-254. (The full essay appears on pp. 231-259.) The delicate depreciation of the importance of *mitzvah* appurtenances and the concomitant emphasis on the interior experience of performing the *mitzvah* characterizes both aggadic and hasidic stories. Elsewhere, I deal with the relationship between a story preserved within the corpus of midrashic literature and a hasidic story that suggests as much (see my Hebrew essay "The Extended 'Hand' of God and the Pilgrim's 'Foot': On Individual, Authentic Sacrifice and 'Seeing God's Face' in an Ancient Story from Palestine and in a Late Hasidic Story," *Kabbalah* 10 [2004], pp. 227–248). In that essay (p. 245, n. 71), I turn readers' attention to the concept of "boundary" that Moshe Weiss uses as part of his argument that hasidic sources like this one (and particularly in the first generations)—even if they cannot reasonably be characterized as antinomian (see below, note 20)— regularly approach the dangerous boundary between normative *halakhah* and its subversion as behavior best characterized as "sinning for its own sake." Weiss also discusses the trepidation inspired in the reader by the sense of danger that results from approaching this kind of border, as he writes: "This sense of an open border is one of the most basic features of hasidic religiosity…[such that] *halakhah* intentionally leads individuals to build within that border. Earlier Hasidism…consciously seeks to bring adherents across that specific boundary. Hasidism [thus] flourishes in the context of danger, and could even be said to urge its adherents forward toward that boundary" (see his *Meḥkarim B'ḥasidut Breslav* [Jerusalem: Mossad Bialik, 1974], p. 101). And see also Micha Ankori, *V'zeh Ha-ya·ar Ein Lo Sof: Mistikah Y'hudit U-p'sikhologiyah Analitit* (Tel Aviv: Ramot, 1991), pp. 168–178.

[18] Regarding equanimity as a spiritual value, the "Testament of the Baal Shem Tov" explains: "*Shivviti* (in Psalm 16:8) refers specifically to equanimity (*hishtavvut*), and the psalmist's point is that he has attained the spiritual level of being able to encounter any happenstance with equanimity" (in *Sefer Shivḥei Ha-besht im Hosafot*, ed. Benjamin Mintz [Jerusalem: Yad Binyamin, 5729 [1968/1969], p. 215). The valorization of equanimity as a spiritual value leads to a clear distinction between the spiritual grandeur of the *tzaddik* who has attained that level of spiritual achievement and regular people: the former is defined as one who is indifferent both to the kind of pleasure after which ordinary

people naturally lust, but also to the kind of pain from which ordinary people naturally flee (cf. Moshe Idel, *Hasidism: Between Ecstasy and Magic* (Albany: State University of New York Press, 1995, pp. 60-61. Many studies consider earlier and late sources in this regard, but I will cite here only several of the most pertinent. Regarding equanimity as a spiritual value in kabbalistic sources, see Moshe Idel's chapter "Seclusion as Concentration in Prophetic Kabbalah and Its Later Manifestations" in his book *P'rakim Ba-kabbalah Ha-n'vu·it* (Jerusalem: Akademon, 1990), pp. 120, 128–133, and 153–157, where Idel references Sufi and Stoic parallels as well. Regarding equanimity specifically in hasidic thought, see Rachel Elior, *Ḥeirut al Ha-luḥot* (Tel Aviv: Misrad Ha-bitaḥon, 5760 [1999/2000]), pp. 153–154; Zev Gries, *Sifrut Ha-hanhagot: Toldoteha U-m'komah B'ḥayyei Ḥasidav shel Ha-ba·al Shem Tov* (Jerusalem: Mossad Bialik, 1989), pp. 210–212; and Yoram Jacobson, *Toratah shel Ha-ḥasidut* (Tel Aviv: Misrad Ha-bitaḥon, 1985), pp. 72–75.

[19] This calls to mind the surprising response of Rabbi Akiva, who chortled with joy when seeing the Temple in ruins: "The sages, when visiting Jerusalem, first went to Mount Scopus, whereupon they rent their garments. And then, approaching the Temple Mount, they saw a fox run out from under the ruins of the Holy of Holies and began, all of them, to weep, but Rabbi Akiva laughed" Sifrei Devarim 43:16 (Siferei on Deuteronomy, ed. Louis Finkelstein [1940; rpt. New York: Jewish Theological Seminary, 1969], pp. 94-95). And see the explanation adduced in the Sifrei itself for Rabbi Akiva's laughter and also the comments of Yuval Shachar in his Hebrew-language essay, "Rabbi Akiva's Take on the Destruction of the Temple and the Establishment of Fasts Commemorating Its Destruction," *Zion* 68:2 (5763 [2002/2003]), pp. 145–165. And see also my "The Extended 'Hand' of God and the Pilgrim's 'Foot'" (referenced in note 17 above), and particularly my comments on pp. 247–248 there about the blessing coined for recitation after experiencing some tragic event.

[20] I wish to stress that there is nothing inherently antinomian about this story; it does not in any way cast aspersions on the importance of fulfilling the commandments or the value of *mitzvah* appurtenances. What the story does teach, however, is that we must not err in thinking that just as our lives in the material world feature the endless acquisition of more and more things, so too should (or at least could) our spiritual journey toward intimacy with the divine realm be facilitated by simply performing *mitzvot* and acquiring more and more *mitzvah* appurtenances. The story seeks to teach that, in the world of the spirit, the process that leads to progress is precisely the opposite—because the spiritual world requires that we swim *against* the current, keeping in mind always that a sense of divine intimacy can never be attained by endlessly piling up things, but only through an individual's total submission to the will of God. See below regarding the correct way to understand the relationship between

tangible objects and the divine realm.

[21] For an exposition of the various Buberian terms that I use in this essay, see my own Hebrew essay, "Introduction to Buber's Teaching," in Aharon Flashman's Hebrew translation of Martin Buber, *I and Thou* (Jerusalem: Mossad Bialik, 2013), pp. 160–231.

[22] Regarding absolute despair as a kind of spiritual diving board capable of propelling the despairing individual to the divine plain, see my Hebrew-language essay "Despair as the Point of Origin for the Construction of the Self," in *Ha-ḥayyim K'ga·agua: K'ri·ot Ḥadashot B'sippurei Ma·asiyot shel Rav Naḥman Mi-bratzlav*, ed. Roee Horn (Tel Aviv: Yediot Aḥaronot, 2010), pp. 79–88; as well as the comments of Aviezer Cohen in his Hebrew-language essay, "Individualization and the Question of the Subject in the *Mei Shilo·aḥ*," in *El Atzmi: Tahalikhei Individuatziah U-ma·avarei Ha-ḥayyim*, eds. Devorah Nov and Baruch Kahana (Jerusalem: Reuben Mass, 2014), pp. 335–348, regarding the opinion of Rabbi Simḥah Bunem of Przysucha (1767–1827) that the "messianic light" can only be created from total despair regarding one's ability to improve behavior so depraved that "even repentance cannot help." Thinking along these lines goes back to Philo of Alexandria, who already in the first century BCE took note of the centrality of despair in the construction of any individual's spiritual self. According to Philo, "there is a great advantage to individuals who know themselves if that self-knowledge rests on a foundation of despair, for despair leads to a renewed understanding of reality in that it functions as an invitation to escape from earlier theories that derive from sensual data and not from pure spiritual illumination" (in Philo's *K'tavim*, trans. Yehoshua Amir and Maren Nihof [Jerusalem: Mossad Bialik, 2012], vol. 5, p. 321, n. 97, a note by the editors).

The Tie That Binds: Ashkenazic Women Stitch Life

Barbara Thiede

The Torah commands Jews to choose life. The command is clear; the means are not. To love God, to hear and obey God's voice, to cleave to the Divine—these are the instructions we are given. Jews must, as always, interpret.

For centuries, the rabbis have insisted that choosing life is, for Jews, based in significant measure on the practice of circumcision (*b'rit milah*)—which the rabbis considered as equal to all other commandments combined.[1] By circumcising their sons, Jewish parents fulfill a command that is fundamental and central to Jewish existence. By doing so, they have heard and obeyed; they have chosen life. For rabbinic tradition, circumcision assures lineage, fertility, salvation, revelation—even life itself.[2] And this is not solely true for the male infant undergoing the procedure: the practice of circumcision saves and gives life to all Israel. On Yom Kippur, God looks at the blood of Abraham's circumcision and grants Israel forgiveness and reprieve from death in the year to come.[3]

The actual rite of *b'rit milah* features liturgical and biblical texts that make the same claim: circumcision assures salvation. After the removal of the foreskin, the *mohel* (the ritual circumciser) announces: "The living God commanded that the beloved of our flesh shall be delivered from the pit, for the sake of God's covenant that God set in our flesh, as it is said, 'I passed by you and saw you wallowing in your blood, and I said to you: In your blood, live; I said to you: In your blood, live'"(Ezekiel 16:6). Though the verse from Ezekiel addresses a menstruant (and uses, accordingly, feminine grammatical forms), the blood invoked is understood, in the liturgical context of a *b'rit milah*, as the blood of circumcision.[4] That blood gives life.

To choose life has been, for centuries of Jewish men, to inscribe the sign of the covenant on the bodies of infant boys. And for Jewish women? Given the paucity of female-authored texts for much of Jewish history, one might think we could never know.

But we can. Jewish women did, in fact, produce texts about circumcision—hundreds, even thousands of them. During the Middle Ages, as rabbis issued rulings forbidding women from participating at all in the ritual circumcision of their sons, women of Ashkenaz (a medieval Jewish name for a collection of German territories) wrote their own *midrashim* on circumcision. Their parchment was the very cloth first used to swaddle their sons just seconds after the foreskin had been surgically removed. These wimpels (as the cloths were known) were later used to bind the synagogue's Torah scrolls, the most sacred ritual items the community possessed. Through symbols, texts, and even wordplay, Ashkenazic women not only wrote a record of their sons' lineage and history, but they also recorded the complex nature of Jewish life in Europe. Synagogue practice grew to include the presentation of the wimpel as a gift to the community, thus introducing new rites into the Torah service that highlighted women's artistic labors and gave them pride of place before the entire community. And wimpels remained a significant part of Ashkenazic culture and practice for over five centuries: in 1964, two decades after the Holocaust, over fifteen hundred Torah scrolls confiscated by the Nazis were sent to London for repair and preservation. Those who unpacked them discovered that hundreds were tied with wimpels commemorating the births of children whose lives were, for the most part, lost in the Holocaust.

Wimpels were made from the cloth that had been used to swaddle the baby just after circumcision. The cloth was cleaned, cut into four strips, and then sewn together. The resulting band was embroidered with the child's birthdate, name, and father's name, as well as the blessing recited twice during the circumcision ceremony: "May he grow to a life of Torah, *huppah*, and good deeds."

Wimpels became a site for exploring a set of associations around circumcision that originated in male-authored texts, from Bible to Zohar. But the women of Ashkenaz did not merely rely on male instruction and direction for their inspiration. Their texts, their embroidered figures, and their creative renderings of folk traditions, legends, songs, and stories were not mere restatements of rabbinic readings. The history of the wimpel is both revealing and instructive: it is a story of resilience, of engagement, and of the ongoing challenge Jews face in interpreting their texts and forming the rites of Jewish life. It provides a deeply nuanced narrative of how Jews have realized the commandment to "choose life so that you and your offspring may live" (Deuteronomy 30:19). The wimpel and its history demonstrate that Jewish culture has never been expressed solely in male-authored texts, but in a richly diverse material culture—one that depended, in significant part, on how Jewish women read the commandments. For the women of Ashkenaz, circumcision retained its life-saving and life-giving powers; their wimpels proclaim that belief, often in ways that were particular to their experience as women in a male-dominated world.

Technically, it is a father's responsibility to circumcise his son—though the *halakhah* permits the father to delegate the responsibility to a professional circumciser instead. This, in fact, became the general practice in Jewish communities. It appears that the rite was initially performed in private homes, which likely encouraged both the presence and participation of women.[5] Circumcision wine was, according to a ninth-century text, given to the mother at the ceremony for the express purpose of speeding her recuperation from the birth.[6] And until the thirteenth century, nearly all authorities in German states permitted a woman to act as a *mohelet* if no Jewish male could be found to perform the circumcision.[7]

During that same century, however, the Maharam (Rabbi Meir ben Barukh of Rothenburg) ruled that a woman sitting among the men at a circumcision was "not a proper custom, even if her husband or her father or her son is the circumciser." The Maharam pointed out that women are not bound by the commandment of circumcision, and therefore should, on no account, be found holding their infants during the procedure. Women, according to the Maharam, had no right to "snatch the commandment from men."[8] About a century later, Rabbi Jacob Segal Molin, known as the Maharil (c. 1363–1427), followed suit, extending his predecessor's judgment to bar women from crossing the threshold of the synagogue door during a circumcision. Instead, a woman (other than the child's mother) was charged with the responsibility of bringing the child to the synagogue, handing the infant to a male functionary at the door, and waiting for the conclusion of the rite to bring the child home. German rabbis succeeded, at least halakhically, in ending all ritual roles for mothers, argues Lawrence Hoffman: "With the Maharil, the circumcision had finally become exclusively male."[9]

We can understand this judgment if we assume that the male rite was the only circumcision rite Jews had created. But to do so would be to inadvertently collude with male perspectives that have dominated the discussion of Jewish history in both rabbinic and academic circles. Such perspectives privilege textual evidence over that produced by material culture. In the process, the very sites women used to explore their relationship to Jewish practice have often been ignored.

So it is, perhaps, no wonder that scholars have for so long failed to notice that the women's handiwork altered and reconstructed liturgical practice in Ashkenaz, for many centuries. By the sixteenth century, the wimpel's popularity had engendered new synagogue rituals that literally tied material evidence of the fulfilled commandment to the scroll in which it was written. The custom of presenting the wimpel to the community during the Torah service is first recorded in the 1530 Augsburg edition of Antonius Margaritha's *Der gantze jüdische Glaube* ("The Entire Jewish Faith").[10] Less than a century later, the ceremony was described in some detail by Yuspa Shammash (1604–1678), who reported that the boy's mother was accompanied by the rabbi's wife and other female dignitaries to the synagogue on the fourth Shabbat after the birth. As her husband stepped forward, the baby's mother sent the embroidered Torah wimpel down from the women's section of the synagogue. The father brought the child to the *bimah* (a raised platform where the Torah would be read), presented the wimpel, and offered it for use as a Torah binder as the child's first "donation" to the community.[11] In some Ashkenazic communities, boys under the age of thirteen gathered at the *bimah* before the Torah reading when a new binder was presented to the synagogue. The binder was unrolled and then tossed among the youngsters. Whoever caught it had the privilege of wrapping the Torah.[12] Wimpels became part and parcel of Jewish liturgical practice throughout much of central and eastern Europe and remained so for centuries, as the binders found on the Torah scrolls confiscated by the Nazis amply proved.

Circumcision was accompanied by a set of rituals designed to invoke the desired outcome: a male child bound to Torah and to Jewish identity. When the wimpel made from the circumcision cloth was wrapped and tied around the Torah scroll during synagogue services, so too, symbolically, was the child. The women of Ashkenaz could not have made it clearer: their sons were bound to Torah.

Admittedly, while women's work was given both public acknowledgement and even a stage for its presentation, the synagogue ritual did not offer the seamstress, the actual agent of this liturgical transformation, the foreground. The community heard the father bless the child and present the wimpel as his son's first donation. A crowd of prepubescent boys waited to catch the wimpel to determine who would bind the Torah scroll after the reading. The scene is entirely male. Nevertheless, the ritual item was a female production: it was created by women, and men then participated in making that production both public and sacred.

When a boy was called to Torah for his first public reading at the time of his bar mitzvah, his wimpel was again used to bind the scroll. The binder was also present at his wedding, stretched between the poles carrying the marriage canopy. The wimpel was clearly regarded as a holy ritual object that deserved the same veneration as manuscripts, prayer books, and Torah scrolls. Torn, damaged, or otherwise unusable wimpels have been found in *genizahs*, synagogue storerooms, alongside sacred texts and scrolls.[13] A product women produced had attained the status of the holy.

The earliest surviving wimpels were found in the Westheim *genizah*.[14] They date to 1592 and 1609, though there is evidence that a binder from 1570 was kept in a synagogue in Worms until the building was destroyed in 1938 by the Nazis during the state-sponsored pogrom known as Kristallnacht.[15] But in an account from 1893, Georg Minden (the president of Berlin's Reform community) presented two wimpels to the *Verein für Volkskunde* (Association for Cultural Studies) for examination. One wimpel was dated to 1490, and the second to 1696. The blessing twice invoked in the male rite was central, as was the child's name, father's name, and date of birth.[16]

A likely origin for the wimpel is to be found in Christian practice:

it appears that German Catholics of the medieval period were in the habit of inscribing pious statements on the *Taufwindel*, a baptismal swaddling cloth.[17] While priests performed the baptism, Christian women managed the task of recording the child's birth on swaddling cloths—a division of labor mirrored in Jewish practice, where the ritual circumciser performed the rite and the operation and women embroidered the cloth.[18] For the Christian community, the *Taufwindel* was not an insignificant product: in 758 CE, when King Pippin named Pope Paul I the godfather for his daughter Gisela, he made the tie official by sending the pope her *Taufwindel*. The latter, apparently, received the swaddling cloth ceremoniously and hung it in the Saint Petronilla Chapel in Rome.[19]

Jewish tradition, of course, provides a different narrative. According to the *Sefer Ha-maharil*, the chief work of the Maharil, the first connection between a boy's circumcision and a holy object used in the dressing of the sacred Torah occurred because, quite simply, a particular set of parents had committed a faux pas:

> It happened one time that Rabbi Jacob Segal Molin…was *sandek* [godfather] and no cloth had been provided to wrap the baby's legs. The rabbi ordered that a *mappah* (binder) be brought from the Torah scroll to be used for the child. He declared this permissible, citing "danger of life"; further, that the binder might be used again without impairing its holiness, provided it had been cleansed of blood. Also, the family should give a donation to charity, so as not to enjoy the use of holy objects free of charge.[20]

The story features a renowned rabbi of Ashkenaz, one who had played a leading role in excluding women from the actual rite of circumcision. Here we begin with a missing cloth and a rabbi who saves the day by permitting a holy ritual object's use for the circumcision rite.[21] The Maharil ruled that a binder which protects and binds the scrolls of the sacred Torah may, after the circumcision is performed, be used to swaddle the child—quite literally holding and protecting the inscription of Jewish identity on his body. Instead of the wimpel standing as the child's donation to the synagogue as a Torah binder, the parents are instructed to make a monetary donation for the use of a Torah binder to swaddle their son.

The story seeks to reverse the more likely trajectory, one in which the swaddling-cloth that bound the child was made into the binder for the scrolls. The rabbinic story that explains the connection of Torah binder to swaddling-cloth gives official sanction and a male authority for a practice the rabbis likely did not initiate.[22] Of course, it is certain that male-authored texts influenced what Jewish women sought to represent on their sons' wimpels. Fertility, lineage, life and death were all features of the historically male conversation around *b'rit milah*, and all were reflected in the choices Jewish women made, the symbols they embroidered, and the folk traditions they created around the wimpel.

The Torah clearly connects circumcision to fertility: it is decreed that those who do not circumcise shall have no progeny (Genesis 17:14). Historians have explored in some detail the connections in the Bible between circumcision and fertility.[23] The women of Ashkenaz made such associations of circumcision and fertility playfully obvious, and they did so employing not a Jewish symbol but a Christian one. Some of the earliest extant wimpels feature the quintessential Christian symbol of fertility, the stork, emerging from the Hebrew letter *lamed* in the word *nolad* ("was born"). The infant's own (future) offspring were evoked: the embroidered cloth that had once bound the child's circumcised organ would depict the future fertility engendered there.

B'rit milah valorized descent through the father rather than the mother. Wimpels accordingly named the child and indicated his lineage through his father's name. Women also include tribal symbols to evoke lines of descent. For example, a Levite's pitcher symbolized the duty of the Levites to wash the hands of the priests before a religious service and signaled the child's membership in the tribe of Levi. Also, the symbol of priestly hands in the position of classic benediction signaled that the child was the descendant of the Aaronid line, the *kohanim*.

For those who could not trace their descent lines to the *kohanim* or the Levites, there were other means to evoke an infant's relationship to ancient tribes. Medieval Jewish texts, from the *Sefer Yetzirah* to the Zohar, associated the months of the year with a given tribe. Mothers of sons born in Nisan might embroider lions on their sons' wimpels because mystical texts associated that month with the tribe of Judah (symbolized by the lion). Likewise, boys born in Kislev, the month associated with the tribe of Benjamin, might feature wolves (the symbol of that tribe). Lineage here was not depicted literally, but it was achieved allusively.

Rabbinic texts equated idolatry with death and worship of the one God with life. To fulfill the commandment of circumcision was, they argued, to separate from death. The foreskin stood for death and the uncircumcised were compared to mourners, associated with death because they were cut off from their kin, and therefore separated from their community, and life.[24]

The importance of circumcision as a sign of life is not in spite of, but rather because of its dangers: circumcision is understood as a personal, bodily sacrifice. Such a sacrifice is inherently dangerous, as the men of Shechem discovered when Jacob's sons took advantage of their weakened state after they had undergone circumcision, and attacked their city and slaughtered them all (Genesis 34:25). Talmudic texts do not shirk from admitting the risk for infant boys, either; rabbinic deliberations include discussions about when circumcision should be postponed or even left unperformed.[25]

The invocation and prayer uttered during the rite, that the child grow up to become a full adult with his own family, would have been a heartfelt one for many centuries. Embroidering the blessing onto the cloth that had been used during the rite constituted a way for women to connect the act with their own "utterance" of the blessing. Their version had a permanence and material reality that would go on public display. The women's recitation of the blessing for a life of Torah, *huppah*, and good deeds would be stitched into the cloth that had been used to bind the wound. It would be seen in the synagogue and materialized as a sacred ritual item meant to hold and protect the sacred text of Torah.

Not surprisingly, given the dangers of circumcision, representations of death also appeared on the wimpels of Ashkenaz in the person of the demoness Lilith, the baby killer who had long been part and parcel of Jewish folk practice and tradition. While rabbinic tradition certainly had much to say about Lilith, rabbinic writings focused on her almost exclusively as a sexual temptress. Jewish women had described her role as a baby killer for centuries—in incantation bowls, on amulets, in magical rituals, and in folk stories.[26] In a wimpel of 1693, the text appears to present a pleasant enough blessing for the newborn: "Abraham, son of Naphtali, may he live, born under a good constellation…" Nonetheless, Lilith is clearly present in the form of a large snake that emerges from the *lamed* in the acronym *shin-lamed-yod-tet* (standing for *she-yihyeh l'orekh yamim tovim*, "may he have a good long life"), directly threatening a baby depicted between a naked woman's legs.[27] Death thus emerges from the prayer for life. Here, Jewish women made their piece of the circumcision rite—the wimpel—speak to their own concerns: namely, the safety and the survival of their sons.

Quite possibly, their depiction of Lilith functioned as a prophylactic against death in much the same way as the actual removal of the foreskin did for male Jewish tradition. The Bible itself provided an origin story clearly associating circumcision with a method of warding off the most murderous intent imaginable—that of the deity. In Exodus 4:24–26, God appears in the dark of the night, intending to murder Moses before he ever gets to Egypt to fulfill his charge. Moses' wife, Zipporah, saves her husband by circumcising their son, apparently holding the sacrificial foreskin to her son's feet, Moses' feet, or God's—the text is very unclear.[28]

For Jewish women to combine a blessing for life with the very image of death was to perform, in embroidery, a similarly apotropaic ritual. Depicting Lilith emerging from the Hebrew acronym *shin-lamed-yod-tet* ("may he live") was to adjure *against* her power; the adjuration was extended in the prayer (that the child grow to a life of Torah, marriage, and good deeds) that had been recited at the rite itself. The foreskin was, in the male rite, the essential sacrifice that would ward against death. The depiction of Lilith on wimpels was, in its own way, a sacrifice as well: it acknowledged her power to threaten the child and yet symbolically presented her with the evidence of the child's blood sacrifice—the cloth on which Lilith appeared had absorbed the actual blood sacrifice of circumcision. The cloth stood for the blood that had been shed.[29] The wimpel depicted how death was to be conquered: Lilith might attack, but the Hebrew prayer would ensure that life would triumph. "May he live" was an adjuration *that* he live.

Apparently, the child's life became so tied up in the wimpel embroidered for him that the women of the community could read his future in the way he reacted to the public presentation of his wimpel. In some communities, when the father gave the wimpel to the community during the Torah service as the child's first donation, the infant in his arms would—at least according to female folklore—reveal his nature by his own reaction. Women of the community "would congratulate the mother, point out remarkable qualities of the boy." If the child gave up his wimpel willingly, he was described as a *Goldkind* ("a golden child"): happy, outgoing, and ready to share. If the child seemed reluctant to give up the binder or if he cried as the gift was made, it was obvious that he was already deeply attached to Torah. He would become a "teacher in Israel."[30] The cloth that had, quite literally, held the evidence of the commandment fulfilled could be used to prophesy the life the child would lead.

Ashkenazic Jewish women produced handiwork recording their readings of the importance of *b'rit milah*; they recorded prayers for their sons' lives, invoked the fertility the rite would ensure, and included particularly female prophylactic images warding off death. Jewish women, through the production of the wimpel, chose life for their progeny. Excluded from male rites of circumcision, they created their own site for a corollary practice: creating works of art that bound their sons first physically and then figuratively to the commandments and the Torah.

When Ashkenazic women embroidered and created, they chose life in ways neither they nor the rabbis could possibly have foreseen. For them, the wimpel was a material manifestation of their adherence to a central commandment, one that would protect their son, future generations, and even Israel itself. They could hardly have predicted that their work would actually save Jewish men's lives—in real time and from genuine threat. In later centuries, though, wimpels served a particularly important purpose when it came to avoiding one of the most onerous and frightening of national duties: conscription. Wimpels were accepted as civil documents, functioning as registers of birth. During the French Revolution and Empire period, French civil authorities relied on wimpels to prove the age of potential recruits.

In one document, the commissioner of the executive authorities in the canton of Soulz (Lower Alsace) acerbically took note of the lack of enthusiasm for the military among the local Jews, and openly suspected that they were taking advantage of his ignorance of Hebrew: "If I am to trust their circumcision registers or the napkin strips on which the year of birth has been noted in Hebrew—that I cannot read and that only a single man, whom I have to trust, in the canton is able to decipher—nobody will be of an age for the first requisition: All are either too young or too old…"[31]

From the Middle Ages on and into even our own time, Ashkenazic women have demonstrated that wimpels could be open to any motif. Bickering chickens, peacocks, and foxes scamper across wimpels. Wimpels even feature puns: when a woman embroidered the letter *nun* in the shape of a fish, she was playing with words; the name of the letter also means "fish" in Hebrew. On one wimpel, a fox stands clutching a stolen goose, a clear reference to the folk song *Fuchs, Du hast die Gans gestohlen, gib sie wieder her* ("Fox, you stole the goose, return it at once").[32] In the early 1800s, Alsatian wimpels consistently include the colors of the French tricolor; often, even the depiction of the *ḥuppah* is adorned with a French flag.[33] From references to local folklore to nationalistic motifs, wimpels demonstrate complex hybrid identities among Jewish communities of Europe.

The rabbis did not appear to find it necessary to limit or legislate concerning the symbols or associations women embroidered onto wimpels, even though they were brought into synagogues and used to wrap the scrolls of the law. Ashkenazic Jewish women appear to have had free reign to design wimpels as they wished, so it may not be so surprising that their descendants have included the depiction of such popular figures as Mickey Mouse on the wimpels they have designed. Today, women in Germany are relearning the craft of making and designing wimpels[34] and Americans post instructions and pictures, and write blog posts, about the wimpels they have created.[35]

We assume that we cannot know how Jewish women thought about Jewish life, Jewish culture, and the Torah's commandments because we lack female-authored texts for much of our history. We are gazing at a lacuna because we are adopting a longstanding rabbinic and academic tradition; we are beginning and ending our explorations with textual evidence, with parchment and manuscripts. But as endlessly rich as our textual inheritance is, there is yet more. When we extend our gaze we see that there is no lacuna—at least not the one we imagine. The material culture that Jewish women produced for centuries was the site for their texts and *midrashim*.

The women of Ashkenaz devoted themselves to realizing the commandment to circumcise in a ritual of their own making. They cut the fabric that had wrapped their infant sons. They cleaned it and created exquisite ritual items that would reflect all the promises associated with *b'rit milah*: the assurance of lineage, fertility, and salvation. For these women, the wimpel was a way to demonstrate that they, too, had chosen life—by stitching it into existence. The outcome was life-giving.

NOTES

[1] In the Mishnah (e.g., at M. Nedarim 3:11), a number of rabbis offer various reasons for the claim that "great is circumcision, for it is equivalent to all the other commandments."

[2] For a few of the many academic treatments of rabbinic texts tying circumcision to each of these outcomes, see Lawrence Hoffman, *Covenant of Blood: Circumcision and Gender in Rabbinic Judaism* (Chicago: University of Chicago Press, 1996), passim; Howard Eilberg-Schwartz, "The Fruitful Cut: Circumcision and Israel's Symbolic Language of Fertility, Descent, and Gender," in his *The Savage in Judaism: An Anthropology of Israelite Religion and Ancient Israel* (Bloomington: University of Indiana Press, 1990), pp. 141–176; David Kraemer, "The Problem with Foreskin: Circumcision, Gender, Impurity, and Death," in his *Reading the Rabbis: The Talmud as Literature* (New York: Oxford University Press, 1996), pp. 109–123; Elliot R. Wolfson, "Circumcision, Vision of God, and Textual Interpretation: From Midrashic Trope to Mystical Symbol," in *History of Religions* 27:2 (November 1987), pp. 189–215; idem, "Circumcision and the Divine Name: A Study in the Transmission of Esoteric Doctrine," *The Jewish Quarterly Review* 78:1/2 (July-October 1987), pp. 77–112; and Daniel Boyarin, "'This We Know to Be the Carnal Israel': Circumcision and the Erotic Life of God and Israel," *Critical Inquiry* 18:2 (Spring 1992), pp. 474–505.

[3] Pirkei D'rabbi Eliezer, chap. 29. Lawrence Hoffman discusses the reasons given in this text to prove circumcision's saving power, including the claim that the Israelites were circumcised the day they left Egypt and mixed the blood of circumcision together with the blood of paschal lamb and smeared it on their doorposts; because of the blood of circumcision, God showed compassion. See Hoffman, *Covenant of Blood*, p. 101.

[4] The verse is meant to demonstrate that Israel will be saved from death "*by virtue of its blood that is shed in covenant*" (ibid., p. 103; italics in original).

[5] For example, a circumcision booklet produced in Italy in 1600 seems to suggest that the actual circumcision took place in a private home while the festivities celebrating the rite took place in the synagogue; the question here is salient, given the Ashkenazic rabbis' move to ensure that the rite would take place in the synagogue where women's presence could be restricted. Even in the Middle Ages there were Sephardic Jews who continued to perform the rite in private residences rather than synagogues. See Eva Frojmovič, "Illustrierte Mohelbücher und Beschneidungsliturgien," in *Mappot…gesegnet, der da kommt: Das Band jüdischer Tradition*, eds. Annette Weber, Evelyn Friedlander, and Fritz Armbruster (Osnabrück, Germany: Secolo Verlag, 1997), pp. 56–57.

[6] Hoffman, *Covenant of Blood*, p. 89.

[7] Abraham Grossman, *Pious and Rebellious: Jewish Women in Medieval Europe*

(Lebanon, NH: Brandeis University Press, 2004), p. 190.

[8] *Sefer Tashbetz Katan* §397. The *Sefer Tashbetz*, a collection of responsa, was written by Samson ben Tzadok, a pupil of Meir of Rothenburg, who died in the late thirteenth century. According to Lawrence Hoffman, the rabbis followed the biblical text in interpreting Israelite history so that circumcision would become the key to the inheritance of covenantal status (*Covenant of Blood*, p. 49). In doing so, the rabbis helped define a rite that would constitute a "ceremonial celebration of the obligation that binds men to each other in rabbinic culture" (p. 80). "Circumcision," he writes, "was no life-cycle ceremony. For a newborn, it was a ritualization of male status within Judaism" (p. 80). By the Middle Ages, Hoffman concludes, "all women, even the child's mother, were forbidden to attend a circumcision; hence the current rite does not recognize the mother at all" (p. 95).

[9] Hoffman, *Covenant of Blood*, p. 205.

[10] Antonius Margaritha was the son of Rabbi Jacob Margoliot of Regensburg, Germany, and a convert to Christianity. See Joseph Gutmann, "Die Mappe Schuletragen" in *Mappot*, p. 66.

[11] Ibid., pp. 66–67.

[12] Ruth Eis, "Introduction," in *Torah Binders of the Judah L. Magnes Museum* (Berkeley: The Judah L. Magnes Memorial Museum, 1979), p. 15. This rite is not the only time that boys took part in rituals related to circumcision. According to Hoffman, boys who were about to become bar mitzvah were, in some cases, active participants in a rite that involved mixing blood from a circumcision with water. The boys dipped their hands in that mixture and then wiped their faces with the liquid (*Covenant of Blood*, p. 105).

[13] Guttman, "Die Mappe Schuletragen," p. 68. Likely, they held this status because they contained the words of *lashon ha-kodesh* and because they tied the Torah, rather than because of their original use at a *b'rit milah*. A *genizah* is a "hiding place," a storeroom where unusable sacred writings are deposited to safeguard them from any desecration.

[14] Ibid., p. 66. The author does not say which Westheim he is referring to, but I suspect he is referring to Westheim bei Hassfurt, located in Bavaria, because he postulates that the custom of creating wimpels began in that region. Obviously, it is a challenge under the best of circumstances to preserve cloth over many centuries; for Europe's Jews, subject to pogroms, massacre and, in the twentieth century, the Holocaust, it proved painfully difficult.

[15] Ibid.

[16] Minden noted essential texts found on wimpels in his summary of the presentation in the club newsletter. These included the name of the child, the date of his birth, and the blessing "may he grow to Torah, *huppah*, and good deeds" ("*Gott lasse ihn gross werden zur Torah, zur Chuppah und zu guten Werken!*").

Minden also described customs around the presentation of the wimpel and its decorations, pointing out that that these customs were still operative in his time. See Georg Minden, "Die Torah-Wimpel oder Mappe: Ein Beitrag zur jüdischen Volkskunde," in *Zeitschrift des Vereins für Volkskunde* 3 (1893), pp. 205–208.

[17] When Georg Minden presented the two Torah wimpels before his club, Dr. Ulrich Jahn noted that Bavarian farmers likewise embroidered the baptismal swaddling-cloths of their children with a "pious saying" ("mit einem frommen Spruch," p. 207, n. 1). Their word for such a cloth, however, was *Fatsche*, a word he traced back to the Latin *fascia* (band, strip, ribbon). Jacob and Wilhelm Grimm's *Deutsches Wörterbuch* (published in 1854) notes the Latin origin for *Fatsche* and *Fätsche* and translates the term with the word *Wiegenband* (meaning "cradle swaddling cloth"). That a Latin term rather than a German one was used for the swaddling cloth may provide some proof of the antiquity of this custom.

[18] Christian influence may be found elsewhere in the development of the rite of *b'rit milah*: Hoffman traces the relationship between the developing role of *sandek* (godfather) in the medieval period to Christian practices. The term *sandek* comes, he argues, from the Greek *anadekomenos*, which means someone who undertakes or promises to do something or to stand surety for (*Covenant of Blood*, p. 203).

[19] Peter Classen, "Bayern und die politischen Mächte im Zeitalter Karls des Grossen und Tassilos III," in *Die Anfänge des Klosters Kremsmünster: Symposion 15–18 Mai 1977*, ed. Siegfried Haider (Linz: Oberösterreichisches Landesarchiv, 1978), pp. 169–187; quotation appears on p. 175.

[20] *Sefer Maharil. Minhagim, Hilkhot Milah*, as cited in Ruth Eis, "Introduction," *Torah Binders of the Judah L. Magnes Museum* (Berkeley: Judah L. Magnes Memorial Museum, 1979), p. 12.

[21] It is difficult to imagine that parents would not have brought a swaddling-cloth to wrap the baby in after the circumcision.

[22] The rabbis of Ashkenaz were sometimes hard-pressed to keep up with the many ways in which Jewish women claimed their right to practice commandments traditionally understood to be incumbent only on men. Grossman has described a veritable "rebellion" on the part of thirteenth-century Jewish women regarding their marital duties (see *Pious and Rebellious*, pp. 231–252). The record is complex and never univocal: some rabbinic authorities legislated on behalf of Jewish women taking on additional commandments, some appeared merely to be reconciling themselves to women's practice, and some actively combatted what they judged arrogant and bizarre behavior. Circumcision was one such site. Possibly, the wimpel was part of a larger set of turf wars over women's presence in synagogues, their potential roles as cantors, or as ritual slaughterers. The Maharam, who was also the first Ashkenazic rabbi to legislate against the pres-

ence of women at *b'rit milah*, used rather unconventional readings of Jewish law to combat this trend. See Grossman, *Pious and Rebellious*, pp. 231–252.

[23] In Genesis 17:14 God informs Abraham that "if any male who is uncircumcised fails to circumcise the flesh of his foreskin, that person shall be cut off from his kin; he has broken My covenant." One meaning of the Hebrew root translated here as "cut off" (*kof-resh-tav*) is "to exterminate." Scholars have explored the likelihood that the term could refer to a divine curse of infertility. For example, Jacob Milgrom writes: "The one who is excised not only suffers the termination of his lineage, but is 'excised' from joining his ancestors" (Milgrom, *Leviticus: A Book of Ritual and Ethics* [Minneapolis: Fortress Press, 2004], p. 257). See also David Biale, *Blood and Belief: The Circulation of a Symbol between Jews and Christians* (Berkeley: University of California Press, 2007), p. 35. Howard Eilberg-Schwartz has produced the most exhaustive exploration of the relationship of circumcision to fertility; see his *The Savage in Judaism*, pp. 141–176. And see also Howard Eilberg-Schwartz, *People of the Body: Jews and Judaism from an Embodied Perspective* (New York: State University of New York Press, 1992), p. 23.

[24] David Kraemer, *Reading the Rabbis: The Talmud as Literature* (New York: Oxford University Press, 1996), p. 113.

[25] See B. Shabbat 134a and B. Pesaḥim 69a.

[26] Rebecca Lesses, "Exe(o)rcising Power: Women as Sorceresses, Exorcists, and Demonesses in Babylonian Jewish Society of Late Antiquity," *Journal of the Academy of Religion* 69:2 (June 2001), p. 367.

[27] My thanks to John Reeves, Blumenthal Professor of Judaic Studies at UNC Charlotte, who pointed out that this was an acronym. A full description of this wimpel can be found in "Fragment of a Torah Binder 1693," in *Mappot… gesegnet, der da kommt: Das Band jüdischer Tradition*, p. 125.

[28] Robert Alter points out that there are three male candidates, given the ambiguity of the pronoun. "He" can include the child, Moses, and God. Alter also notes that "here circumcision serves as an apotropaic device, to ward off the hostility of a dangerous deity by offering him a bloody scrap of the son's flesh, a kind of symbolic synecdoche of human sacrifice." He goes on to describe relationships that have been long noted between this story and the narrative of the tenth plague, in which sacrificial blood must be smeared on the lintel to ward off the death of the firstborn. See Robert Alter, *The Five Books of Moses: A Translation with Commentary* (New York: Norton, 2004), pp. 330–331, n. 24. William Propp also explores these scenes and comes to similar conclusions; see his *Anchor Bible Exodus 1–18: A New Translation with Introduction and Commentary* (New York: Anchor Bible series, 1999), pp. 233–238, 437.

[29] Minden describes the wimpels he presented as being bloodstained, but other descriptions of wimpels do not indicate the presence of bloodstains.

[30] Eis, *Torah Binders*, p. 14.

[31] Freddy Raphaël, "Am Shawess bréngt mein Jénigle die Mappe in d'Schüle," in *Mappot*, p. 74.

[32] Ibid., p. 77.

[33] Ibid., p. 78. After Germany annexed the region in 1870, wimpels continued to promote and acknowledge the French heritage of those who created them. One wimpel features a saber fight between a French soldier and a spike-helmeted Prussian. Both figures emerge out of the two *lameds* in the name of the Hebrew month Elul. The designer clearly indicates whom she supports; at the end of the binder a victorious French soldier stands ever so proudly, holding, of course, the blue-white-red flag. German Jews responded in kind with wimpels that depicted triumphant German soldiers. See Eis, *Torah Binders*, pp. 63 and 68.

[34] See Annette Wollenhaupt, "Heilige Handarbeit Mainz: Frauen aus der Gemeinde besticken einen Torawimpel," in *Jüdische Allgemeine* (February 02, 2006), available online at www.jgmainz.de/akt-20060216-handarbeit.htm. For the most part, the women who gather to learn the art seem to be Russian Jewish émigrées to Germany.

[35] See, for example, http://tinyjudaica.com/making-a-mappah/, http://www.jewishtreats.org/2015/11/bound-to-torah-german-wimple-custom.html, and http://www.debimishael.com/files/wimpel_information.pdf.

Free Will: Is There Anything Free About It?

Michael Graetz

The effort to produce a meaningful definition of free will is legendary; the parallel effort to unravel the various theological and philosophical problems associated with the concept is seemingly endless. I wish to confine my treatment here, however, to the use of the concept as an indisputable axiom of *halakhah*. And it *is* an axiom in that the halakhic system appears to require a doctrine of reward and punishment in order to be able to determine guilt or innocence at all. (On this notion, see below in detail.) And the doctrine of free will is also essential to the creation of relationships between people (for example, in the context of marriage), because it enables the court to adjudicate problems as they arise in a relationship.

The creation of the modern social science of psychology is clearly the greatest challenge to the way freedom of will was defined in earlier generations—that is, primarily philosophically. What is will? Is every action that a person does consciously chosen by the person doing it as a function of some mental function known as will? Surely the default answer to that question in the context of the history of Jewish thought is yes. The assumption that every person is possessed of a will that he or she activates when choosing what to do was an unchallenged axiom of how human beings (and not solely Jews) understood themselves to function in the world.

It is also clear, conceptually and ethically, that a system of laws—and the whole concept of punishing wrongdoers for their transgressions—needs such a concept to justify its enforcement, and we shall soon see how the enforcement of law was justified in classical rabbinic sources precisely with reference to the free will of the wrongdoer. Nor is the obvious corollary to that principle—that a person who was coerced to do something cannot be considered liable for his or her actions—foreign to our classical sources. The insight of modern psychology that there are an almost limitless number of forces (including some that individuals are rarely or even never aware of) impacting on each decision that a person makes thus poses a serious challenge to the traditional doctrine and in a sense calls into question the meaning of the adjective "free" when used to qualify human will. I hope to show that rabbinic literature developed an approach that attempted to discover exactly which elements of a person's choice were most likely free, thus paving the way for determining guilt or innocence based not on some amorphous concept of "will," but rather on a more specific part of the thought process—namely, intention.

Freedom versus Coercion

The major philosophical debate over the existence of freedom of choice has two parts. The first concerns the precise relationship between coercion and freedom at the time an action is undertaken by an individual, and the second concerns the vexing theological doctrine of divine omniscience that appears to imply that since God knows what will happen in the future, assigning freedom of will to human activities must be, at best, a chimera. And this is not an abstruse idea: if divinely foreseen means being divinely ordained (and how can it not?), then how can anything that happens not be God's own fault?

Interestingly, the first problem mentioned above can be addressed without reference to God at all, in that modern psychology has produced a long list of coercions that invisibly and imperceptibly impact human actions. Indeed, any one of these coercive forces might be adduced in court to absolve—and, in some cases, even to justify—the most heinous crimes. We will see that this issue is raised in halakhic discussions as well and is addressed in halakhic methodology.

The second problem is also addressed, at least to some extent, in early halakhic literature. However, it is only really treated seriously much later on in the context of Jewish philosophic literature, and remains outside of the scope of this essay.

Early Halakhic Treatment of Divine Foreknowledge

Beginning even before the destruction of the Second Temple and lasting until the dawn of the fifth century CE, the principal expression of the philosophical question is Rabbi Akiva's famous remark that "everything is foreseen, and yet permission [to freely choose] is given, and [thus] the world can be judged by the amount of goodness, according to a majority of good deeds" (M. Avot 3:15).[1] Although the remark served in early and late rabbinic literature as the platform for philosophical discussion about the human ability to act freely, it remains seriously cryptic.

At the very least, Akiva is describing a paradox rather than a simple doctrine. Each deed is foreseen, he claims, yet, at the same time, permission—presumably to do it or to not do it—is extended to all. To illustrate the inscrutable nature of this statement, we only have to take a look at its subsequent presentation in contemporary sources.

One ancient source, Avot D'rabbi Natan (a kind of midrash on Pirkei Avot), rephrases the lesson to read that "everything is foreseen and everything is revealed, yet everything [unfolds] according to a person's knowledge."[2] Yet another passage in that same work reads as follows: "Everything is foreseen and revealed, and yet depends upon the deed. A net is spread out over all of life, [yet] the judgment is one of truth, and the shop is always open, the table set, the account book open—with a hand [always] writing upon it, the shopkeeper extends credit, and the collector is alive and strong."[3] The image here of God as a shopkeeper who extends credit to the customers, but who always collects that which is due, actually affords us a way to understand the paradox. God's foreknowledge, the text appears to be implying, is not exactly a function of the individual's choice, but rather of that individual's need. God offers unbound credit, but the amount that a person takes is a completely free choice.

More interesting is the following source, also from the Avot D'rabbi Natan:

> Everything is foreseen, and yet permission [to freely choose] is given. And so did the sages declare that, from the minute that Adam sinned, the desire of his heart [*tzafui libbo*], which was a light of wisdom, was diminished such that his descendants now know not what tomorrow will bring, as is written: "Do not rejoice over tomorrow, for you know not what the day will bring" (Proverbs 27:1)....And how do we know that the human capability to foresee the consequences of an action—the light of wisdom—was diminished? As it is written: "A man is besotted and does not understand; he is [correctly] likened to the animals" (Psalm 49:13).[4]

The first thing to note is that the word *tzafui*, which in the texts cited is translated as "foreseen," is here interpreted as knowing the consequences of an action! That is, the action is *not* foreseen—and *is* freely chosen—but what can be known in advance, at least theoretically, are simply an action's possible consequences. The text here is thus talking about the meaning of predicting consequences based on known data. And, indeed, we might imagine that the first part of the statement simply means that "everything is possible" as a result of a given choice of a course of action. Before the sin in the Garden of Eden, human beings were aware of what would or could occur as a result of their deeds, but after the sin this light of wisdom was dimmed. In modern terms, each person in Eden—and there were only two—was blessed with complete psychological awareness of all the forces that inhered in any decision made, but this awareness was lost after the expulsion from paradise.

But, what about the second part of the statement in this text from Avot D'rabbi Natan? A bit later in the passage, the word *r'shut* (translated here as "permission [to freely choose]") is also re-interpreted: "What is *r'shut*? It is network, kingship, and power embedded in human rule of the earth, as is written: 'A rope is laid for him on the ground...(Job 18:10).'" Thus the passage also talks of the traps that a wicked person does not see, a net (*reshet*, evoking the word *r'shut*) of consequences spread out to trip one up. So this source turns our enigmatic statement into something else: a lesson that teaches us that, since forces beyond our control are at work, everything is possible as a result of even apparently unrelated actions.

Thus, at least according to the sources adduced above, freedom of choice is crucial to the human condition because it justifies the rabbinic doctrine of reward and punishment. Furthermore, it is axiomatic that humans are granted free will in matters of good and evil.

Freedom of Action in Halakhic Sources

People can be held to be culpable of transgression not only on the assumption that they know the dos and don'ts of the Torah, but also only if they have freely chosen to transgress what they know to be forbidden. In the account of the giving of the Torah to Israel and the people's acceptance of it in the Book of Exodus, it appears that the Torah is accepted freely and unconditionally by Israel. It would be hard to read the text other than as a story of a nation exercising its free will to bind itself in loyal covenant to its God.

But this notion is challenged by a rabbinic midrash in which the script is entirely different. In this scenario, God lifts Mount Sinai over the heads of all the people and makes them "an offer they cannot refuse." Rabbi Akiva interprets the verse in question ("the people stood at the bottom of the mountain," Exodus 19:17) to mean that God actually lifted the mountain over their heads and said to them, "If you accept the Torah all will be well, and if not this will be your graveyard."[5] The talmudic passage continues that this is great news for all of Israel, because it implies that no person can be held accountable for transgressing a covenant entered into under duress. But, as it happens, later (in the days of Mordecai and Esther) Israel recants and accepts its obligations freely, thereby making themselves and their descendants liable to prosecution for breaking its laws.

As noted above, the assumption of a person's freedom to choose his or her actions freely is necessary in order to justify any possible system of valuation of the action as either good or bad: even qualifying an action as good, as deserving of reward, as bad, or as deserving of punishment, relies on the concept that the chooser of the action acted freely. The rabbis did not shy away from the natural corollary of such a principle, which asserts that there is no moral legitimacy to imposing punishment, on anyone if a person acted under duress. The same would hold true, as Alex Blum makes clear, if God's omniscience is presumed to include events still in the future.[6] Perhaps that is the main reason that there is no conception of divine foreknowledge in the Bible.

The halakhic system does, however, accept that a person may not be liable for a given action because of outside coercion. If there is any hint of coercion, then a transaction is not deemed binding and whatever relationship it called into existence is considered void. For example, a couple is validly married only when neither of them is coerced to enter into the marriage.[7] And the same is true of divorce, even though in classic *halakhah* divorce may only be initiated by the husband.

Freedom of Choice as the Standard of Right and Wrong in the Light of Coercion

Let us examine the rabbinic approach to free will, reward, and punishment in a case complicated by coercion. The classic halakhic discussion of this issue is found in the Talmud at B. Nazir 23a–b:

> Rabbah bar Bar Ḥana, quoting Rabbi Yoḥanan, said: The verse "For the ways of the Eternal are right and the just do walk in them, whereas transgressors stumble in them" (Hosea 14:10) may be illustrated by the following example. Two men roast their paschal lambs. One eats it with the intention of fulfilling the precept and the other eats it with the intention of having an ordinary meal. To the one who eats it to fulfill the precept, "and the just do walk in them" [applies]; but to the one who eats it to have an ordinary meal, "whereas transgressors stumble in them" [applies].

The rabbis understand the verse from Hosea as saying that two people can perform the same action, which involves the performance of a commandment, yet one of them is deemed righteous while the other is evil. How can this be? The first example illustrating this is the commandment of eating the paschal lamb, and the distinction is based upon each person's intent in eating this meal. But the passage continues with a rebuttal of this example:

> Resh Lakish remarked to him: Do you call such a man wicked? Granted that he has not fulfilled the precept in the best possible manner, but he has at least carried out the Passover rite.

The point should be clear: the second person has fulfilled the ritual imperfectly, but he cannot be labelled wicked if he has fulfilled all of its halakhic requirements. The Talmud seems to accept this point as valid, and then proposes a second example:

> Rather, it should be illustrated by two men, each of whom had his wife and his sister staying with him. One chances upon his wife [and has intercourse with her] and the other chances upon his sister [and has intercourse with her]. To the one who chances upon his wife, "and the just do walk in them" [applies], but to the one who chances upon his sister, "whereas transgressors do stumble therein" [applies].

This example is also rebutted, because the Talmud needs an example of two people doing the exact same thing, with one of them considered righteous and the other wicked—whereas in this case, the two are each doing a different thing:

> But are the cases comparable? We speak [in the verse] of one path, whereas here [in the example given] there are two paths.

Finally, an example is given that answers the question, and in so doing creates a whole category that refines the question, seeing intention as being the main factor in judging whether an action is righteous or wicked:

> Rather it is illustrated by Lot when his two daughters were
> with him. To these [the daughters], whose intention was
> to do right, "the just do walk in them" [applies]; whereas to
> [Lot himself], whose intention was to transgress, "whereas
> transgressors do stumble therein" [applies].

This example is of different people participating in the same incestuous
act, an egregious transgression. Yet one of the parties participating in
the act is deemed wicked, while the other is labelled righteous—a
perfect illustration of the verse! Note that the determinant here is the
intent of the doer of the deed. Thus, intention is a necessary factor
in determining if an act is wicked or just, and not only freedom of
choice. In this case both parties acted with full freedom of choice,
but their intentions were diametrically opposed! The daughters
thought that all humanity had been destroyed, and they were needed
to carry on the line of humanity. Lot was merely a lecherous old man
engaging in incestual sex because the opportunity to do so presented
itself. The passage continues:

> But perhaps it was his intention also to do right? [Do not
> think this for a moment, for] Rabbi Yoḥanan has said: The
> whole of the following verse indicates [Lot's] lustful character.
> "And Lot lifted up" (Genesis 13:10) is paralleled by [and thus
> meant to bring to mind the verse regarding the lustful wife
> of Joseph's master Potiphar], "And his master's wife lifted
> up her eyes upon Joseph" (Genesis 39:7). "His eyes" [in the
> Lot story] is paralleled by [and intended to bring to mind
> the verse regarding Delilah, for whom Samsom ill-advisedly
> lusted], "for she has found grace in my eyes" (Judges 14:3).
> "And beheld" [in the Lot story] is paralleled by [and intended
> to bring to mind the verse recording Shechem's lustful desire

for Dinah], "And Shechem the son of Ḥamor beheld her" (Genesis 34:2). "All the *kikkar* ['plain'] of the Jordan" [in the Lot story is intended to recall the verse from Proverbs that talks about men lusting for prostitutes], "For on account of a harlot, a man is brought to a *kikkar* ['loaf'] of bread" (Proverbs 6:26). And "it was well watered everywhere" [in the Lot story is meant to call to mind the verse from Hosea that records Israel's infidelity to its God], "I will go after my lovers, that give me my bread and my water, my wool and my flax, mine oil and my drink" (Hosea 2:7).

The attempt to rebut this example, perhaps by arguing that Lot too had worthy intentions, is denied with many texts that all show his lustful character. His true intent is discerned by examining all his past deeds and their connection to other, similarly evil, deeds.

One last attempt is made to exonerate Lot by asking if he was perhaps a victim of coercion, which would rule out defining his deed as meaningfully wicked. He was, after all drunk at the time, and perhaps did not know what he was doing:

> But was [Lot] the victim of compulsion? It had been taught on behalf of Rabbi Yosei son of Rabbi Ḥoni that the dot over the letter *vav* [meaning "and"] in the word *u-v'kumah* ["and when she arose"] occurring in [the story of] the elder of Lot's daughters is to signify that it was her lying down that he did not notice, but that he did notice when she arose. But what could he have done, since it was all over? The difference is that he should not have drunk wine the next evening [too, when his younger daughter came to seduce him].

The answer is that although Lot was perhaps compelled by drink on the first night, he should have then abstained on the second night. He was thus certainly guilty of incest on the second night, even if he may not have been on the first.

In the continuation of this talmudic discussion, we read a summary statement that fixes Lot's guilt:

> Rava (but some say Rabbi Isaac) expounded as follows: What is the significance of the verse "He that separates himself seeks his own desire and snarls against all sound wisdom" (Proverbs 18:1)? "He that separates himself seeks his own desire" refers to Lot, while "and snarls [*yitgalla*] against all sound wisdom" tells us that his disgrace was publicized [*nitgallah*] in the synagogues and houses of study, as we have learnt: "An Ammonite and a Moabite are forbidden [in marriage] and the prohibition is permanent."[8]

And then we are given yet other cases where the same transgression is considered in one case to be righteous, and in another case to be wicked:

> Ulla said: Both Tamar [as described at Genesis 38:14] and Zimri [as described at Numbers 25:14] committed adultery. Tamar committed adultery and gave birth to kings and prophets, but Zimri committed adultery and on his account many tens of thousands of Israel perished (Numbers 25:9).[9]

And, finally a general rule is pronounced:

> Rabbi Naḥman ben Yitzḥak said: "A transgression performed with good intention is better than a precept performed with evil intention."

The Place of Intention in Determining Reward and Punishment

The talmudic passage cited at length above establishes that the main factor in determining the righteousness or the evil of an act, in terms of law, is not the act but the actor. In the specific case under discussion, all the actors are presumably deemed to have transgressed because all chose to engage in uncoerced incestuous relations. And, indeed, the conclusion is just that: the factor that determines reward or punishment must always be the intention of the actor in choosing the act. As Alex Blum explains, "The answer must be that in the space in which we are free, we predict a future that we intend, or our friends think that we intend to bring about."[10] Freedom is thus necessary to justify reward or punishment, but what is most unaffected by outside coercion is intention. Thus, the basis for reward and punishment is intention and not an ethereal function called "will."

One may actually claim that halakhic sources posit free will as an obvious precondition for a working system of law and takes its existence (and its reality) as axiomatic. As a passage preserved in the Talmud at B. Shabbat 88a made clear, without free will there is no basis for law at all. Coercion directly hobbles or may even destroy free will, and in that case the law must mitigate punishment for an act when the actor's free will has clearly been compromised.

Indeed, intention can alter the way any action is judged. This is because the only factor that may be described as "free," with no coercion, is intention. Intention can alter the very basic values of the system. In the words of the rabbis (quoted above), "A transgression performed with good intention is better than a precept performed with evil intention."

A particularly poignant and full illustration of this principle is found in a responsum of Rabbi Jacob Ettlinger (1798–1871).[11] Rabbi Ettlinger was asked by Rabbi Mendel Friedlander, a Hungarian rabbi, about an unusual case of a woman whose husband had gone away on business and left her on her own. A man in torn clothes who was clearly hungry had come to her house, and he asked her for shelter. Having mercy on him, she let him stay in an empty room. He stayed in the room and acted in an ascetic fashion, even engaging in self-flagellation. In the end, he took advantage of her innocence and kindness by declaring to her that he was the prophet Elijah who had come to prepare a messiah for the world, and that she would bear this child. He gave her a chest that he claimed contained a large sum of money to be used for the rearing of the child, and he convinced her to have adulterous sex with him. She reluctantly agreed to this, considering that her actions would bring salvation to humanity. After having relations with him, the man vanished. She opened the chest, saw that it was empty, and then realized that she had been deceived. When her husband returned she tearfully told him this story. Rabbi Friedlander testified that he had investigated the wife's tale thoroughly, and he believed her to be telling the truth. The husband asked what he should do with his wife.

Rabbi Ettlinger answers that it is a difficult question. The *halakhah* is clear that, because of the actions involved, the man should be prohibited from returning to his wife. Yet he wished to find a way for them to put the past behind them and resume their previously happy life together as husband and wife.

Ettlinger at first considered relying on the Shulḥan Arukh, which states clearly that if a woman merely *says* that she has had adulterous relations with another man, and if there are no witnesses that she actually did have such relations, then we may allow her to return to her husband—since we posit that she may well have merely been fantasizing about another man.[12] The problem with relying on this *halakhah* to allow her to return to her husband, however, is that she insisted that she did not fantasize about this man at all, but was duped by his behavior and his appeal to her good nature. Rabbi Ettlinger then explored a more creative direction to allow the woman to return to her husband. He saw the sexual activity as forced, as a rape in which the woman had no possibility of exercising her free

choice to desist from engaging in sexual relations with her guest, because his elaborate story had so influenced her that her free will was
obviated by her desire to save the world. (This is similar to how we
view members of cults, who have been brainwashed into giving up
their money or their lives for a "higher" cause.) According to Rabbi
Ettlinger, the woman believed that this act of intercourse was a *mitzvah* that had been vouchsafed to her personally as a way of bringing redemption to the world. In this way, her mind was coerced into
believing that something she certainly knew was a transgression was
actually a positive commandment that she was being called upon to
fulfill. Her fervor to keep a commandment was used as a force of coercion against her. And if she was coerced, concluded Ettlinger, then
she could not be considered liable for the punishments associated
with this transgression. It was her intention that removed the stigma
of adultery (and its repercussions) from her action.

What Are We Choosing with Our Free Choice?

And thus we reach my main question regarding free will: What is it
exactly that we are freely choosing? In light of the sources adduced
above, I can answer: Free will is invariably (and only) a function of
intention; what people endowed with freedom of choice can choose
freely is the intention with which they inform the actions they
undertake. Our sources raise the possibility that the action itself
(such as eating the paschal lamb) is what is chosen, and so one who
follows the rules has kept the *mitzvah* even if one's intention was just
to have a good meal. But I believe this approach is refuted in the texts
cited above, which suggest that the true value of any action, good or
evil, is specifically *not* determined by the action itself but rather by
the intention the individual undertaking it invests in it. No *mitzvah*

may be fulfilled absent the proper intention.

Rabbi Abraham Joshua Heschel, in his monumental work *Torah Min Ha-shamayim* (a survey of the schools of thought in early rabbinic literature), concentrates on the two schools of the founding sages Rabbi Akiva and Rabbi Ishmael. In addition, he refers to other significant differences between the Torah of the sages of the Land of Israel and those of Babylonia. This very point concerning intention is at the heart of one of the most interesting disputes in rabbinic literature, namely: Does every *mitzvah* require its doer to have proper intention, in order for the *mitzvah* to be properly fulfilled?

In the introduction to *Torah Min Ha-shamayim*, Heschel explains that one of the major differences between the sages of the Land of Israel and those of Babylonia was their attitude toward *halakhah* and *aggadah*.[13] In the Land of Israel, *halakhah* and *aggadah* were considered to be two parts of a larger whole, and should therefore be imagined as always working together to create Jewish religion. In Babylonia, on the other hand, *aggadah* was a light diversion to the *halakhah*, with only peripheral value to the main part of the Torah.

Regarding intent, Heschel quotes Rabbi Shimon ben Yoḥai, one of the great sages of Roman Palestine in his day, who said that the goal of Jewish life is to develop *yirat shamayim*, reverence for the Divine; whereas Ulla, one of the great sages of Babylonia, taught that the only place for God in this world is within the four ells of *halakhah*.[14] In the same vein, the metaphor from the Land of Israel for studying Torah is playing music: Rabbi Yoḥanan, an important Palestinian sage, said that learning must be musical; whereas Abbaye, a major teacher of Babylonia, disagreed.[15]

Heschel develops this contrast between Israel and the Diaspora by connecting the opposition to music with the dispute over enjoyment that comes from fulfilling the commandments. Midrash Tehillim, an ancient Palestinian book of homilies on the Psalms, proposes that one should seek joy in performing a *mitzvah*, whereas Rava, a Babylonian, teaches that "the commandments were not given for enjoyment."[16]

Heschel presents a critical example of difference in religious psychology with many implications for practice of religion in general. In the Land of Israel, Resh Lakish says that "the [meaningful] performance of the commandments requires that they be done with [full] intent."[17] Rava of Babylon, on the other hand, says that they do not. In addition, Heschel points out that the verse that discusses how to proceed "if a matter is beyond your ken" (Deuteronomy 17:8) was taken as aggadically in the Land of Israel, but as *halakhah* to be followed in Babylon. He also cites the dispute about parting from a friend with *d'var halakhah* or *d'var aggadah* (that is, with a lesson about law or a homiletical teaching without legal importance), which he takes to imply that the sages of the Land of Israel functioned under the influence of a kind of prophetic mode of thought, whereas the sages of Babylonia decreed that one must even address God "in the language of *halakhah*."[18]

Heschel presents the religious approach of the Land of Israel as pursuing some sort of balance between *halakhah* and *aggadah*, as seeing the two parts of potentially unified religious life.[19] He did not see it as the "golden mean" promoted by Maimonides. But his vision of balance between opposing forces, of a sense of spiritual equilibrium between *halakhah* and *aggadah*, is the key to Heschel's philosophy of how to live a full, rich, and meaningful Jewish life. He implies that this can be done only in the Land of Israel, where one can fully open oneself up to poetry and *aggadah*—both of which disciplines were conceived and developed in the Land of Israel.

Heschel also analyzes the method of Torah study in the Land of Israel and finds it lively and inspiring. On the other hand, Rabbi Zeira (one of the few sages who left Babylonia and chose instead to live in the Land of Israel) and his pupil Rabbi Yirmiyah both see the study of Babylonia as dark and uninviting.[20]

As concrete examples of the wholeness of *halakhah* and *aggadah*, Heschel discusses the notion that the saving of a life overrides the normal strictures that delimit activity on Shabbat, as well as the parallel lesson that the preservation of human dignity overrides any of the Torah's negative commandments.[21] The very concept of overriding firm legal rulings for the sake of a greater value can only be based on intent. Indeed, the examples seen above from Tractate Nazir and Rabbi Ettlinger's responsum fit into this pattern perfectly.

Heschel quotes an unexpectedly wide range of stories about rabbis being tempted by the devil or by evildoers disguised as beautiful women or as harlots. One of those stories relates how Rabbi Akiva once actually cried over an issue of misplaced intent.[22] Another, also featuring Rabbi Akiva, reads as follows:

> Rabbi Akiva used to scoff at transgressors. One day Satan appeared to him as a woman on the top of a palm tree. Grasping the tree, he went climbing up: but when he reached half-way up the tree, he [Satan] let him go, saying: "Had they not proclaimed in heaven 'Take heed of Rabbi Akiva and his learning,' I would have valued your life at two *ma·ah*."[23]

Akiva's story is followed by a similar ones about Pelimo, Rabbi Ḥiyya bar Abba (whose wife tempted him disguised as a famous harlot), and Rabbi Ḥiyya ben Ashi (who was so afraid of temptation that he avoided sexual relations with his wife). Most interesting of all is the account of how Akiva wept for those whose intent almost brought them to transgression.[24]

Each story features a sage struggling to overcome his intention to sin. Since the intention in these cases is the opposite of that in the passage from Tractate Nazir or the responsum of Rabbi Ettlinger (both of which were discussed above), the moral lesson is highlighted.

But the process, deciding on how to act based on achieving an act which makes a specific intention a reality, and the judgment of the outcome, namely that even if act is a normally forbidden act it is justified because of the intention, are the same.

The effort to find a way to affirm the notion of absolute divine omniscience with respect to the future and the total freedom of the individual to act as he or she wishes will ultimately lead nowhere, which is why our sages generally ignored on both sides of this conundrum, or at least the side which in a given case would seem impossible without even trying to negotiate its straits. On the other hand, the question of a person's intentions in performing a *mitzvah* or in avoiding transgression, is a subject that can be freely discussed as part of the sages' overall effort to add meaning to our actions.

In all the rabbinic sources discussed above, a sense of the successful integration of actions and values, both informed by a critical stance toward our intentions and our desires, is what appears to be demanded of those who would serve God through the medium of *mitzvot*. In other words, human beings can be aware of their intentions if they wish to be, and in particular those driven by potentially coercive desires. Thus, intention is the foundation upon which moral independence must rest.

I believe that the introduction of intention as a concept into rabbinic *halakhah*—a concept that does not seem to be biblical—was one of the great creative revolutions of the sages of Jewish antiquity. They revoked a simple behaviorist model for keeping the laws of the Torah blindly and slavishly, and established instead the model of an arena in which coercive desire struggles with the intention to live a godly life in order to make choices worthy of a Jewish individual.

NOTES

[1] The Hebrew reads *ha-kol tzafui v'ha-r'shut n'tunah u-va-tov ha-olam niddon v'ha-kol l'fi rov ha-ma·aseh.*

[2] Avot D'rabbi Natan, text A, chapter 39. To whom this remark should be attributed is unclear. Depending on whether the editor meant to connect it to what precedes it or follows, it could be either Rabbi Eliezer the son of Rabbi Yosei the Galilean or Rabbi Yishmael the son of Rabbi Yosei. The Hebrew reads *ha-kol tzafui v'ha-kol galui v'ha-kol l'fi da·ato shel adam.* The word translated here as "knowledge" could also mean "idea" or "understanding."

[3] Avot D'rabbi Natan, text A, ch. 44; attributed to Rabbi Eliezer, the son of Rabbi Yosei the Galilean.

[4] Ibid., Addition 2 to Version A chap. 8, ed. Schechter (ed. Vienna, 5647 [1886/1887]), p. 162.

[5] B. Shabbat 88a.

[6] Alex Blum in *Organon F 19* (2012), no. 1, pp. 55–57.

[7] Cf. Mishnah Kiddushin, chapter 2.

[8] Quoting B. Yevamot 76b. The Torah specifies that the nations of Moab and Ammon were descended from Lot through his incestuous union with his daughters.

[9] Regarding Tamar giving birth to kings and prophets, cf. B. Sotah 10b.

[10] See above note 6, and cf. B. Shabbat 88a.

[11] Jacob Ettlinger, *She'eilot U-t'shuvot Binyan Tziyyon* (ed. Altona, 5628 [1867/1868]), responsum 154, pp. 65b–66b.

[12] S.A. Even Ha-eizer 115:6.

[13] Abraham Joshua Heschel, *Heavenly Torah: As Refracted Through the Generations,* trans. Gordon Tucker (New York: Continuum, 2007), pp. 1–4.

[14] *Torah Min Ha-shamayim* (London: Soncino, 1968), p. xvii. Notes to the Hebrew original reference passages left untranslated in the English edition.

[15] *Heavenly Torah*, pp. 14–15.

[16] Ibid., p. 15.

[17] Ibid.

[18] Ibid., pp. 15–16.

[19] Heschel relies on this sense of balance in his book on Shabbat, but here we see that his thoughts apply broadly to Judaism as a religion .

[20] *Heavenly Torah*, p. 16.

[21] Saving a life (*pikku·ah nefesh*): cf. Tosefta Shabbat 15:17, B. Yoma 84b, and many other passages; human dignity (*k'vod ha-b'riyyot*): cf. B. Eruvin 41b, Berakhot 19b, and many other passages. The notion of aggadic values justifying overriding *halakhah* is an important feature in Heschel's Hebrew pamphlet *Pikku·ah N'shamah* (New York: Baraniel Press, 1949).

[22] *Torah Min ha-Shamayim*, vol. 1, p. 137–138, and sources cited there. The original source is in the extra-talmudic tractate called Semaḥot, ed. Higger (New York: De-Bei Rabanan, 1931), p 125.

[23] B. Kiddushin 81a–b. A *ma·ah* is unit of a coin, in this case a coin of 100 units.

[24] The original sources are B. Kiddushin 81a–b, Sifrei Bemidbar §153, and T. Nazir 3:14.

Translation
Grant peace everywhere goodness and blessing,
Grace, lovingkindness and mercy to us and unto all Israel

Transliteration
Sim shalom tovah u-v'rakhah
ḥein va-ḥesed v'raḥamim aleinu ve-al kol Yisrael amekha

שִׂים שָׁלוֹם*

שִׂים שָׁלוֹם טוֹבָה וּבְרָכָה
חֵן וָחֶסֶד וְרַחֲמִים עָלֵינוּ וְעַל כָּל יִשְׂרָאֵל עַמֶּךְ

---

www.BlechTapes.com

a focused YouTube channel

Benjamin Blech Exegesis

on 10-theme Mesorah Matrix

sequence of 12 twenty-minute tapes:

intro + 10 themes + outro

www.UnifyingScienceSpirituality.com

About the Contributors

Reuven P. Bulka, C.M., is Rabbi Emeritus of Congregation Machzikei Hadas in Ottawa, Ontario, Canada. He chairs the Trillium Gift of Life Network that is responsible for organ and tissue donation and transplantation in all of Ontario, and he is President and CEO of Kind Canada Généreux. Rabbi Bulka is the author or editor of close to forty volumes on a wide range of topics. His most recent book, *Honeycombs* (written with his granddaughter Rikki Ash), deals with a novel way to understand the Amidah. He and his wife Leah share many generations of children.

Nina Beth Cardin, a Conservative rabbi living in Baltimore, is an author and activist who works in the intersection of faith and sustainability.

Martin S. Cohen is the rabbi of the Shelter Rock Jewish Center in Roslyn, New York, and one of the senior editors of the Mesorah Matrix series. He is the author of *Our Haven and Our Strength: The Book of Psalms* (Aviv Press, 2004), *The Boy on the Door on the Ox* (Aviv Press, 2008), four books of essays, and four novels. Rabbi Dr. Cohen served as senior editor of *The Observant Life*, published in 2012 by the Rabbinical Assembly. His new translation and full-length commentary on the Torah are forthcoming.

Michael J. Cook, Ph.D., is Bronstein Professor of Judeo-Christian Studies, Hebrew Union College, Cincinnati, and the only American rabbi with a full professorial Chair in New Testament. He has served on the Executive Board of the Central Conference of American Rabbis and many advisory groups in Jewish-Christian relations. Aside from his widely used *Modern Jews Engage the New Testament* (Jewish Lights, 2012), his publications treat Jewish views of Jesus, Paul, Jewish symbols in Christian art, anti-Semitism, and the Talmud in Gospel study.

Elliot N. Dorff is Rector and Distinguished Service Professor of Philosophy at American Jewish University and Visiting Professor at UCLA School of Law. Rabbi Dorff chairs the Conservative Movement's Committee on Jewish Law and Standards, and he is a past president of the Society of Jewish Ethics, the Academy of Jewish Philosophy, the Jewish Law Association, the Academy of Judaic, Christian, and Islamic Studies, and Jewish Family Service of Los Angeles. Of the twelve books and over 200 articles he has written on Jewish thought, law, and ethics, his book most germane to the essay printed in this volume is *Matters of Life and Death: A Jewish Approach to Modern Medical Ethics* (Jewish Publication Society, 2003).

Aubrey L. Glazer, Ph.D. (University of Toronto) is Affiliated Scholar at the Herbert D. Katz Center for Advanced Judaic Studies of the University of Pennsylvania and director of *Panui*, an open contemplative space for researching, reflecting and teaching Jewish mysticism in a dynamic and authentic way to build a conscious, compassionate community. As a graduate of the Institute for Jewish Spirituality, Aubrey continues practicing and co-leading Jewish meditation retreats. His published reflections on contemporary spirituality include *Mystical Vertigo* (2013); *Tangle of Matter & Ghost: Leonard*

Cohen's Post-Secular Songbook of Mysticism(s) Jewish & Beyond (2017); and *God Knows Everything Is Broken: The American Gnostic Songbook of Bob Dylan* (2018).

Edwin C. Goldberg is the Senior Rabbi, Temple Sholom of Chicago. He has published a number of books and articles on the subject of rabbinic literature and liturgy. Rabbi Goldberg has a Doctorate of Hebrew Letters from Hebrew Union College-Jewish Institute of Religion.

Elaine Goodfriend teaches at California State University, Northridge, in the Department of Religious Studies and the Program for Jewish Studies. She earned her Ph.D. in Near Eastern Studies from the University of California, Berkeley, and her chief interests are biblical law and ancient Israelite history. Elaine has contributed entries to several works, including *Anchor Bible Dictionary* (Doubleday, 1992), *The Oxford Handbook of Jewish Ethics and Morality* (Oxford University Press, 2013), and the forthcoming *Food and Jewish Traditions.*

Michael Graetz worked as assistant to the editor-in-chief of *Encyclopedia Judaica*, for which he wrote articles on modern Jewish thought. He was a senior lecturer in Jewish thought at Kaye College in Beer Sheva and is Rabbi Emeritus of Magen Avraham congregation in Omer, a suburb of Beer Sheva. He was one of the founders of the Masorti Movement and the Schechter Rabbinical school in Israel. His works may be found at https://michaelgraetz.com/.

Daniel Greyber is rabbi at Beth El Synagogue in Durham, North Carolina and the author of *Faith Unravels: A Rabbi's Struggle with Grief and God* (Resource Publications, 2012). He recently served as Team USA Rabbi at the 20th World Maccabiah Games in Israel. Formerly a Jerusalem Fellow at the Mandel Leadership Institute, a faculty member at the Ziegler School of Rabbinic Studies in Los Angeles, and the Executive Director of Camp Ramah in California, Rabbi Greyber's articles have been featured in a wide range of Jewish publications.

Zvi Grumet is a master teacher, creative educational thinker, and innovative Tanakh scholar whose teaching over the past three decades has inspired students and communities in the US and Israel, and throughout the English-speaking world. He engages his listeners in a close reading of the biblical text, bringing its characters alive and bringing out the compelling nature of the biblical message. Rabbi Grumet earned his rabbinic ordination and Ed.D. at Yeshiva University, and then dedicated the first eighteen years of his career to teaching Torah and leading educational institutions in the US. Rabbi Grumet currently teaches at Yeshivat Eretz Hatzvi in Jerusalem and other university-level programs in Israel. He is a senior staff member at The Lookstein Center for Jewish Education, where he is editor of *Jewish Educational Leadership* and generates initiatives to help advance Jewish education on four continents. Rabbi Grumet's books include *Moses and the Path to Leadership* (Urim, 2014) and *Genesis: From Creation to Covenant* (Maggid, 2017).

James Jacobson-Maisels is the founder of Or HaLev: A Center for Jewish Spirituality and Meditation, and has been studying and teaching meditation and Jewish spirituality for over fifteen years. Rabbi Dr. Jacobson-Maisels teaches Jewish thought, mysticism, spiritual practices, and meditation at the Pardes Institute of Jewish Studies, Haifa University, and Yeshivat Hadar, and in a variety of other settings around the world as well. He strives to integrate his study and practice and to help teach and live Judaism as a spiritual discipline.

Admiel Kosman, a renowned poet, is Professor for Jewish Studies at Potsdam University as well as the academic director of Geiger College, a training school for liberal rabbis, in Berlin. He is the author of several books and many articles in the field of talmudic research and of collections of Hebrew verse, and he also writes a regular column for *Haaretz* in which he interprets traditional stories in a postmodern light. His latest academic book is *Gender and Dialogue in the Rabbinic Prism* (Walter de Gruyter, 2012), and his most recent collection of poetry is *Approaching You in English: Selected Poems* (Zephyr Press, 2011).

Alex Maged holds an M.A. in Bible from Yeshiva University's Bernard Revel Graduate School of Jewish Studies, where he studied as a Wexner Graduate Fellow. He has taught Torah in communities across North America and has published widely on Tanakh and Jewish thought in journals such as *Kol Hamevaser* and *The Jewish Bible Quarterly*. In 2013, he founded *WhatsPshat.org*, where he shares essays on the weekly Torah portion with a community of over 1,300 subscribers.

Gidon Rothstein studies Judaism, trying to see where and how it can add productively to people's lives. Rabbi Rothstein currently blogs and podcasts A Responsum a Day, finding responsa written on each day of the Jewish calendar, five days a week at ou.org and once a week on torahmusings.com.

Barbara Shulamit Thiede is a faculty member of the Department of Religious Studies at the University of North Carolina at Charlotte. She teaches Hebrew Bible, Jewish history, the history of anti-Semitism, and the legacy of the Holocaust for both the undergraduate and graduate programs. In addition, she also offers a range of classes in Hebrew Bible and Jewish history for ordination programs at ALEPH, the Alliance for Jewish Renewal, and serves as a member of the ALEPH Academic Vaad. The spiritual leader for Temple Or Olam in Concord, North Carolina, Rabbi Dr. Thiede blogs at adrenalinedrash.com.

Kim Treiger-Bar-Am has taught law at various institutions in Israel and England. She made aliyah to Israel after her studies of philosophy and law at Yale, and later wrote her doctorate in law at Oxford. Her main research and teaching interests extend to the intersection between speech rights and the rights of authors and artists under copyright doctrine. She is currently writing a book on positive freedom in Jewish and Kantian thought in which she shows how the values of Judaism and the democratic values of the State of Israel accord with each other.

Mark Washofsky, the Solomon B. Freehof Professor of Jewish Law at Hebrew Union College-Jewish Institute of Religion in Cincinnati, served as chair of the Responsa Committee of the Central Conference of American Rabbis from 1996 to 2017. He writes on the history of *halakhah*, the nature of rabbinical decision-making, and issues of medical ethics in Jewish law. He is the author of *Jewish Living: A Guide to Contemporary Reform Practice* (URJ Press, 2010) and of *Reform Responsa for the Twenty-First Century* (CCAR Press, 2010), the latest printed collection of Reform responsa.

Shira Weiss is the author of *Joseph Albo on Free Choice: Exegetical Innovation in Medieval Jewish Philosophy* (Oxford University Press, 2017) and *Ethical Ambiguity in the Hebrew Bible* (Cambridge University Press, 2018), as well as articles in various academic journals. She holds a Ph.D. in medieval Jewish philosophy and has been awarded fellowships from the NEH and The John Templeton Foundation.

MESORAH MATRIX

10-BOOK SERIES
150+ Essayists

dimensions of

Spirituality & Kedushah

THE SPARK OF THE INFINITE DIVINE

Mesorah Matrix
Series

David Birnbaum

Editor-in-Chief

MESORAH MATRIX

2015

2015

2016

2016

2017

2017

2018

2018

2019

2019

200+ original essays

jewish thought & spirituality

150+ global thought leaders

a decade-long unified endeavor

MESORAH
MATRIX

10-BOOK SERIES
150+ Essayists

Sanctification

Tikkun Olam

Birkat Kohanim

The Kaddish

Modeh Ani

Havdalah

Search for Meaning

U-VACHARTA BA-CHAYIM

Ehyeh asher Ehyeh

V'Shamru

THE SPARK OF THE INFINITE DIVINE

Mesorah Matrix Series

Sanctification ("Kedushah")

Tikkun Olam ("Repair the World")

Birkat Kohanim (The Priestly Blessings: a contemporary take)

The Kaddish (specifically, The Mourner's Praise of God)

Modeh Ani (The solo daily morning prayer of Gratitude)

Havdalah (separating Holy from Secular: Sabbath > secular)

Search for Meaning (pegging-off of Viktor Frankl's classic)

U-VACHARTA BA-CHAYIM (The 613th precept-Choose Life)

Ehyeh asher Ehyeh ("I Will Be That Which I Will Be" – at the Burning Bush)

V'Shamru (The Sabbath)

21st CENTURY PUBLISHING

David.Birnbaum.NY@gmail.com

www.NewParadigmMatrix.com

MESORAH MATRIX
VOLUME 1

David Birnbaum / Mesorah Matrix Series

LIGHTS OF CREATION & TRANSCENDENCE

Sanctification

Editors

David
Birnbaum & Benjamin
Blech

LEAD ESSAY: **Jonathan Sacks**

New Paradigm Matrix™

EXPLORING HIGHER DIMENSIONS

MESORAH MATRIX
V O L U M E 2

TIKKUN OLAM

JUDAISM, HUMANISM & TRANSCENDENCE

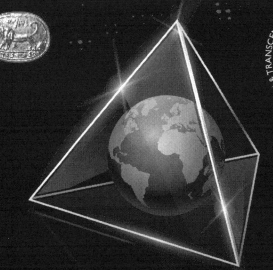

David Birnbaum / Mesorah Matrix Series
LIGHTS OF CREATION & TRANSCENDENCE

Editors

David
Birnbaum & Cohen
Martin S.

Associate Editor: **Saul J. Berman**

New Paradigm Matrix™

EXPLORING HIGHER DIMENSIONS

VOLUME 3

BIRKAT KOHANIM

David Birnbaum / Mesorah Matrix

FLIGHTS OF CREATION & TRANSCENDENCE

EXPLORING HIGHER DIMENSIONS

Editors

David
Birnbaum & **Cohen**
Martin S.

Associate Editor: **Saul J. Berman**

New Paradigm Matrix®

VOLUME 4

KADDISH

Editors

David
Birnbaum & Cohen
Martin S.

Associate Editor: **Saul J. Berman**

New Paradigm Matrix™

EXPLORING HIGHER DIMENSIONS

LIGHTS OF CREATION & TRANSCENDENCE / David Birnbaum / Mesorah Matrix Series

Modeh Ani

THE TRANSCENDENT PRAYER OF GRATITUDE

Editors

David
Birnbaum & Martin S. **Cohen**

Associate Editor: **Saul J. Berman**

New Paradigm Matrix™

EXPLORING HIGHER DIMENSIONS

LIGHTS OF CREATION & TRANSCENDENCE

David Birnbaum

Mesorah Matrix Series

HAVDALAH

Editors

David
Birnbaum & Cohen
Martin S.

Associate Editor: **Saul J. Berman**

EXPLORING HIGHER DIMENSIONS

New Paradigm Matrix™

MESORAH MATRIX

VOLUME 7

LIGHTS OF CREATION & TRANSCENDENCE

David Birnbaum | Mesorah Matrix Series

SEARCH FOR MEANING

Editors

David
Birnbaum & Martin S. **Cohen**

Associate Editor: **Saul J. Berman**

New Paradigm Matrix™

EXPLORING HIGHER DIMENSIONS

MESORAH MATRIX

VOLUME 8

David Birnbaum / Mesorah Matrix Series

LIGHTS OF CREATION & TRANSCENDENCE

U-VACHARTA BA-CHAYIM

EXPLORING HIGHER DIMENSIONS

Editors

David
Birnbaum & **Cohen**
Martin S.

Associate Editor: **Saul J. Berman**

New Paradigm Matrix ®

MESORAH
MATRIX
VOLUME 9

LIGHTS OF CREATION & TRANSCENDENCE / Mesorah Matrix Series

David Birnbaum

Ehyeh
asher
Ehyeh

Editors

David
Birnbaum & Cohen
Martin S.

New Paradigm Matrix™

EXPLORING HIGHER DIMENSIONS

MESORAH
MATRIX
VOLUME 10

LIGHTS OF CREATION & TRANSCENDENCE
David Birnbaum / Mesorah Matrix Series

EXPLORING HIGHER DIMENSIONS

U'shamru

Editors

David
Birnbaum & Martin S. **Cohen**

New Paradigm Matrix™

ESSAYISTS

Avivah Zornberg
Author

London, UK

David Ellenson
HUC-JIR

New York, NY

Saul Berman
Y.U. / Stern

New York, NY

Jonathan Sacks
United Hebrew
Congregations
London, UK

James Kugel
Bar Ilan University

Ramat Gan, Israel

Shalom Carmy
Yeshiva University,
Tradition Magazine
New York, NY

Rachel Barenblat
Bayit

Williamstown, MA

Rachel Friedman
Lamdeinu

New York, NY

W. Zeev Harvey
The Hebrew University of Jerusalem
Jerusalem

Rachel Adelman
Hebrew College

Newton Centre, MA

Shlomo Riskin
Ohr Torah Stone Colleges
Efrat, Israel

Mark Goldfeder
Emory University

Atlanta, GA

Hillel Goldberg
Intermountain Jewish News
Denver, CO

Lawrence Schiffman
NYU
New York, NY

Alan Cooper
Jewish Theological Seminary
New York, NY

Yonatan Feintuch
Bar Ilan University

Tel Aviv, Israel

Jacob Schacter
Yeshiva University

New York, NY

Aryeh Cohen
American Jewish
University
Los Angeles, CA

Avram Reisner
Chevrei Tzedek
Congregation
Baltimore, MD

Elliot Dorff
American Jewish
University
Los Angeles, CA

Michael Graetz
Congregation Eshel
Avraham
Omer, Israel

Steven Kepnes
Colgate University

Hamilton, NY

Reuven Bulka
Congregation
Machzikei Hadas
Ottawa, Canada

Adena Berkowitz
Kol Ha-neshamah

New York, NY

Alan Mittleman
Jewish Theological
Seminary
New York, NY

Tzvi Sinensky
Rosh Beit Midrash

Lower Merion, PA

Bradley Artson
American Jewish
University
Los Angeles, CA

Jill Jacobs
T'ruah: The Rabbinic
Call for Human Rights
New York, NY

Michael Broyde
Emory University

Atlanta, GA

Noam Zion
Hartman Institute

Jerusalem

Sid Schwarz
CLAL

New York, NY

Rahel Berkovits
Pardes Institute

Jerusalem

Howard Addison
Temple University

Philadelphia, PA

Robert Harris
Jewish Theological
Seminary
New York, NY

Samuel Lebens
Rutgers University

New Brunswick, NJ

Richard Hidary
Congregation
Shearith Israel
New York, NY

Jonathan Schorsch
Universität Potsdam
Potsdam
Germany

Eliezer Shore
Hebrew University
of Jerusalem
Jerusalem

Roberta Kwall
DePaul University
Law School
Chicago, IL

Alon Ferency
Heska Amuna
Synagogue
Knoxville, TN

Aubrey Glazer
Congregation Beth
Shalom
San Francisco, CA

Rebecca W. Sirbu
Rabbis Without
Borders, CLAL
New York, NY

Geoffrey Claussen
Elon University

Elon, NC

Jeremy Gordon
New London
Synagogue
London, U.K.

Shoshana Klein
Poupko
Ahavath Torah
Englewood, NJ

Michael
Wasserman
The New Shul
Scottsdale, AZ

Daniel Greyber
Beth El Synagogue

Durham, NC

Gail Labovitz
American Jewish
University
Los Angeles, CA

James Jacobson-Maisels
Or HaLev, Center for Jew-
ish Spirituality & Meditation
New York, NY

Yeshaya Dalsace
Dor Vador Com-
munaute Massorti
Paris, France

Kari Tuling
Congregation
Kol Haverim
Glastonbury, CT

Karyn Kedar
B'nai Jehoshua
Beth Elohim
Deerfield, IL

Nina Cardin
Rabbinical
Assembly
New York, NY

Aryeh Klapper
Center for Modern
Torah Leadership
Sharon, MA

Jonathan Wittenberg
New North London
Synagogue
London, UK

Michael Knopf
Temple Beth-El

Richmond, VA

Rivon Krygier
Congregation
Adath Shalom
Paris

Elie Spitz
Congregation
B'nai Israel
Tustin, CA

Ira Bedzow
Aspen Center for
Social Values
Aspen, CO

Yitzchak Blau
RCA

Jerusalem

Alfred Cohen
YU High School

New York, NY

Elliot Cosgrove
Park Avenue
Synagogue
New York, NY

Yehonatan
Chipman
Hitzei Yehonatan
Israel

David Flatto
Penn State Law

University Park, PA

Shohama H. Wiener
Temple Beth-El

City Island, NY

David Evan Markus
Temple Beth-El

City Island, NY

Nathaniel Helfgot
Yeshivat Chovevei
Torah
New York, NY

Cass Fisher
University of South
Florida
Tampa, FL

Admiel Kosman
Postdam University

Germany

Simcha Krauss
Eretz Hatzvi

Jerusalem

Melanie Landau
Monash University

Australia

Vernon Kurtz
North Suburban
Synagogue Beth-El
Highland Park, IL

Rolando Matalon
B'nai Jeshurun

New York, NY

Shmuly Yanklowitz
Valley Beit Midrash
President & Dean
Scottsdale, AZ

Peter Knobel
Beth Emet

Evanston, IL

Harvey Meirovich
Zacharias Frankel
College
Berlin, Germany

Aryeh Frimer
Bar-Ilan University

Ramat Gan

Martin Lockshin
York University

Ontario, Canada

Shai Cherry
Shaar Hamayim

Del Mar, CA

David Shatz
Yeshiva University

New York, NY

Jeremy Rosen
Persian Jewish
Center
New York, NY

David Greenstein
Congregation
Shomrei Emunah
Montclair, NJ

Avraham Walfish
Herzog College and
Michala Jerusalem
Tekoa, Israel

David Mescheloff
RCA

Israel

Barbara Thiede
UNC Charlotte

Concord, NC

Lawrence Troster
GreenFaith

Highland Park, NJ

Ruth Walfish
Herzog College and
Michala Jerusalem
Tekoa, Israel

Lenn Goodman
Vanderbilt
University
Nashville, TN

Dan Ornstein
Ohav Shalom

Albany, NY

Dena Freundlich
Ma'ayanot AMIT

Jerusalem

Elaine Goodfriend
California State
University
Northridge, CA

Berel Dov Lerner
Western Galilee
College, Herzl Inst
Northern Israel

Orna Triguboff
Neshama Life
Organisation
Sydney, Australia

Nehemia Polen
Hebrew College

Newton Centre, MA

Mark Greenspan
Oceanside Jewish
Center
Oceanside, NY

Richard Claman
Zeramim Journal

New York, NY

Avi Olitzky
Beth El Synagogue

St. Louis Park, MN

Michelle J. Levine
Stern College for Women
Yeshiva University
New York, NY

Yehuda Gellman
Ben-Gurion
University
Negev, Israel

Herbert Bronstein
Lake Forest
College,
Lake Forest, IL

Avraham Feder
Beit Knesset
Moreshet Yisrael
Jerusalem

Elyse Goldstein
City Shul

Ontario, Canada

Kerry M. Olitzky
Big Tent Judaism

New York, NY

Dalia Marx
Hebrew Union
College
Jerusalem

Jason Rubenstein
Mechon Hadar

New York, NY

Herbert Yoskowitz
Adat Shalom
Synagogue
Farmington Hills, MI

Mark Sameth
Pleasantville Com-
munity Synagogue
Westchester, NY

Catharine Clark
Congregation
Or Shalom
London, Ontario

Jacob Adler
Temple Shalom of
Northwest Arkansas
Fayetteville, AR

Jonathan Jacobs
John Jay College,
CUNY
New York, NY

David Kunin
Beth Shalom
Synagogue
Edmonton, AB

Michael Marmur
Hebrew Union
College
Jerusalem

Mordechai Luria
Institute for Jewish
Ideas & Ideals
New York, NY

Noah Farkas
Valley Beth Shalom

Encino, CA

Alex Maged
Yeshiva University

New York, NY

Hayyim Angel
Yeshiva University

New York, NY

Elie Kaunfer
Mechon Hadar

New York, NY

Alex Sztuden
The Herzl Institute

Jerusalem

David Golinkin
Schechter Institute
of Jewish Studies
Jerusalem

Mark Washofsky
Hebrew Union
College
Cincinnati, OH

Edwin C. Goldberg
Temple Sholom of
Chicago
Chicago, IL

Baruch Frydman-Kohl
Beth Tzedec
Congregation
Toronto, Canada

Ora Horn Prouser
Academy for
Jewish Religion
Yonkers, NY

Howard Wettstein
University of
California
Riverside, CA

Zvi Grumet
Yeshivat Eretz
Hatzvi
Jerusalem

Erica Brown
The Jewish
Federation
Rockville, MD

Meesh Hammer-Kossoy
Pardes Institute
of Jewish Studies
Jerusalem

Michael J. Cook
Hebrew Union
College
Cincinnati, OH

James Diamond
University of
Waterloo
Ontario, Canada

Shira Weiss
Ben Gurion
University
Beer Sheba, Israel

Gidon Rothstein

Bronx, NY

Ariel Mayse
Stanford University
Stanford,
California

Dr. Elyssa Wortzman
Mindful art-based
spiritual education
San Francisco

Ellen LeVee
Spertus Institute

Chicago, IL

Kim Treiger-Bar-Am
Tel Aviv

Israel

David Maayan
Boston College

Newton, MA

Senior Editors

Benjamin Blech
Yeshiva University

New York, NY

Martin S. Cohen
Shelter Rock,
Jewish Center
Roslyn, NY

21st CENTURY PUBLISHING

David.Birnbaum.NY@gmail.com

www.NewParadigmMatrix.com

Sanctification

'Sanctification'
from Essay by Chief Rabbi Lord Jonathan Sacks

... And there is the priestly task of kedushah, sanctifying life by honouring the sacred ontology, the deep moral structure of the universe, through the life of the 613 commands, a life of discipline and self-restraint, honesty and integrity, respect and love, the code set out in the chapter of the Torah that opens with the momentous words, "Be holy for I, the Lord your God, am holy." Other cultures and faiths drew inspiration from its wisdom and prophetic traditions, but kedushah remained a specific Jewish imperative that made us different. Even so, it contains a message for the world, which Jews bear witness to whenever and wherever they remain faithful to it.

Our vocation remains, to be mamlechet cohanim vegoi kadosh, "a kingdom of priests and a holy nation."

— The Ethic of Holiness, August 2012

to view series updated authors list,

see www.MesorahMatrix.com

Mesorah Matrix Series

Editors

David Birnbaum

Martin S. Cohen

Benjamin Blech

Editor

- born in Zurich in 1933, is an Orthodox rabbi who now lives in New York City.

Rabbi Blech has been a Professor of Talmud at Yeshiva University since 1966, and was the Rabbi of Young Israel of Oceanside for 37 years. In addition to his work in the rabbinate, Rabbi Blech has written many books on Judaism and the Jewish people and speaks on Jewish topics to communities around the world.

Benjamin Blech
Yeshiva University,
"Understanding
Judaism"

Education

Rabbi Blech received a Bachelor of Arts degree from Yeshiva University, a Master of Arts degree in psychology from Columbia University, and rabbinic ordination from the Rabbi Isaac Elchanan Theological Seminary.

Milestones

Rabbi Blech is the author of twelve highly acclaimed and best selling books, with combined sales of close to half a million copies, including three as part of the highly popular Idiot's Guide series. His book, *Understanding Judaism*: The Basics of Deed and Creed, was chosen by the Union of Orthodox Jewish Congregations as "the single best book on Judaism in our generation".

Wikipedia online, http://en.wikipedia.org/wiki/Benjamin_Blech (accessed November 8, 2012)

Martin S. Cohen

Martin S. Cohen

Martin S. Cohen has been a Senior Editor of the inter-denominational Mesorah Matrix series since 2012.

From 2000-2014, he served as Chairman of the Publications Committee of the quarterly journal *Conservative Judaism*, which was under the joint auspices of the JTS (Jewish Theological Seminary) and the RA (Rabbinical Assembly) during that span.

Rabbi Cohen also served as the senior editor of *The Observant Life*, a compendium of Jewish law, custom published by the Rabbinical Assembly in 2012.

Martin's weekly blog can be viewed at www.TheRuminativeRabbi. blogspot.com. He serves as rabbi of the Shelter Rock Jewish Center in Roslyn, New York.

Rabbi Cohen was educated at the City University of New York and at Jewish Theological Seminary of America, where he was ordained a rabbi and received his Ph.D. in Ancient Judaism. He is the recipient of fellowships at the Hebrew University (Jerusalem) in 1983 and Harvard University in 1993.

Martin Cohen has taught at Hunter College, the Jewish Theological Seminary of America, the Institute for Jewish Studies of the University of Heidelberg, as well as at the University of British Columbia and the Vancouver School of Theology.

His published works include *The Boy on the Door on the Ox* (2008) and *Our Haven and Our Strength: A Translation and Commentary on the Book of Psalms* (2004).

Rabbi Cohen is currently writing a translation and commentary on the Torah and the Five Megillot.

Saul Berman
Mesorah Editor

Saul J. Berman is one of the world's leading Jewish intellects.

He is an American Jewish scholar and Modern Orthodox rabbinic.

Rabbi Berman was ordained at Yeshiva University, from which he also received his B.A. and his M.H.L. He completed a degree in law, a J.D., at New York University, and an M.A. in Political Sciesnce at the University of California, Berkeley, where he studied with David Daube. He spent two years studying mishpat ivri in Israel at Hebrew University of Jerusalem and at Tel Aviv University. He did advanced studies in Jewish Law at Hebrew University and Tel Aviv University Law Schools. Since 1971 Rabbi Berman serves as Associate Professor of Jewish Studies at Stern College for Women of Yeshiva University. Rabbi Berman was Rabbi of Congregation Beth Israel of Berkeley CA (1963-1969), Young Israel of Brookline, MA (1969-1971) and of Lincoln Square Synagogue in Manhattan (1984-1990.) Since 1990 he has served as an Adjunct Professor at Columbia University School of Law, where he teaches a seminar in Jewish Law. Aside his academic appointments, from 1997 until 2006.

Rabbi Berman is a contributor to the *Encyclopedia Judaica* and is the author of numerous articles which have been published in journals such as *Tradition, Judaism, Journal of Jewish Studies, Dinei Yisrael*, and others.

Rabbi Berman was the founder and director of the Edah organization for the promotion of Modern Orthodoxy. Edah was ultimately absorbed into Yeshivat Chovevei Torah.

He is married to Shellee Berman; they have four children and seven grandchildren.

Saul Berman
Yeshiva University,
Stern College

Wikipedia online, http://en.wikipedia.org/wiki/Saul_Berman (accessed February 15, 2013) + The Tikvah Center for Law & Jewish Civilization online, http://www.nyutikvah.org/fellows/saul_berman.html (accessed February 15, 2013)

Shalom Carmy
Contributing Editor

Shalom Carmy is an Orthodox rabbi teaching Jewish Studies and philosophy atYeshiva University, where he is Chair of Bible and Jewish Philosophy at Yeshiva College. He is an affiliated scholar at Cardozo Law School of Yeshiva University. He is also Editor of Tradition, an Orthodox theological journal.

Shalom Carmy
Yeshiva University,
Tradition Magazine

A Brooklyn native, he is a prominent Modern Orthodox theologian, historian, and philosopher. He received his B.A. in 1969 and M.S. from Yeshiva University, and received his rabbinic ordination from its affiliated Rabbi Isaac Elchanan Theological Seminary, studying under Rabbis Aharon Lichtenstein and Joseph Soloveitchik. He has edited some of R. Soloveitchik's work for publication. Carmy has written many articles on Biblical theology, Jewish thought, Orthodoxy in the 20th century, and the role of liberal arts in Torah education. He edited "*Modern Scholarship in the Study of Torah*: Contributions and Limitations" (ISBN 1-56821-450-2), "*Jewish Perspectives on the Experience of Suffering*", as well as several other works. He writes a regular personal column in *Tradition*, and contributes regularly on Jewish and general subjects to *First Things* and other journals. In addition to his exegetical and analytic work, Carmy's theological contribution is distinguished by preoccupation with the way religious doctrine and practice express themselves in the life of the individual.

http://en.wikipedia.org/wiki/Shalom_Carmy (accessed May 7, 2014)

David Birnbaum

Saul Berman

Benjamin Blech

Martin S. Cohen

Shalom Carmy

Mesorah Matrix
SENIOR EDITORIAL BOARD

LIGHTS OF CREATION & TRANSCENDENCE

David Birnbaum

Mesorah Matrix Series

The spines of ten books, left to right:

Sanctification — VOLUME 1 — ESORAH MATRIX — Birnbaum & Blech — New Paradigm Matrix — 2015

TIKKUN OLAM — VOLUME 2 — ESORAH MATRIX — Birnbaum & Cohen — New Paradigm Matrix — 2015

BIRKAT KOHANIM — VOLUME 3 — ESORAH MATRIX — Birnbaum & Cohen — New Paradigm Matrix — 2016

KADDISH — VOLUME 4 — ESORAH MATRIX — Birnbaum & Cohen — New Paradigm Matrix — 2016

Modeh Ani — VOLUME 5 — ESORAH MATRIX — Birnbaum & Cohen — New Paradigm Matrix — 2017

HAVDALAH — VOLUME 6 — ESORAH MATRIX — Birnbaum & Cohen — New Paradigm Matrix — 2017

SEARCH FOR MEANING — VOLUME 7 — ESORAH MATRIX — Birnbaum & Cohen — New Paradigm Matrix — 2018

U-VACHARTA BA-CHAYIM — VOLUME 8 — ESORAH MATRIX — Birnbaum & Cohen — New Paradigm Matrix — 2018

Enyeh asher Enyeh — VOLUME 9 — ESORAH MATRIX — Birnbaum & Cohen — New Paradigm Matrix — 2019

U'Shamru — VOLUME 10 — ESORAH MATRIX — Birnbaum & Cohen — New Paradigm Matrix — 2019

March 2018

www.MesorahMatrix.com

www.NewParadigmMatrix.com

Washofsky
Cohen
Kosman
Graetz
Poupko
Treiger-Bar-Am
Maged
Rothstein
Thiede
Jacobson-Maisels
Greyber
Dorff
Goodfriend
Cook
Grumet
Goldberg
Cardin
Bulka
Weiss
Glazer

For the mountains shall erode

and the hills indeed collapse,

but My grace towards you shall never waver.

- Isaiah 54:10

כִּי הֶהָרִים יָמוּשׁוּ

וְהַגְּבָעוֹת תְּמוּטֶינָה

וְחַסְדִּי מֵאִתֵּךְ לֹא יָמוּשׁ

יְשַׁעְיָהוּ 54:10 –

21st CENTURY PUBLISHING

David Birnbaum
Editor-in-Chief

New Paradigm Matrix
att: David Birnbaum
Tower 49
12 E 49th St.
11th Floor
New York, NY 10017

David.Birnbaum.NY@gmail.com

$16.00 / book

U-vacharta Ba-chayim

ISBN 978-0-9961995-5-1